THE POETICS OF IMPERSONALITY

THE POETICS OF IMPERSONALITY

T.S. ELIOT AND EZRA POUND

MAUD ELLMANN

Lecturer in English, University of Southampton

Harvard University Press
Cambridge, Massachusetts
1987

Printed in Great Britain

10 9 8 7 6 5 4 3 2 1

Library of Congress Cataloging-in-Publication Data

Ellmann, Maud, 1954–
The poetics of impersonality.
Includes bibliographies and index.
1. American poetry—20th century—History and criticism. 2. Self in literature. 3. Identity (Psychology) in literature. 4. Persona (Literature) 5. Eliot, T. S. (Thomas Stearns), 1888–1965—Criticism and interpretation. 6. Pound, Ezra, 1885–1972—Criticism and interpretation. I. Title.
PS310.S34E45 1987 821′.912′09353 87-7422
ISBN 0-674-67858-3

To my mother and father

Contents

Preface

The theory of impersonality has a long and distinguished genealogy, but it is Eliot who resurrected it for modernism. Pound espoused the theory, too; but more importantly he put it into practice in *The Cantos* by submerging his identity in masks, citation, *bricolage*. Indeed, both poets spent their careers devising disappearing tricks and new varieties of scriptive self-occlusion. Even in its early days, however, the doctrine of impersonality was inconsistent and eclectic. It derives from many sources, philosophical, poetic, and political: and it can mean anything from the destruction to the apotheosis of the self. It conceals an ideological tension as well as a conceptual instability, and for this reason it continually slips into the ethics of "personality" it was designed to supervene. This book, therefore, involves two different but overlapping projects. On the one hand, it traces the vicissitudes of impersonality in the *theories* of Eliot and Pound; but it also studies how their poems "murder and create" their fictive selves. For these texts *manufacture* forms of subjectivity, rather than *reflecting* personalities already made. As Mallarmé says, "Devant le papier, l'artiste *se fait*."[1] In the case of modernism, "il se *dé*fait", too: and it is crucial to discern both moments of this disengendering. For Pound and Eliot, poetry becomes the workshop of the self, where personal identity is both constructed and dismantled.

* * *

An earlier version of this book was submitted as a D.Phil. thesis at Oxford in 1982. I should like to thank my supervisor, John Bayley, for his advice and encouragement, and also my examiners, Terry Eagleton and Graham Martin, for their scrupulous reading. My work on Eliot was made possible by Mrs Valerie Eliot, who directed me to his unpublished manuscripts. Mrs Eliot has copyright to all these papers, and she has kindly given me permission to quote from them. Equally, Mary de Rachewiltz has taken a friendly interest in my work, and has generously permitted me to quote from Pound's unpublished letters. Joseph Bristow, Lucy Ellmann, and Lindsay Smith helped with the later stages of the thesis, and Danuta Waydenfeld has given me great support throughout. Derek Attridge and Isobel Armstrong read the thesis and showed me how to change it into a book, while Sandra Kemp advised me on the style. My father, too, has always been most generous with his advice and encouragement. I have also had the privilege of discussing the issues of the book with Anne Janowitz, Colin McCabe, Andrew Parker, Jean-Michel Rabaté, Eve Kosofsky Sedgwick, Frank Stack, John Wilkinson, and Ann Wordsworth.[2] Most of all, I should like to thank Robert Young, who has seen the book through all its incarnations, and given me invaluable advice at every stage.

Notes

1. Mallarmé, *Correspondance*, Vol. I, 1862–71 (Paris: Gallimard, 1959), p. 154.
2. I regret that Rabaté's excellent book, *Language, Sexuality and Ideology in Ezra Pound's Cantos* (Albany, New York: State University of New York Press, 1986) was published too late for me to cite it.

Principal Short Forms of Citation

A
Ezra Pound. *Antheil and the Treatise on Harmony*. Chicago: Pascal Covici, 1927. Repr. New York: Da Capo Press, 1968.

ABCE
Ezra Pound. *ABC of Economics*. London: Faber, 1933.

ABCR
Ezra Pound. *ABC of Reading*. London: Routledge, 1934. Repr. London: Faber, 1951.

ASG
T. S. Eliot. *After Strange Gods: A Primer of Modern Heresy*. London: Faber, 1934.

BN
T. S. Eliot. *Burnt Norton* (1935). References to this poem and to the other *Four Quartets* will be designated by the appropriate abbreviation, followed by the section in Roman numerals, followed by the line number.

C
Ezra Pound. *The Cantos*. New York: New Directions, 1970. Most references to *The Cantos* will omit the *C*, and will consist of the number of the Canto in Roman numerals followed by the page number in the New Directions edition.

CC
T. S. Eliot. *To Criticise the Critic, and Other Writings*. London: Faber, 1965.

CE
Henri Bergson. *Creative Evolution*. Trans. Arthur Mitchell. London: Macmillan, 1911.

CEP
Ezra Pound. *Collected Early Poems*. Ed. Michael King. London: Faber, 1977.

CPP
T. S. Eliot. *The Complete Poems and Plays*. London: Faber, 1969.

CSP
Ezra Pound, *Collected Shorter Poems*. London: Faber, 1968.

CUP
Cambridge University Press.

CWC
Ernest Fenollosa. *The Chinese Written Character as a Medium for Poetry*. Ed. Ezra Pound. 1936. Repr. San Francisco: City Lights, 1968.

Draft
T. S. Eliot. Draft of a paper on Bergson. MS (1910–11), b. MS Am 1691 (132), Houghton Library, Harvard University, Cambridge, Mass.

DS
T. S. Eliot. *The Dry Salvages* (1941). *CPP* 184–90. See note to *BN*.

EC
T. S. Eliot. *East Coker* (1940). *CPP* 177–83. See note to *BN*.

English 26
T. S. Eliot. Undergraduate lectures (Harvard): English 26: English Literature from 1890 to the Present Day.

Essai
Henri Bergson. *Essai sur les données immédiates de la connaissance*. Paris: Librairie Felix Alcan, 1896.

GB
Ezra Pound. *Gaudier-Brzeska: A Memoir*. New York: New Directions, 1970.

GK
Ezra Pound. *Guide to Kulchur*. London: Faber, 1938. Repr. London: Peter Owen, 1952.

I
Ezra Pound. *Impact: Essays on Ignorance and the Decline of American Civilization*. Ed. Noel Stock. Chicago: Henry Regnery, 1960.

Illeg. exc.
Illegible excision (in manuscript).

L
Ezra Pound. *Selected Letters: 1907–41*. Ed. D. D. Paige. 1950. Repr. New York: New Directions, 1971.

LA
T. S. Eliot. *For Lancelot Andrewes: Essays on Style and Order*. 1928. Repr. London: Faber, 1970.

LE
Ezra Pound. *Literary Essays*. Ed. T. S. Eliot. London: Faber, 1954.

LG
T. S. Eliot. *Little Gidding* (1942). *CPP* 191–8. See note to *BN*.

M&M
Henri Bergson. *Matter and Memory*. Trans. Nancy Margaret Paul and W. Scott Palmer. London: Allen and Unwin, 1911. Repr. 1919.

MN
Ezra Pound. *Make it New*. New Haven: Yale University Press, 1935.

NDC
T. S. Eliot. *Notes towards a Definition of Culture*. London: Faber, 1948.

Notes
T. S. Eliot. *Notes on Lectures of Henri Bergson*. MS (Paris, 1910–11), b. MS Am 1691 (130). Houghton Library, Harvard University, Cambridge, Mass.

P
Ezra Pound. *Personae: Collected Shorter Poems.* London: Faber, 1952.

PP
T. S. Eliot. *On Poetry and Poets.* London: Faber, 1957.

PS
Ezra Pound. Postscript to *The Natural Philosophy of Love*, by Rémy de Gourmont. Trans. Ezra Pound. London: Casanova Society, 1926.

RKP
Routledge and Kegan Paul.

RS
"Ezra Pound Speaking": Radio Speeches of World War II. Ed. Leonard W. Doob. Westport, Connecticut and London: Greenwood, 1978.

SE
T. S. Eliot. *Selected Essays.* London: Faber, 1932. 3rd edn, 1975.

SE
The Standard Edition of *The Complete Psychological Works of Sigmund Freud.* Trans. James Strachey. London: Hogarth, 1953–74. References to the Standard Edition will be followed by the volume number in Roman numerals, followed by the page number.

SP
T. S. Eliot. *Selected Prose.* Ed. Frank Kermode. London: Faber, 1975.

SPr
Ezra Pound. *Selected Prose 1909–1965.* Ed. William Cookson. London: Faber, 1973.

SR
Ezra Pound. *The Spirit of Romance.* 1910; rev. edn, London: Peter Owen, 1952.

SW
T. S. Eliot, *The Sacred Wood*. 1920; 2nd edn, London: Methuen, 1928.

TFW
Henri Bergson. *Time and Free Will: An Essay on the Immediate Data of Consciousness*. Trans. F. L. Pogson from *Essai sur les données immédiates de la connaissance*; 4th edn, London: Allen and Unwin, 1921.

TLS
Times Literary Supplement.

TWM
Wyndham Lewis. *Time and Western Man*. London: Chatto and Windus, 1927.

U
James Joyce. *Ulysses*. 1922. Harmondsworth: Penguin, 1969.

UPUC
T. S. Eliot. *The Use of Poetry and the Use of Criticism*. 1933. Repr. London: Faber, 1964.

WL Fac
T. S. Eliot. *The Waste Land: A Facsimile and Transcript of the Original Drafts Including the Annotations of Ezra Pound*. Ed. Valerie Eliot. London: Faber, 1971.

Acknowledgements

The author gratefully acknowledges permission to reprint extracts from the following:

Ezra Pound, *COLLECTED SHORTER POEMS*, London: Faber, 1968 (US title PERSONAE). Copyright © 1926 by the Ezra Pound Literary Property Trust. All rights reserved.

Ezra Pound, *COLLECTED EARLY POEMS*, edited by Michael King, London: Faber, 1977. Copyright © 1926, 1935, 1954, 1965, 1967, 1971, 1976 by the Ezra Pound Literary Property Trust.

Ezra Pound, *THE CANTOS OF EZRA POUND*, New York: New Directions, 1970. Copyright © 1934, 1937, 1940, 1948, 1956, 1959, 1962, 1963, 1968, 1972 by the Ezra Pound Literary Property Trust.

Reprinted by permission of Faber and Faber Ltd, London and New Directions Publishing Corporation, New York.

Excerpts from "The Death of Saint Narcissus" and "The Hollow Men" from *POEMS WRITTEN IN EARLY YOUTH*, by T. S. Eliot, Faber: London, 1967, Farrar Straus, 1967. Copyright © 1967 by Valerie Eliot. Reprinted by permission of Faber and Faber Ltd., London and Farrar Straus and Giroux, Inc., New York.

Extracts from Unpublished Material, by T. S. Eliot. Reprinted by permission of Mrs. Valerie Eliot and Faber and Faber Ltd., London © Valerie Eliot, 1987.

Extracts from *COLLECTED POEMS, 1909–1962*, by T. S. Eliot, London: Faber, 1963. Copyright 1935, 1936 by Harcourt Brace Jovanovich, Inc. Copyright © 1964 by T. S. Eliot. Reprinted by permission of the publishers.

From "Burnt Norton", "East Coker", "Little Gidding" and "The Dry Salvages", in *FOUR QUARTETS* by T. S. Eliot, London: Faber, 1944, Harcourt Brace, 1943. Copyright 1943 by T. S. Eliot, renewed 1971 by Esme Valerie Eliot. Reprinted by permission of the publishers.

From *SELECTED ESSAYS* by T. S. Eliot, London: Faber, 1932, Third Edition, 1975. Copyright 1950 by Harcourt Brace Jovanovich, Inc. Renewed 1978 by Esme Valerie Eliot. Reprinted by permission of the publishers.

From *THE FAMILY REUNION*, London: Faber, 1939, Harcourt Brace, 1939. Copyright 1939 by T. S. Eliot, renewed 1967 by Esme Valerie Eliot. Reprinted by permission of the publishers.

INTRODUCTION

Ego Scriptor

As a lone ant from a broken ant-hill
From the wreckage of Europe, ego scriptor.

Ezra Pound, Canto LXXVI 458

Ego scriptor: I, the writer. This dictum flouts the ethic of impersonality, for it denies that artists should efface themselves behind their work. Rather, Pound asserts that he alone, in the wreckage of Europe, can salvage his identity through writing. On a closer look, however, his bravado begins to falter. For one thing, he is imprisoned in a cage at Pisa, a traitor to his "half-savage country", the United States: and it is from this American detention camp that he surveys the ruins of the West. Moreover, this nugget of self-certainty floats in the detritus of the *Pisan Cantos*, forsaken and incarcerated in non sequiturs. By using Latin to declare himself, Pound vaunts his credentials as a European (a moment later, he scorns the barbarians in Greek), and he resurrects his selfhood with the ancients. Yet a mask intervenes at the very moment of his self-creation, together with a touch of Babel. I write, therefore I am: but I write in the language of another, a dead language which my formic voice can scarcely animate.

In a nearby fragment, Pound hints that the writer is marooned in language, rather than authenticated by his verse:

a sinistra la Torre
seen through a pair of breeches. (LXXIV 431)[1]

Here, all that remains of the ant and his ego is the passive verb "seen", signifying a perspective rather than a subject, the narrow limits of a point of view. The legs of a guard become the window to the world, hinting that knowledge is enframed by power, and the observer trapped in the very systems that he scrutinises. Is it Pound, here, who is looking at the tower, or have the tower and the forked sentry fastened their panoptic gaze on *him*? The syntax cuts both ways: "seen through a pair of breeches", Europe and its scriptor disassemble one another. In the *Pisan Cantos*, the poem itself becomes a cage, for the poet has immured himself into his writing and the histories he demolishes as he records. The writer here is *written*, scripted in the text he writes, unable either to possess or to escape his personality.

Ego Absconditus

T. S. Eliot's theory of poetic impersonality has baffled many of his readers, and it even irked its own inventor. He first announced the doctrine in 1919, in the essay "Tradition and the Individual Talent" (a title Pound no doubt would have considered "possumish".) Yet the bolder slogans of the times, like "vorticism", have receded into curiosities, the dinosaurs of literary evolution; whereas the doctrine of impersonality still perplexes and unnerves interpreters. Philip Le Brun, for instance, remonstrates that "Eliot cannot possibly mean what he seems to mean by his theory of artistic impersonality."[2] Similarly, Kristian Smidt dismisses the poetics of impersonality as "a phantom and an illusion."[3] According to F. R. Leavis, Eliot's doctrine is a "wholly arbitrary dictum", whose "falsity and gratuitousness . . . are surely plain enough." "Tradition and the Individual Talent" seems to him contrived to elicit "awed confusion" rather than to justify its terms.[4]

The difficulty is that Eliot and Pound both advocate impersonality (though Eliot more tenaciously than Pound), yet both resist its implications, too. Their theory diverges from their practice, but the theory also contradicts itself: and they often smuggle personality back into their poetics in the very terms they use to cast it out. Eliot, for instance, insists that poetry originates in personal emotion, implying that the author's subjectivity pervades the text, yet at the same time he deplores this intervention. Pound, on the other hand, argues that poetry should be as objective as science: yet like many scientists he fails to see how deeply the subject is entoiled in the object he observes. As poets, both efface themselves through masks, personae, and ventriloquy, and the polylogue within their texts impugns the self's domain. As critics, both suspect that writing is an act of self-estrangement—an agon with the other, the unconscious, and the dead—yet neither is willing to dethrone the author without salvaging a good deal of his former privilege. Although they hesitate about the poet's role, grudging to relinquish his centrality, they both admit with Yeats that the living person differs from the writing self, and differs radically from the personality composed upon the page. A poet, says Yeats, "never speaks directly": "he is never the bundle of accident and incoherence that sits down to breakfast; he has been reborn as an idea, something intended, complete." But Yeats also argues that the poet "writes always of his personal life", so that the poem still originates in the experiencing subject, "completing" rather than dislodging him.[5] This subterfuge is typical of Eliot and Pound's poetics too. In spite of these inconsistencies, however, the notion of impersonality is crucial to modernist aesthetics, and it is more valuable to trace the logic of its contradictions than to flounder "in the hope of straightening things out."[6] Pound warns in *The Cantos* that "definition can not be shut down under a box lid" (LXXVIII 479): and the meaning of impersonality lies in the very struggle of its own enunciation.

That struggle, however, did not begin with modernism. Eliot and Pound deployed the doctrine in their campaign against Romanticism, but it is probable that they derived it from the very poets they attacked. The Romantic notion of inspiration, for example, implies that the poet is the instrument of forces which transcend his personality. Another precedent is Keats's view that the poet has "no identity", but is continually "filling some other Body"—beyond the confines of his private self.[7] Many critics would argue that modernism as a whole repressed Romanticism rather than transcending it.[8] Nonetheless, Eliot and Pound had urgent reasons for burying their antecedents even if they never fully exorcised their ghosts. Eliot, for instance, argues that Romantic poets were so engrossed in making themselves *present* in their verse that they neglected the lessons of the *past*. Romanticism preached originality, exuberance and novelty where Classicism had demanded order, discipline and canonicity. And where Romanticism stressed the relativity of moral and aesthetic values, Classicism insisted on impersonal authority in both domains. For Pound as for Eliot, the only antidote to the "slither" of Romantic individualism was a fierce renunciation of the self.

Both poets, however, are more eager to divulge what impersonality is not than what it is. Does it mean decorum, reticence, and self-restraint? Does it imply concealment or extinction of the self? Or does it mean the poet should transcend his time and place, aspiring to universal vision? These are just a few of the confusing ways that Pound and Eliot manipulate the term. In every case, however, the writer has the power to *decide* to overcome himself. But there is a darker innuendo in the theory—that poetry is necessarily impersonal, because the act of writing is impelled by forces which elude the author's consciousness. Poetry writes itself—and the poet is a mere amanuensis, whether his dictation comes from God, the unconscious, the tradition, or the dead. Besides, he must contend with language, and mediate his private self through public words, however supple and intimate his form. In this sense the poem depersonalises the poet rather than confirming his identity. At its most radical, Eliot claims, impersonality poses a threat to the "substantial unity of the soul" (*SE* 19). This hyperbole, however, typifies the slippage of his terms: for in this case "personality" denotes the theological soul, but in other cases it refers to the philosophical subject, psychological consciousness, legal individual, or grammatical first person, depending on the pressures of the argument. My book explores the way these meanings implicate each other, rather than imposing boundaries that Eliot and Pound preferred to blur.

Why did impersonality emerge as a doctrine when it did,

and why did it become a watchword for the modernists? One reason was that it served to screen the poet from the prying forms of criticism which accompanied the rise of popular psychology. Since the 1880s, readers had begun to search the text for the confessions of the author rather than the truths of the external world. As Allon White has pointed out, "There was a direct threat in this form of attention": and poets grew furtive to defend themselves against their readers' scrutiny.[9] If any indiscretions crept into their verse they could always disown them as "impersonal". Eliot once told John Hayward that he had "personal reasons" for asserting his impersonality, and this probably means that he was able to confess more freely if he disavowed those confessions as his own.[10] However, this coyness does not explain why his polemic for impersonality became so urgent, so vociferous. The reason is primarily political: for the doctrine emerged as the equivalent in art to a crusade against Romantic individualism in society. It was T. E. Hulme who imported this crusade to England from the reactionary *philosophes* of L'Action française: "la tendance fortement antiromantique et le classicisme de l'Action française", in the words of its spokesman Pierre Lasserre.[11] In "A Tory Philosophy", Hulme argues that the classical spirit "shows itself in the belief that there are certain rules which one must obey. . . . The idea of a personal inspiration jumping all complete from nature . . . is ridiculous to it."[12] In other words, the classical poet must obey the rules established from without rather than the impulses suggested from within. L'Action française and its official journal were dedicated to the restoration of the monarchy, and they argued that political reform entailed a unilateral purgation of the intellect. Later, Eliot and Pound also found it empowering to operate on this extended front, and to explore the interpenetration of cultural domains. In their work, the banner of impersonality unites the realms of poetry, aesthetics, philosophy and politics, and each instils the others with a borrowed vehemence.

Humanist critics resist the theory of impersonality because they sense the anti-liberalism which inspired it. But Marxist critics have renewed hostilities against the author, closely followed by post-structuralists. Both these latter movements are opposed to liberalism, too, but they are even more opposed to Pound and Eliot's authoritarian alternatives. They construe the literary text as a democracy, governed equally by reader and by writer, or by the language which confers these offices upon them both. Roland Barthes, for instance, declares the author dead, but he announces the birth of the reader in his stead, who inherits all the old prerogatives. On the other hand, Michel Foucault believes that the author has only recently been born, however phantasmal his existence. A parvenu in history, he is a figment of the law of copyright.[13] Similarly, semiotics subordinates the author to his language, as if he were concocted by the signifiers he manipulates. Marxism subordinates him to his history and to the institutions which engineer his subjectivity. Psychoanalysis subjects him to his own libido, to the wishes he reveals but cannot know.

Strangely enough, these critiques have only brought the author more into the limelight, where he obstinately fails to vanish into history, discourse, institution, or desire, in spite of all epistemological assaults. In fact, he thrives on the chastisement. And the very disciplines which undermine the self are forever searching for the secret of its animation. Despite their anti-humanism, for example, Althusserians in Britain have been puzzling for many years about the "constitution of the subject": as if to rescue subjectivity from the excesses of their own critique. In *After Strange Gods*, Eliot defines this kind of double-think as "blasphemy". "No one can possibly blaspheme", he says, "unless he profoundly believes in that which he profanes" (*ASG* 52). A double negative, blasphemy denies its own denials. In this case, the repudiation of the personality revives its power, together with the metaphysics which enshrines it. "Chase away subjectivity, it returns at a gallop", Georges Poulet remarks.[14] However, what returns is never quite the same as what was jettisoned.

Eliot's criticism dramatises these duplicities. In his Introduction to Valéry's *Le Serpent*, for instance, he scolds the critics for snooping into authors' personalities, rather than the authors for exposing them to view. "To English amateurs", he complains, "inclined to dismiss poetry which appears reticent, and to peer lasciviously between the lines for biographical confession, such an activity [as Mallarmé's] may seem no other than a *jeu de quilles* . . .". Be this as it may, "To reduce one's disorderly and mostly silly personality to . . . a *jeu de quilles* would be to do a most excellent thing . . .".[15] Here Eliot reduces impersonality into a question of decorum rather than a challenge to the very notion of the self, as he asserts in "Tradition and the Individual Talent" (*SE* 19). The starting-point of poetry remains the poet's personality, however stringently he chooses to "reduce" it. He wills his own invisibility. There is no suggestion here, as there is in Mallarmé, that the creative process necessarily undoes the self.[16] Instead, the poet now resembles God in nature, untouched by the energies he has unleashed: as Joyce says, the artist "remains within or behind or beyond or above his handiwork, invisible, refined out of existence, paring his fingernails."[17] Furthermore, Eliot implies that the poet's reticence actually safeguards his identity, as if impersonality were the formaldehyde that preserves the self against dispersion through "effusion". "We forget", Eliot complains, "that Browning and Shelley and Byron, for all their effervescence, give us less of themselves than do Turgenev or Flaubert."[18] Because Romantic poets give themselves away, their personalities volatilise and effervesce, while a classical "reserve" defends the self from such expenditure. Surreptitiously, this economy empowers the very subject that it promised to disarm.

Pound's poetics also demonstrate this circularity. Although he aspires to impersonality as the acme of his craft, he sometimes hints that it is poetry's most intimate deficiency. His article on "Vorticism" of 1914 embraces both positions:

> In the "search for oneself," in the search for "sincere self-expression," one gropes, one finds some seeming verity. One says "I am" this, that, or the other, and with the words scarcely uttered one ceases to be that thing.
>
> I began this search for the real in a book called *Personae*, casting off, as it were, complete masks of the self in each poem. I continued in a long series of translations, which were but more elaborate masks.
>
> Secondly I made poems like "The Return," which is an objective

> reality and has a complicated sort of significance. . . . Thirdly, I have written "Heather," which represents a state of consciousness, or "implies," or "implicates" it. . . .
>
> These two latter sorts of poems are impersonal. . . .[19]

Here Pound implies that every moment transfigures personality. Thus the self has vanished by the time that it is named, and hundred new identities have risen and fallen in its place. Elsewhere, however, he rejects this notion of the self as a "morass of Berkeleyan-Bergsonian subjectivo-fluxivity."[20] In this passage, too, he soon abandons the pursuit of self. Having rejected his personae and translations as more or less elaborate masks, Pound asserts that "The Return" and "Heather" are "impersonal". Within a few paragraphs, the search for self has turned into an odyssey to anonymity.

Both Eliot and Pound demote the self in favour of tradition, which they insinuate is on the wane. They may be right: for modernism fights its battles over subjectivity because it has deprived itself of almost any other ground. György Lukács, for example, complains that modernism focusses exclusively upon the self, denuding personality of every social and historical appurtenance.[21] And the more the text revolves around the self, the more fragmentary that self appears. Personality is reduced to the sheer instance of enunciation, as in Beckett's play *Not I*, where the only speaker is a disembodied Mouth babbling wildly in the darkness. When self is most itself, least lumbered with otherness, it paradoxically grows other to itself: "not I".

Eliot once described *The Cantos* as a "reticent autobiography", and this formula applies to much of his own poetry, particularly to *The Waste Land* or the *Four Quartets*.[22] All these texts are "personal" in form, for they concentrate upon the poet's consciousness. At the same time, however, they disguise that consciousness in masks and taciturnities. In this sense they undermine both self and selflessness. For example, the duration of *The Cantos* grew identical to Pound's, so that the text could only terminate when *he* did; and he pushed its inception back, as well, until it almost coincided with his own beginnings.[23] As Eliot writes, "*The Cantos* . . . are wholly himself . . .".[24] Yet the poem broods upon the self only to conspire in its ruin: "my errors and wrecks lie about me" (CXVI 795). Poetry becomes the work of mourning for the author's missed appointment with himself. In the same way, Eliot concedes that every poem is an "epitaph", an obituary to the consciousness in which it was conceived (*LG* V 12). The very instrument of self-discovery turns out to be the wedge that severs self from self.

A.E.I.O.U.

In *Ulysses*, Stephen Dedalus wonders whether he still owes George Russell (whose mystic name was AE) the pound he borrowed from him five months previously. "Wait", he thinks. "Five months. Molecules all change. I am other I now. Other I got pound." Since the body alters every moment, weaving and unweaving its own substance, there is no assurance that the I that borrows is the I that owes. In a world without history, all debts would be cancelled. But Stephen continues:

> But I, entelechy, form of forms, am I by memory because under ever-changing forms.
> I that sinned and prayed and fasted.
> A child Conmee saved from pandies.
> I, I and I. I.
> A.E.I.O.U. (*U* 189–90).

If I am I by memory, personal identity depends upon the continuity of time, binding what I might become to what I have already ceased to be. In Stephen's formula, the self can never be a single I, for personality unfolds in time; but memory inserts a comma in between the I that was and the I that is, rather than a full stop and annihilation. History, Stephen finds, is rather an expensive luxury—"A.E.I.O.U." But he prefers to be indebted than unselved.

Eliot and Pound concur with Joyce that personal identity depends upon the possibility of history; for only if one is tomorrow what one was a day ago can one claim to have and be a self. This is crucial, for the definition of *im*personality depends upon the nature of the self to be dethroned. Now Wyndham Lewis asserted that Eliot, Pound, Joyce, Stein, and most of the other writers of the avant-garde were bewitched by the popular philosophy of time. He blamed Henri Bergson, its inventor, for the way that they equivocate about the self. Bergson devised his theory of duration to prove the continuity of personality: for he believed that time is cumulative rather than linear, and that the present is "swollen" with the past. Like Stephen, Bergson attributes personal identity to memory; but, in his philosophy, the I that was interpenetrates the I that is without the slightest gap or punctuation. He denounces the linear idea of temporality as a "bastard concept", engendered by confusing space with time.[25] This mistake has blinded Western thought to personality: for its philosophers have either given up the subject in despair, or rescued it posthumously through the apotheosis of the "soul". Whether they idealise or deny the self, they all treat time as a trajectory of points in space, discrete, deprived of rhythm, shot with gaps. According to Bergson, personality unrolls continuously like a wave; but space dismembers consciousness into a "Series/Of intermittencies"—to use Pound's phrase.[26] In temporal terms, each existence has its own rhythm, its unique *durée*; but space reduces time into a common currency, by measuring it out in calendars or clocks or coffee-spoons.

In *Time and Western Man*, Lewis sneers at this philosophy of time because it does away with permanent, immortal values to celebrate the fugitive sensations of the inner world. All solid, spatial, and objective truths disintegrate into a solipistic flux. In spite of Bergson's fetish for uniqueness, the distinction between self and other disappears, and for this reason Lewis complains that the "time-book must always be obsessed with the personality of the author', whatever "superficial doctrine" of impersonality he holds (*TWM* 271). However, the same logic that glorifies the self condemns it to disband among its yesterdays. Thus "you are a *history*", Lewis mocks: "there must be no Present for you" (*TWM* 181). While Bergson merges self and world into an oceanic flux, Lewis insists that personality depends on fixity (*TWM* 192):

> although it is true that a pig would be a strange pig who dreamt himself a cat, or a cat that allowed the psychology of the horse to overpower it, and so forgot it was a cat, for this life, at least, a man still is the most detached and eclectic of creatures. But if his life is centred upon some deep-seated instinct or some faculty, he will find a natural exclusiveness necessary to proper functioning. For our only terra firma in a boiling and shifting world is, after all, our "self." That must cohere for us to be capable at all of behaving in any way but as mirror-images of alien realities, or as the most helpless and lowest organisms, as worms or as sponges. . . . when it comes to the pinch, I will side and identify myself with the powerfullest Me. . . . (*TWM* 5–6)

It was this pinch which Bergson thought essential to avoid.

This is not the place to dispute the coherence of Lewis's critique, nor to point out that his own aesthetic values often chime with those that he derides: in particular, his unconfessed yet unreformed allegiance to personality. However, *Time and Western Man* does take its culture's mental temperature, as it were: a culture in which Bergson's influence was as pervasive as Sartre's in the 1950s, and even more than Derrida's today. As Hulme puts it in 1911:

> There have been stirring times lately for those peculiar people amongst us who take an interest in metaphysics. We have not been able to buy even a sporting evening paper without finding in it an account of a certain famous philosopher. . . . One began to imagine that one would someday see the newsboys running along the street with the flaring placards, "Secret of the universe discovered: special interview. . . .[27]

In 1913, the time-philosophy was still notorious enough for Eliot to quip: "The landscape is decorated with Bergsonians in various degrees of recovery from intellect."[28] His own access to Bergson was more direct than Pound's, since he attended his lectures on personality in Paris in 1910–11 and underwent a "temporary conversion" to his thinking.[29] The first chapter of this book analyses these lectures through Eliot's own records and proceeds to trace his disillusionment with Bergsonism: for his exasperation with the time-philosophy was crucial to the theory of impersonality.[30] Part of that irritation had to do with Bergson's voguishness, and it is significant that he defected from Bergson to F. H. Bradley, the most cloistered and unpublic of philosophers. As for Pound, he rejected Bergson much as he repudiated

Nietzsche, because he was disgusted with the "clatter" that surrounded them.[31] In the Anglo-Saxon world, fashion is the kiss of death to a philosophy: it was to take Nietzsche half a century to recover from his popularity, and Sartre has only recently become passé enough to be respectable. However, it is not only arrogant but impossible to sweep aside the modes of thought which dominate one's time and to remain untainted by its "episteme". By arguing that Eliot did not erase all traces of his contact with the time-philosophy, I do not mean that Bergson had greater influence upon his thought than other thinkers he more readily acknowledged, like Bradley, William James, Russell, Moore or Husserl. My point is rather that the doctrine of impersonality was launched specifically as an attack on Bergsonism, and that its context is crucial to its form.

Goethe once said that "There is nothing to which one is more severe than the errors that one has just abandoned."[32] Because Eliot and Pound opposed impersonality to their own rejected Bergsonism, the doctrine remains in an uncanny intimacy with the values they intended to dislodge. Donald Davie argues that modern criticism became Bergsonian through Hulme, who had imported his philosophy to the Poets' Club long before importing its detractors.[33] It is here that Pound would have imbibed its values, which were individualist, anti-traditional, expressive, and intuitive, as opposed to the authoritarian beliefs that soon supplanted them. Pound was still enraptured with Bergsonian values in 1914 when he changed the name of *The New Freewoman* to *The Egoist*, in homage to "the individualist principle in every department of life."[34] It was the ideologues of L'Action française who inspired Hulme's rejection of Bergson, and Pound was soon to follow suit. Lasserre attacked the time-philosophy for three related reasons: in the first place, Bergson encouraged individualism, and he did so by falsifying time, for instead of recognising that the past is the museum of man's errors, he insisted on the possibility of change. Finally, Bergson was a Jew, which to Lasserre's mind accounted for his subjectivism and made his popularity particularly pernicious.[35]

Michael H. Levenson's *Genealogy of Modernism* traces

these antecedents so exhaustively that there is little point in recapitulating his research. He argues persuasively that "modernism was individualist before it was anti-individualist, anti-traditional before it was traditional, inclined to anarchism before it was inclined to authoritarianism."[36] In other words, modernism came into being through its own repudiation of itself. But Levenson is more concerned to show how the modernists forgot their history than to show how that history remembered them. For the past that modernism was so eager to obliterate deranges its precepts from within. Often Pound and Eliot reject the terms without relinquishing the structure of their trashed illusions. And it is this structure that my book explores, as opposed to any dubious economy of influence: a structure of intransigent exclusions, vexed by the return of the repressed. In particular, the opposition between time and space resurfaces in Eliot and Pound, and it engenders many others of its kind, so that their work unfolds as a contagion of antitheses. Like Bergson, they honour time with metaphors of speech, denouncing space with metaphors of writing. Jacques Derrida has used this particular opposition to disclose the "violent hierarchies" which structure Western thought, exalting speech over writing as presence over absence, mind over matter, inside over outside, self over other. According to Derrida, speech has been preferred to writing because the spoken word guarantees the presence of the speaker to the interlocutor. In this way, it nurtures the delusion that communication can occur without adulteration, loss, delay. Writing threatens this immediacy, because it simulates speech, but disappropriates the subject of his words. It *distances* the writer from the reader, *defers* his meaning, and betrays the *difference* between himself, his intentions, and his words. In this sense, writing *is* space (or "spacing", in Derrida's neologism), for it has come to represent the fierce intrusion of extension into speech, in the form of difference, deferral, distance, dissimulation, death.

Derrida traces these superstitions back to Plato, so Bergson is a latecomer in this dynasty. But almost any modern philosophical idea could boast this pedigree. The idea of impersonality, for instance, finds a spot in *The Republic*, and every age of criticism has rediscovered it in one form or another.[37] But it is more revealing to explore the differences which constitute the history of a thought than to dispatch it to its ancestors. The meaning of an idea depends upon the way it filters through the ethos of the era. For instance, Eliot condemns the time-philosophy because it smacks of liberal individualism. But Lewis thinks it nurtures the herd-instinct and could munition a totalitarian regime. Similarly, the theory of impersonality resembles the critique of authorship today, yet the former was the doctrine of the right, the latter of the left. For Eliot, impersonality implied a reinstatement of traditional authority; for Barthes, the deconstruction of authority *per se*.

It is important, therefore, to examine the new ways that Pound and Eliot constellate the old ideas of time and space, speech and writing, personality and impersonality. For it is the form of their enunciation, rather than their abstract sense, that gives these ideas their vitality. Lewis originally called *Time and Western Man* "The Politics of the Personality", but either title would apply, because the questions of the self and temporality are inextricable.[38] My book modifies the earlier title to hint that Eliot and Pound implicate the politics of time in their poetics of impersonality. In fact, the idea of impersonality leads a double or "diphasic" life in their aesthetics.[39] Both writers had formulated the idea by the second decade of the century, but it is in the 1930s, and particularly in 1933, that they explicitate its politics. Eliot, for instance, comes to see the cult of author-worship as the latest of the golden calves engendered by the "heresy" of liberalism. In an unconscious parody of Marxist explanation, Pound blames heresy on economic factors, specifically on the growth of usury. But his conclusions are similar to Eliot's: that modern culture has succumbed to a relentless drive to counterfeit its racial heritage. Writing, space, and personality connive with heresy to stifle the values that they simulate, divesting speech, tradition and community of all authority. The theory of impersonality is one of the main strategies these poets use to preach a "revolution" which would turn the world full circle back to speech and time. In fact, they use the same "logocentric" weapons to attack personality that

Bergson uses to defend it, for they share his dread of writing and commit themselves with growing urgency to a return to speech. Both champion an oral culture, in order to restore hegemony and to dispel the *difference* that they call "personality".

This book gives greater weight to Eliot because he broached the theory of impersonality, and he defended it more systematically than Pound. After an introduction to Bergson, the first chapter analyses Eliot's formulations of impersonality, and shows how he conscripts the doctrine into his radical conservatism in 1933. The second, third, and fourth chapters consist of readings of his poems, examining the ways that they compose and discompose the self. It is impossible to say precisely how "impersonal" these poems are, for the more the poet tries to hide himself the more he seems to give himself away. In later life, for instance, Eliot looks back upon *The Waste Land* as a "personal . . . grouse against life . . . a piece of rhythmical grumbling."[40] At the same time, however, this poem violates the very notion of a private self, for its speaker is invaded by the dead, hypnotically repeating the voices of the past. Caught in an infinite quotation, the "I" is exposed as a grammatical position, rather than the proof of the presence of the author. That Eliot was feeling gloomy when he wrote the poem tells us something about *him*, but very little of the forms of subjectivity that he composed.

To explore these forms, it is fruitful to combine a historical perspective with the kind of critical suspicion that one learns from Freud. But rather than imposing Freud's ideas on Pound and Eliot's, or treating the Standard Edition as a canonical text, I have tried to show how poetry and psychoanalysis disclose the strangeness of each other. Whereas psychoanalytic critics usually cast the poem as the patient, self-blinded by its own reticences, this book urges that the poem may interpret its interpreter. The issue here is essentially one of translation: for traditionally criticism redescribes the text in other terms, be they psychoanalytic, moral or historical, assuming that its core of sense remains inviolable. Recent critics have attacked this view, insisting that meaning is a practice rather than an essence, and that the text's significance inheres in the language which expresses it. It is to defend this view that I allow the poems themselves to provide the idiom of their interpretation, complying with the mimicry which they solicit by redeploying their texture and their metaphors.

The structure of the early chapters of this book reflects disparities between the prose and poetry of Eliot. In Pound, however, it is impossible to keep the two apart. As he tells Louis Zukofsky in an unpublished letter, "My poetry and my econ/are NOT separate or opposed. essential unity."[41] His whole opus subverts the distinction between interpretation and creation: and in "Date Line" he asserts that poetry itself is just the highest form of criticism (*LE* 75). Bearing this in mind, the last two chapters of this book explore his poetry, politics and criticism in conjunction, to detect their mutual encroachments. Chapter Five follows the vicissitudes of his early theories of impersonality; but it also analyses his early lyrics and "Hugh Selwyn Mauberley", to see how they undo the selves that they contrive. The sixth chapter explores the personality that Pound constructed in *The Cantos*, tracing the aesthetic, economic and metaphysical assumptions that colluded in its tragic form. This poem shows that Pound could not escape his subjectivity, for he leaves his mark upon the text in the form of an unconscious autograph. In fact, his presence in the poem compares to Bloom's in *Ulysses*, whose name embarks upon an odyssey through puns, misprints, anagrams and floral synonyms. Another analogy may be found in Jung's amusing and uncanny observation that Freud, whose name means "joy", founds his theory in the pleasure principle; Jung, meaning young, in the doctrine of rejuvenation; Adler, meaning "eagle," in the will to power. Jung proceeds to mystify this insight, but there is nothing really esoteric in the autobiographical imperative (the "compulsion of the name", in Stekel's phrase) that shapes these theories, for it grounds them in their history and the materiality of words.[42] As we shall see, this compulsion informs Pound's theory too, for it is in his economics that he literally *makes his name*.[43] However, this self-inscription bears no relation to the unified transcendent consciousness that the nineteenth century had understood as "personality".

Instead, Pound shows that the author is a function of his signature, produced within a certain moment, medium, milieu. In the end, his work insinuates that "personality" is nothing but the mystified effect of the demonic insistence of the name.

Curiously, Stephen Dedalus makes a similar discovery in the midst of proving his identity through memory. For there is another plot embedded in his meditation which unravels in the antics of the words. *Thematically*, Stephen establishes his selfhood to his satisfaction. But *performatively* Joyce reduces personality to the instance of saying "I"—a "paper-*I*"—and then disseminates this letter through the alphabet.[44] Whether personal identity triumphs or collapses here depends upon the difference between speech and writing. Spoken, A.E.I.O.U. admits the "immense debtorship for a thing done", and reaffirms the self through history (*U* 199). Written, the I dissolves into the asemantic play of letters. In Eliot and Pound, speech and writing also come to signify the battle between self and self-oblivion. As much as they denounce personality, they dread its dissolution even more: and the very history that they shore against their ruins conspires in their disremembering.

Notes

1. The reference is to Dante's *Paradiso*, Canto 8, stanza 2. Because of his fascist broadcasts for Rome Radio, Pound was imprisoned in 1945 on a charge of treason at the U.S. Army Detention Training Centre (D.T.C.) near Pisa, where he drafted *The Pisan Cantos*. For about three weeks he was incarcerated in a cage measuring six by six and a half feet.
2. "T. S. Eliot and Henri Bergson", *Review of English Studies*, New Series 18 (1967), 282.
3. *Poetry and Belief in the Work of T. S. Eliot* (Oslo, 1949; repr. London: RKP, 1961), p. xii.
4. F. R. Leavis, "T. S. Eliot as Critic", in *Anna Karenina and Other Essays* (New York: Pantheon, 1952), pp. 180, 179.
5. Yeats, "A General Introduction for my Work" (1937), in *Essays and Introductions* (London: Macmillan, 1969), p. 509.
6. See Richard P. Blackmur, "In the Hope of Straightening Things Out", in *T. S. Eliot: A Collection of Critical Essays*, ed. Hugh Kenner (Englewood Cliffs, N.J.: Prentice-Hall, 1962), pp. 138–9.

7. Keats, Letter to Richard Woodhouse, 27 October 1818, in *Letters of John Keats*, ed. Robert Gittings (London: OUP, 1970), p. 157.
8. See George Bornstein, *Transformations of Romanticism in Yeats, Eliot, and Stevens* (Chicago and London: University of Chicago Press, 1976); C. K. Stead, *The New Poetic: Yeats to Eliot* (London: Hutchinson, 1964); Edward Lobb, *T. S. Eliot and the Romantic Critical Tradition* (London: RKP, 1981); Gregory S. Jay, *T. S. Eliot and the Poetics of Literary History* (Baton Rouge and London: Louisiana State University Press, 1983), pp. 5, 27.
9. See Allon White, *The Uses of Obscurity: The Fiction of Early Modernism* (London: RKP, 1981), pp. 46–7.
10. Letter to E. M. Forster, 1930; in E. M. Forster Collection, King's College, Cambridge.
11. Pierre Lasserre, "La philosophie de M. Bergson", *L'Action française*, Vol. 27, no. 246 (15 March 1911), p. 173.
12. T. E. Hulme, "A Tory Philosophy" (1912), in Alun R. Jones, *The Life and Opinions of T. E. Hulme* (London: Gollancz, 1960), p. 190.
13. Barthes, "The Death of the Author", in *Image—Music—Text*, trans. Stephen Heath (New York: Hill and Wang, 1977), pp. 142–8; Foucault, "What is an Author?" in *Language, Counter-Memory, Practice: Selected Essays and Interviews*, ed. D. Bouchard (Ithaca, N.Y.: Cornell University Press, 1980).
14. Quoted in David Carroll, *The Subject in Question: The Languages of Theory and the Strategies of Fiction* (Chicago and London: University of Chicago Press, 1982), p. 14.
15. Eliot, "A Brief Introduction to the Method of Paul Valéry", in *Le Serpent* by Paul Valéry, trans. Mark Wardle (London: R. Cobden-Sanderson, 1924), p. 12.
16. See, for instance, Mallarmé, *Oeuvres complètes*, ed. Henri Mondor and G. Jean-Aubry (Paris: Gallimard, 1945), p. 366: "L'oeuvre pure implique la disparition élocutoire du poète, qui cède l'initiative aux mots. . . ."
17. James Joyce, *A Portrait of the Artist as a Young Man* (1916; New York: Viking, 1970), p. 215. Notice that the word "within" suggests that the artist still inhabits his handiwork, incorporated rather than expunged.
18. *Le Serpent*, p. 12.
19. Ezra Pound, "Vorticism", *Fortnightly Review*, NS 96 (1914), 463–4; repr. *GB*, p. 85.
20. Pound, "Epstein, Belgion, and Meaning", *Criterion*, 9 (1930), 474.
21. György Lukács, *The Meaning of Contemporary Realism*, trans. Jack and Necke Mander (London: Merlin, 1963), pp. 20–7.
22. Eliot called *The Cantos* an "objective and reticent autobiography", in "The Method of Mr. Pound", *The Athenaeum* (24 October 1919), p. 1065; cited by Ronald Bush, *The Genesis of Ezra Pound's Cantos* (Princeton: Princeton University Press, 1976), p. 5.
23. In 1936 Pound claimed that *The Cantos* originated in a talk with Joseph Ibbotson, who was his teacher at Hamilton College from 1903: see Noel Stock, *The Life of Ezra Pound* (San Francisco: North Point Press,

1982), p. 19.
24. Eliot, Introduction to *Selected Poems of Ezra Pound* (London: Faber, 1928), p. 12.
25. Quoted by Stephen Kern in *The Culture of Time and Space, 1880–1918* (Cambridge Mass.: Harvard University Press, 1983), p. 45.
26. See Pound, *Hugh Selwyn Mauberley: Life and Contacts*, lines 375–6: *P* 213.
27. T. E. Hulme, "A Personal Impression of Bergson", first published in *The Saturday Westminster Gazette*, 18 November 1911; repr. in Jones, *The Life and Opinions of T. E. Hulme*, pp. 205–8.
28. Eliot, [The Relation between Politics and Metaphysics], MS, b.MS Am 1691 (130), p. 2: in Houghton Library, Harvard.
29. Quoted by Edward J. H. Greene, *T. S. Eliot et la France* (Paris: Boivin, 1951), p. 10. See also Eliot's "Lettre d'Angleterre [III]", trans. G. D'Hangest, *Nouvelle revue française*, 11 (1923), p. 260: "je peux témoigner de l'importante influence qu'ont eu sur mon developpement intellectuel *L'Avenir de l'intelligence* et *Belphégor* (non que je veuille classer ensemble Maurras et Benda), et de même, sans doute, à une certaine époque, *Matière et mémoire* . . .". The odder ensemble is Benda and Bergson, since Julien Benda spent most of his life attacking Bergson: e.g. Benda, *Une philosophie pathétique* (Paris: Cahiers de France, 1913), etc.
30. Notes on lectures of Henri Bergson, MS (Paris, 1910–11), b.MS Am 1691 (130), Houghton Library, Harvard: henceforth cited as Notes; Draft of a Paper on Bergson (1910–11) b.MS Am 1691 (132), Houghton: henceforth cited as Draft. Lyndall Gordon dates the Draft as 1913–14: see *Eliot's Early Years* (Oxford and New York: OUP, 1977), p. 41n.
31. See Pound, *Hugh Selwyn Mauberley: Life and Contacts*, line 319.
32. Quoted by Michael H. Levenson, *A Genealogy of Modernism: A Study of English Literary Doctrine 1908–1922* (Cambridge: Cambridge University Press, 1984), p. 91. The following paragraph is much indebted to Levenson's detailed and perceptive historical work.
33. Donald Davie, *Articulate Energy* (London: RKP, 1955), pp. 6, 13.
34. Pound and others, *The New Freewoman*, 1, no. 13 (15 December 1913), p. 244; quoted by Levenson, *A Genealogy of Modernism*, p. 71.
35. See Lasserre, "La philosophie de M. Bergson", pp. 178 and *passim*. In an ominous anticipation of the Nazis, Lasserre complains that the renovation of Church doctrine has fallen into the hands of the "juif Bergson" (p. 181). While Hulme introduced Lasserre to England and to Pound, Irving Babbitt transported his philosophy to Harvard where he taught the young T. S. Eliot in 1909–10: see Herbert Howarth, *Notes on Some Figures Behind T. S. Eliot* (Boston: Houghton Mifflin, 1964), pp. 127–35.
36. Levenson, *A Genealogy of Modernism*, p. 79.
37. See *The Republic*, Bk. III, in the *Collected Dialogues of Plato*, ed. Edith Hamilton and Huntingdon Cairns (Princeton: Princeton University Press, 1963), pp. 638–9.

38. Lewis wrote to Pound on 29 April 1925, that he was at work on "The Politics of the Personality": see *Pound/Lewis: The Letters of Ezra Pound and Wyndham Lewis*, ed. Timothy Materer (New York: New Directions, 1985), p. 145. See also Lewis's letter to Charles Whibley of 1925 in *Letters*, ed. W. K. Rose (London: Methuen, 1963), p. 155, where he explains that "The Politics of the Personality" "traces the systematic crushing of the Subject in favour of the propaganda of collectivism . . .".
39. I take the term "diphasic" from Freud: see *Three Essays on the Theory of Sexuality*, SE VII 200.
40. See *WL Fac*, p. 1.
41. Letter to Zukofsky, TS [March? April? 1935], Pound Archive, Beinecke.
42. Jung is actually paraphrasing Stekel's work on the "compulsion of the name": see Carl Jung, *Synchronicity: An Acausal Connecting Principle*, trans. R. F. C. Hull (1952; London: RKP, 1972), p. 15n.
43. Compare Derrida, *Spurs: Nietzche's Styles*, tr. Barbara Harlow (Chicago: Chicago University Press, 1979), p. 105: "Somewhere here, beyond the mythology of the signature, beyond the authorial theology, the biographical desire has been inscribed in the text. The mark which it has left behind, irreducible though it may be, is just as irreducibly plural."
44. See Roland Barthes, "From Work to Text", in *Image—Music—Text*, p. 161.

PART I

T. S. Eliot

CHAPTER I

The Loop in Time

A locus to loue, a term it t'embarass,
These twain are the twins that tick Homo Vulgaris.
Joyce, *Finnegans Wake*, p. 418, lines 24–5

After his first year as a graduate student in philosophy at Harvard, Eliot travelled to Paris to continue his studies at the Sorbonne. Here he attended Bergson's lectures on personality throughout the winter of 1910–11, and underwent what he later described as a temporary conversion to Bergsonism.[1] This conversion was indeed short-lived, and within a few months Eliot had rejected Bergson's "meretricious captivation" for the "melancholy grace" of Bradley.[2] Nonetheless, he transcribed the Paris lectures scrupulously, and when he returned to Harvard he drafted an attack against the time-philosophy, as if to finish off the exorcism.[3] This chapter uses these unpublished papers to examine Bergson's conception of the self and Eliot's growing disillusionment with it.

Dust in Sunlight and Memory in Corners

In his lectures, Bergson argues that philosophers since Zeno have misconstrued the self because they have confused duration with extension, treating mental states in spatial terms. In their thinking, consciousness becomes a mere mosaic, rather than an interpenetrative movement.[4] This category error leaves philosophers with two alternatives: empiricists like Hume dismiss the unity of personality as a delusion, while idealists conjure up the phantom of the soul to counteract its spatial fragmentation. Now, according to Eliot, Bergson strives to "occupy a middle ground" between these two positions (Draft 1).[5] On the one hand, he attempts to unify the self against the "thousand sordid images" which constituted personal identity for Hume. But he reproaches the idealists, too, because they mystify the self, withdrawing it from life and temporality. As Eliot notes on 20 January, "les conclusions de l'école empiristique sont toujours que le moi est inconnaissable." Idealists, on the other hand, can only "superposer ce qu'ils appellent une unité" (Notes 7). Although Kant also criticised both these positions, his "transcendental synthesis of apprehension" strikes Bergson as an empty, supererogatory unity.[6] Like the idealists he attacks, Kant preserves the supposition of the self only by abstracting it from time. As Eliot records, "son unité est au dehors, un *lien*, un *fil*, que nous surajoutons." It is, moreover, a "unité vide" (Notes 16). All these false unities and the false fissures that they strive to heal arise when space usurps the empery of time. Bergson insists that personality does not transcend experience, but finds its wholeness in the very midst of Hume's "poussière" (Notes 6).[7]

According to Eliot, Bergson began his lectures by criticising Hume's attack on personal identity in the *Treatise of Human Nature*.[8] Hume argues that the self is "nothing but a bundle or collection of different perceptions", and since these alter minute by minute, he derides the notion of a stable self. The mind is a "theatre" where each perception frets its hour, and impressions "pass, re-pass, glide away, in an infinite variety of postures and situations." Moreover, Hume warns that the "comparison of the theatre must not mislead us."

> They are the successive impressions only, that constitute the mind; nor have we the most distant notions of the place, where these scenes are represented, or of the materials, of which it is compos'd.[9]

In the Appendix to the *Treatise*, however, Hume "avoue sa

faiblesse", and admits he has neglected the "principle of connexion" binding these perceptions into the bundle that we call the self (Notes 3).[10] How does he end up this impasse? Bergson thinks that Hume went wrong when he assumed that all "perceptions are distinct": for this belief led him to discredit personality when he had really stumbled on the secret of its unity (Notes 3).[11] In Bergson's view, the flux of mental life is indivisible, and it is in the seamless flow from state to state that the unity of consciousness resides. As Eliot puts it in his Notes: "L'unité du moi c'est la continuité de la transition" (Notes 5). It is as if the intellect dreamt up discontinuity in a perverse impulse to negate *itself*.

It is the faculty of attention that Bergson blames for spatialising time. Like a camera, attention reifies the moment, reducing the continuum of time to broken "stills". It proceeds by spasms—"Efforts périodiques mais discontinus"—and each instant is enclosed in its own solitude, because attention, when it blinks, assumes a corresponding gap in time (Notes 23). Because Hume fastened his *attention* on the self, instead of trusting to his *intuition*, identity disintegrates before his gaze. But Hume is not alone in this mistake. According to Bergson, western thought in general treats consciousness as if it were a cinematic screen where moods defile in *montage* (Notes 7).[12] Neutral and homogeneous, time becomes the backdrop of the stage of life, rather than its living bioplasm. Bergson, on the contrary, insists that "La matière de la durée c'est la durée même." The duration of the snail, for instance, differs qualitatively from our own: "la durée de l'escargot est très différente de l'aspect que prend notre durée." Each existence has its own inimitable tempo. Real time—"c'est *les durées*"—for time consists of the unfolding of innumerable histories (Notes 24).

Behind these errors lie mixed metaphors, for language constantly confuses time with space. The very structure of the sentence separates the subject and the object from the *movement* which constitutes them both. Attention, in this respect, is grammar's henchman, for its pulsations interrupt the flux, chopping time into a series of adjacencies. "L'attention immobilise" (Notes 5). Bergson urges that mobility is *simpler* than stasis, time than space: "L'immobilité est . . . le composé, et le mouvement, le simple."[13] Zeno got things back to front when he transformed the arrow's fluid movement into a trajectory of instants, paralysed. Such dismemberments can only be conceived when space has infiltrated time.

Against this tradition, Bergson proposes a redemptive vision of the self. But he does not see his task as one of refutation, for he believes that a continuity of intuition moves the history of philosophy, and it is only language which conceals this truth. The *idea* of personality, for instance, existed among the Greeks, but they lacked the words to bring it to the light: "Les grecs n'avaient pas de termes pour la personnalité mais ils avaient approfondi la chose" (Notes 11). Just as personal identity achieves itself in the process of its own becoming, so the *idea* of personality endures through all the superficial detours of philosophy. Diversity, discontinuity, belong to the divisive kingdom of *expression*, rather than the unified reality of *thought*. "Little words that cut up the thought, dismember it", Lily Briscoe muses in *To the Lighthouse*: such is the way that language anatomises time.[14] As soon as we name a process, we arrest it: "en réalité, le nom et la définition sont comme des étiquettes collées sur quelque chose qui change . . .".[15] Meaning lies "au-dessus du mot et au-dessus de la phrase", eluding the rigidities of language: "le sens . . . est moins une chose pensée qu'un mouvement de pensée, et moins un mouvement qu'une direction."[16] To intuit this direction, it is necessary to abandon words as so many dead leaves floating on the surface of a pool ("feuilles mortes sur l'eau de l'étang").[17] Every word or symbol severs the *durée*: and it is in this crack that space extrudes, in its double violence of fragmentation and fixation. Indeed, Bergson's attitude to language corresponds so intimately to his view of space that it becomes impossible to tell if space is responsible for words or words for "spacing".[18]

When philosophers transform the mind into a theatre, it is as if extension had invaded psychic life.[19] It is not by chance, moreover, that this metaphor implicates space with *representation*: for Eliot points out in his unpublished paper on Bergson that "space intervenes" whenever time is represented, symbolised (Draft 5). Indeed, by condemning spatial time as a "temps symbolique", Bergson hints that the spatial and symbolic are inseparable evils (Notes 25). Real time resists all representation: but as soon as we stop *living* time to *represent* it, we let Gerontion's "windy spaces" in. For Bergson, words and symbols do not just stand for space but actually perform its mutilations, by introducing gaps and glaciations. He compares them to money, which transforms all things into commodities, regardless of their difference and particularity (Notes 25). In the same way, spatial time becomes the currency through which experience must pass, to be converted in the process into space's terms. The multitudinous rhythms of duration perish in this neutral "cash" of time.

It is important, moreover, that Bergson's images for representation are generally *visual*, whether they be the screen, the stage, the photograph, or the picture-frame. In all these metaphors, it is the *eye* that spatialises. The ear, that Eliot later calls the "murmuring shell of time", can reunite what vision has dissevered (*DS* III 25). In terms of language, Bergson exalts the spoken word over the dissections of the alphabet, for he believes that writing spatialises speech. In music, too, the written note perverts the temporal into the simultaneous: and a handful of arbitrary characters replaces the inimitable movement of the phrase. Space disfigures time in the same way: "comme la mélodie est symbolisée par les notes, les chiffres de musique. C'est une représentation de temps dans l'espace: c'est le temps espace; non pas le temps" (Notes 26). Bergson argues that the charm of poetry and music derives from the temporality of sound, while writing petrifies this rhythm. "The most living thought becomes frigid in the formula which expresses it. The word turns against the idea. The letter kills the spirit", he laments, an unaccustomed frequency of full stops disrupting the continuity of his own prose (*CE* 134). What the *durée* evolves, the letter devolves. Silently, relentlessly, the writing that is space converts all singularities into its own sweeping and indifferent terms.

Since it is in duration that the authentic personality is to be found, space necessarily belies the self. In "Prufrock", for example, the "eyes that fix you in a formulated phrase" fix you in space and fix you in language, and correspond to the paralyses of spatial time (56). Even in self-contemplation we are forced to represent ourselves, so that extension encroaches on our inner world. In another lecture course on "Personality" delivered at Edinburgh, Bergson says:

> the unity of our person (which appears to us the essential element of our personality) eludes us just when we think we grasp it. So long as we make no effort to perceive it, we feel it is there, but, as soon as our consciousness thinks that it beholds it, it is confronted with only an infinity of separate psychical states—a multiplicity. It therefore seems as if the unity of the person exists only so long as it is not perceived.[20]

Whenever we attempt to "grasp" or "apprehend" ourselves, the very words imply that we arrest our temporality. We can only really know the self through intuition, and when we pass from intuition to expression we have already compromised with space. Ultimately, the time-philosophy defines personality as the resistance to our own attempts to know it.

This account of time traps Bergson in a paradox, for even to have *written* it is to have made a pact with space. Moreover, the quantitative terms of space contaminate his rhetoric of temporality, and it is here that Eliot detects a flaw in his philosophy.[21]

To Keep Our Metaphysics Warm

Eliot repudiated Bergsonism with greater zeal than he had ever urged his creed, but he attacked it so relentlessly that it must have remained a powerful threat. In 1924 he urges Bradley's rigour against Bergson's voluptuosities; by 1928, he is equating the time-philosophy with the laxities of "Romanticism in literature" and "democracy in government".[22] However, he had broken with Bergson as early as 1915, when he praises Pound in an unpublished letter for resisting the temptation to "hitch up" Vorticism to Bergson's philosophy. Indeed, he scorns the notion of combining art and philosophy at all:

> I distrust and detest Aesthetics, when it cuts loose from the Object and vapours into the void, but you have not done that. The closer one keeps to the Artist's discussion of his techniques the better, I think. And the only kind of art worth talking about is the art one happens to like. There can be no contemplative or easy chair aesthetics, I think; only the aesthetics of the person who is about to do something.[23]

Later, Eliot was often to disclaim the philosophical dimension of his criticism ("I have no general theory of my own"), and to argue for a "workshop" rather than an easy chair aesthetics. Yet although such statements may reveal the *motives* of his thought they obfuscate its *content* (*UPUC* 143; *PP* 106). Philip Le Brun has argued that the time-philosophy haunts Eliot's aesthetic thought, and that Bergson is the victim of a cover-up.[24] However, it is more important that Eliot resisted him, for we are not concerned with influence but struggle.

The struggle begins in 1911, when Eliot drafted his critique of Bergsonism. The attempt to occupy a "middle ground between idealism and realism" strikes him as the "crux of the *affaire bergsonienne*" (Draft 1, 20). However, it is only in *Matière et mémoire* (1896) that Bergson reaches this position. In his first book, the *Essai sur les données immédiates de la connaissance* (1888), the distinction between time and space is absolute—and it is here that Eliot begins. In the *Essai*, Bergson insists that only matter is extended, while consciousness dwells in time, accumulating memory as it unfolds. It is in time, therefore, that the truer personality resides. But a degraded simulacrum of the self, the "moi sociale", participates in the determined realm of space, trapped in language and automatised like clockwork. According to Bergson, the "moi profond" alone enjoys the freedom of the world of time (*TFW* 128–39).

However, in *Matière et mémoire*, and later in *Creative Evolution*, he recants this hierarchy. He now denies that mind preceded matter, but he denies priority to matter too. Indeed, it is the very notion of priority that must be overhauled, the mistaken notion that "it is necessary to posit from all eternity either material multiplicity itself, or the act of creating this multiplicity, given in block in the divine essence." These are the realist and idealist views, respectively. Opposing both,

Bergson fuses mind and matter in the notion of an overarching movement: "Everything is obscure in the idea of creation if we think of *things* which are created and a *thing* which creates. . . . There are no things, there are only actions" (*CE* 254). Eliot describes this action as "Movement without a *that* which moves: *pure* movement"—and he sets out to prove its impossibility (Draft 11).

First, he objects that Bergson constantly resorts to spatial terms though he insists that consciousness is purely temporal. Thus his own rhetoric betrays him, despite his vigilance against the spatialising powers of the word. How can he make his case for time when he, too, speaks only Space? In fact, Bergson himself admits that he has not yet kicked the "habitude profondément enracinée" of translating time into the dialect of space.[25] Eliot argues that this "hesitation" between space and time vitiates his argument for the freedom of the *moi profond*: "in reality, the superficial [illeg.exc.] personality is just as *free* (or the reverse) as the more profond, and certainly much more rational" (Draft 9).

Bergson recognised this hesitation in himself, and rather than overcoming it he transformed his whole philosophy to accommodate it. In *Matière et mémoire*, the distance that excluded mind from matter closes in. Bergson now insists that matter has duration, too, and consciousness is tainted with extension. "What we are asked to regard as the fundamental self in D.I.", Eliot explains, turns out to be "the fundamental *world* in M&M" (Draft 10–11). Bergson abandons the Cartesian myth of unextended mind, and at the same time attributes memory to matter. For these proportions fluctuate according to a *movement* that encompasses them all. He now refers to time and space as "tension" and "extension", to stress that they differ only in degree. As he puts it in *Creative Evolution*: "Neither is space so foreign to our nature as we imagine, nor is matter as completely extended in space as our senses and intellect represent it."[26] It is this notion that Wyndham Lewis pillories in *Time and Western Man*:

> Chairs and tables, mountains and stars, are animated into a magnetic restlessness and sensitiveness, and exist on the same vital terms as

> men. . . . The *more* static, the more solid, the more fixed, the *more* unreal; as compared with the vivacious, hot, mercurial broth of an object. . . . If [a time-philosopher] could he would lead a revolt of the upholstery. . . . In this way we get rid of that embarrassing thing, the "mind," which gives us (compared to mere tables, chairs or even vegetables and dogs) a rather unfortunately aristocratic colour. Bearing "minds" about with us is all very well: but . . . would it not appear rather conceited, as swagger or swank, from the point of view of an observant tea-pot? (*TWM* 449, 453, 456, 458).

By undoing the antithesis of space and time, Bergson unsettles all his other oppositions. Language, which he had formerly assigned to the degraded realm of space, now contains a "residue" of time (*CE* 252). Speech is language in a state of "tension", while writing is the form words take in the last disintegrations of extension:

> When a poet reads me his verses, I can interest myself enough in him to enter into his thought, put myself in his feelings, live over and over again the simple state which he has broken into phrases and words. I sympathise then with his inspiration, I follow it with a continuous movement which is, like the inspiration itself, an undivided act. Now, I need only relax my attention, let go the tension that there is in me, for the sounds, hitherto swallowed up in the sense, to appear to me distinctly, one by one, in their materiality. . . . In proportion as I let myself go, the successive sounds will become more individualised; and as phrases were broken into words, so the words will scan in syllables which I shall perceive one after another. Let me go further still in the direction of dream: the letters themselves will become loose and seem to dance along, hand in hand, on some fantastic sheet of paper. . . . The further I pursue this quite negative direction of relaxation, the more extension and complexity I shall create . . . (*CE* 220).

As consciousness relaxes, the letters dance out of their words, and meaning diffuses into multiplicity. According to Bergson, personality swerves between the same extremes. For consciousness arrives only at the moments of the greatest tension, while extension dissipates the self in dream:

> The more we succeed in making ourselves conscious of our progress in pure duration, the more we feel the different parts of our being enter into each other, and our whole personality concentrate itself into a point, or rather a sharp edge, pressed against the future and cutting into it unceasingly. It is in this that life and action are free. But suppose we let ourselves go and, instead of acting, dream. At once the self is scattered;

> our past, which till then was gathered together into the indivisible impulsion it communicated to us, is broken up into a thousand recollections made external to one another. They give up interpenetrating in the degree that they become fixed. Our personality thus descends in the direction of space (*CE* 212).

Dissolving into memories, personality descends into a form of writing, and it must return from dream to speech before the fragments of its history reunite. Yet speech and writing, action and dream, no longer nullify each other, but coalesce into a cycle which encompasses them all.

This is where Eliot thinks that Bergson's middle ground breaks down. He argues that the time-philosophy has found a new way of restating an idealist and even absolutist argument that quantity is quality, space time, and matter mind—"from the point of view of eternity." This means that "the theory of durations, which promised to abolish the timeless and eternal, has only reinaugurated it in a new form." Bergson cannot brush eternity aside so easily: for Eliot, the *durée* is "simply not final" (Draft 10, 18, 22). In his opinion, Bergson fails to deduce consciousness from motion, and thus reduces the mind to "a matter of rhythm" (Draft 18). Despite his celebration of the self, Bergson has undermined the very ground of personal identity, a paradox that Lewis seized upon.

A Phalanstery of Selves

In the time-philosophy, "You become no longer one, but many", Lewis complains. "What you pay for the pantheistic immanent oneness of 'creative', 'evolutionary' substance, into which you are invited to merge, is that you become a phalanstery of selves" (*TWM* 175). He insists that separation is the secret of personal identity, whereas Bergson thinks that the self attains its principle only when its boundaries dissolve. Its essence lies in the one impulse, which, "passing through generations, links individuals to individuals, species with species, and makes the whole series of the living one immense wave flowing over matter . . ." (*CE* 263). The truth of life is the *élan vital*, which sluices through the definitions space cuts out of time. According to Lewis, this theory undermines the individual and elevates the herd, in spite of all the adulation Bergson heaps on personality. The more individualist you are in Bergson's sense, "the less 'individualist' you will be in the ordinary political sense" (*TWM* 25). As Bergson himself demands, "Who can tell where individuality begins and ends . . .?" (*CE* x). While the time-philosophy scorns divisions as figments of the spatialising mind, Lewis insists that separation is crucial to personality.

Lewis also ridicules Bergson's distrust of language: for if there were no words to capture the fugitive sensations of the self, personality would disappear into the silence of duration. But Bergson argues that each word estranges self from self, reducing all that is unique to personality to common terms. What we *think* belongs to space and to the language of the other, but what we *are* belongs to time. Lewis turns this notion upside-down, and asserts that all the crimes that Bergson blames on space should really be transferred to time. For example, Bergson denounces the "moi social" as a shadow of a self, an automaton in the bureaucracy of spatiality. Yet the *moi profond*, the truer self, is doomed to deliquesce into the flux. Similarly, Bergson offers unexampled liberty to personality; yet the other side of freedom is the bewildering liquidity in which the self must always differ from itself: "where you are is where you are not", as Eliot will later write (*EC* III 46).[27] What is more, Lewis argues that the time-mind reveals itself to be the "*time-denying* mind", because it does away with all chronology (*TWM* 24). The present and the past change places: it is the present which is always passing and the past which gnaws into the present, to borrow Bergson's striking metaphor.[28] Lewis remonstrates that "We have indeed *lost our Present*: in a Bergsonian attempt to crush all the Past into it, and too much of the Future at a time, as well" (*TWM* 238). In fact, the time-philosophy leaves personality few options, all of which oblige it to renounce itself. Either we enslave ourselves to space and language, which belie the volatile essence of our souls; or else we slump into the silence of the *durée* and thus become a "thoroughfare" for the *élan vital* (*CE* 135). Between these, personality becomes a "history", but a history without chronology, mixing memory and desire in "un présent qui meurt et se renaît à toute instant . . ." (Notes 24). Whichever path it takes, the self advances toward oblivion; and the very words which celebrate the personality attend—indeed, effect—its dissolution.

The Spectres Show Themselves

> When the loop in time comes—and it does not come for everybody—
> The hidden is revealed, and the spectres show themselves. . . .
>
> Eliot, *The Family Reunion*

"A man of ideas needs ideas, or pseudo-ideas, to fight against", Eliot writes, thinking of his feud with Bergsonism.[29] For he disputes the notion that an artist can succumb to influence without a struggle, any more than he can sweep aside his literary ancestry. Similarly, Harold Bloom has argued that "a poem is not writing but *rewriting*"; a poem is "a psychic battlefield", in which the poet wrestles with the dead for every trope he chooses—or refuses.[30] In "Tradition and the Individual Talent", Eliot argues that the voices of the past re-echo even in the writer's most distinctive idiom, and this principle extends to his own prose. It is in the theory of impersonality that his contest with the time-philosophy resumes.

Eliot first launched this theory in 1919, when he published "Tradition and the Individual Talent" in *The Egoist* (an odd arena for attacking egoism, but symptomatic of the doctrine's ambiguities).[31] He renewed the battle in 1933, conscripting his earlier aesthetics into the service of his radical conservatism. *The Use of Poetry and the Use of Criticism* came out in this year, and so did *After Strange Gods*, a work which he was later to repent, partly because it was his most intemperate assault on personality. Besides these published works, he lectured on "The Varieties of Metaphysical Poetry" at Johns Hopkins in January 1933, and in the spring he proceeded to Harvard to teach "English Literature from 1890 to the Present Day."[32] In an amusing letter, Pound warns William Carlos Williams of Eliot's imminent return to native shores:

> Dear Walruss:
> Murry Xmas.
> I read that Possum is to BBBB Poesy Prof. at Hawvud.
> ha haw haw vud
> An a great joke on ole Eliza Schelling and Frozen mug Penniman/
> haw hawhawVUD.
> I trust you will be nice to our sad sad friend Mr Eliot an' help him to bear his cross i na Jheezus = like manner.
> At any rate a great step fer murkn kulchuh, from the Storks and Ausslanders.
> I think you might bury yr/ differences and send him a nice little note of welcome (especially as he aint yet got there).
> A decent; discriminating retroactive academicism is something solider to rebel AGAINST tha the mush of Canby's and incertitudes of Ausslanders.[33]

It is intriguing that Eliot suppressed all these works, though some more rigorously than others. He did "not repudiate" "Tradition and the Individual Talent", but in 1964 he regrets that the essay has become the inevitable choice of his anthologists. He disclaims it as a "product of immaturity", "perhaps the most juvenile" of his works.[34] Moreover, he refused to reprint *After Strange Gods*, embarrassed by its anti-Semitism: and in spite of its impatience with the cult of self, he came to regard it as too personal! As he explains to Pound in 1959:

> "After Strange Gods" is not a good book. Intemperate and unjust, and expresses emotional state of its author rather than critical judgment. "The Use of Poetry" is not good either, except in a few isolated paragraphs. I let "After Strange Gods" go out of print.[35]

Why, then, should we concern ourselves with works that Eliot deplored? It may be that his embarrassment is the barometer of their significance. "Tradition and the Individual Talent" remains the most daring and most difficult of his pronouncements on impersonality. In the 1930s, he revives the doctrine of impersonality as an antidote to false mythologies, the most insidious of which is Bergsonism. Ironically, however, these attacks on "heresy" were later to be vilified by Eliot himself, as heresies against the orthodoxy of his meaning. It is as if the inquisition must anathematise itself, having turned into a stranger god than any of the golden calves it sought to extirpate. The next part of this chapter examines "Tradition and the Individual Talent" in the context of his works of 1919–22, showing how his other theories influence his creed of self-denial. Then we turn to 1933, where his "intemperance" reveals that personality cannot be kept at bay, for it is implicated in the very act of writing.

The Time of Tension

"Tradition and the Individual Talent" divides into two parts, which correspond to its two instalments in *The Egoist*. The first part looks outward to tradition, but the second part turns inward to the author, if only to dispute his claims to authorship. This structure links the questions of personality and history, but also opens up a certain breach between the two.[36] Eliot advances through a series of paradoxes. Newness without novelty—imitation without repetition: any poet "over the age of twenty-five" must meet these contradictory requirements. He must, moreover, be both conscious and unconscious, and though he must "have emotions", he must also know what it means to escape them (21). He must learn his craft from the tradition, but that tradition is defined by what it isn't, rather than by what it is. The very term connotes an absence and a silence: "In English writing we seldom speak of tradition, though we occasionally apply its name in deploring its absence" (3). Moreover, Eliot defines tradition as a heritage that cannot be inherited; it grows, but it does not mature; it is complete at any moment, yet at every moment it transfigures its amoebic form (14–15). Tradition, Eliot says, "involves . . . the historical sense" (14), which is deeper than the knowledge of chronology, for dates and facts may be abused as "means of disowning the past" (*DS* II 41). It is the *presence* rather than the pastness of the past that he insists upon (14). In fact, he believes that the poet is embraced by his tradition whether he schools himself in it or not: but if the past is inescapable, it also represents a fund of erudition which requires ceaseless labour. Its constituents are always changing, for "Tradition cannot mean standing still", as he reiterates in 1933. "The very word implies a movement" (*ASG* 23–4). The word "tradition" has its own tradition, and Eliot hints that the ghosts of former meanings, like "delivery", "surrender", and "handing down", linger in the term's semantic fabric. In other words, tradition posts the past into the present. At the same time, each new work changes the works that have preceded it, and rather than a linear development, literary history becomes an open-ended dialectic, where past and future works react on one another, continually turning into something other than themselves.

Le Brun argues that Eliot is reconstructing literary history in the light of Bergson's notion of duration, where the past invades the present but the present also interpenetrates the past, reshaping what has been in the image of what is yet to come.[37] This conception endangers the very notion of priority, for the presence of the present is eroded, and the past becomes the echo of the future, rather than its point of origin. Moreover, the authority of the original is undermined, for the meaning of a work depends on its posterity, and alters under the compulsion of the new. However, now that we have traced the argument to the point where something quite extraordinary is happening, it is necessary to backtrack and confront the ways that Eliot puts reins on relativity.[38]

If tradition does away with absolutes, implying the provisionality of meaning, history, and value, its own monopoly of literature remains unquestioned, imperturbable. Tradition has no outside. Patiently digesting differences, the old incorporates the new. In fact, the search for novelty strikes Eliot as a perilous pursuit, more likely to "discover the perverse" than the "really new" (21, 15). The presence of the past has now become authoritarian, though Eliot conceals its iron hand by sentimentalising its paternalism. If he suggests that literary history is a play of differences with no fixed terms, no stable legislature, he now submerges this suspicion in the rhetoric of organicism. He speaks as if tradition had emerged according to the laws of nature, rather than through the social, economic and political exclusions which institute the canon by expelling any works that challenge its hegemony. Spongeous and capacious, tradition absorbs all friction into the serenity of its organic form. As Terry Eagleton puts it:

> Eliot's "Tradition" is a labile, self-transformative organism extended in space and time, constantly reorganised by the present; but this radical historical relativism is then endowed with the status of absolute classical authority.[39]

By urging historical awareness, Eliot questions the stability of literary values, but he never contests the boundaries of that awareness nor challenges its mythic unity.

His notion of impersonality is equally equivocal. He argues that the poet, in his confrontation with tradition, submits to a "continual extinction" of the self (17). Does this mean that the author surrenders his identity to the demonic repetition of the past, reduced to the amanuensis of the dead? This would be the most unsettling interpretation: and Eliot hints it when he says that "not only the best, but the most individual parts of [a poet's] work may be those in which the dead poets, his ancestors, assert their immortality most vigorously" (4). By deferring to tradition, the author loses his command over his texts, for their meanings alter every moment. However, Eliot subsumes those changes into the organic whole of history; and he implies that the author gains his place with the immortals at the price of the suppression of himself. In this way, the artist universalises his identity at the very moment that he seems to be negated.

This dialectical reversal, like other strategems, defends the essay from the vertigo of its own insights. At another moment, Eliot ventures that the doctrine of impersonality is "perhaps related to the metaphysical theory of the substantial unity of the soul"—but he then abruptly halts at the "frontiers of metaphysics" (19, 21). Elsewhere he claims that "the difference between art and the event is always absolute" (19); yet he spends half the essay contriving a chemistry which would account for the catalysis between the two. The prose abounds with qualifiers, postponing definitions with promises of future clarity: "I do not mean"; "we do not quite say"; "I am alive to the usual objection . . ."; "there remains to define this process"; "To proceed to a more intelligible exposition . . ." (14–16). Yet the more the essay redefines its terms, the more they seem to lose their anchorage.

For Eliot works figuratively, and despite his philosophical vocabulary the play of metaphor deranges the machinery of logic. At one stage, for example, he defines impersonality as "self-sacrifice", a saintly renunciation of the self (17). This conception ennobles rather than degrades the poet, who remains the unitary source of messages, however frugally dispensed. "Depersonalization" (17), on the other hand, implies that the poet forfeits personality as soon as he begins to write, as the remorseless condition of his medium. Yet when Eliot speaks of a "continual extinction of personality" (17), he hesitates between these humanist and anti-humanist alternatives. The theory of tradition means that every word the author writes infringes on his own identity, for it is impossible to tell where repetition ends and his originality begins. But he undergoes extinction in his art only to enjoy distinction in eternity, and "loss is his gain", as Joyce once said of Shakespeare's self-restraint (*U* 197). "In each major area of discussion", John Chalker has observed, "personality is left behind defeated, only to reappear at a later stage and in a different form. The characteristic movement is circular . . .".[40] In "Tradition and the Individual Talent", the terms "self-sacrifice", "depersonalization", and "continual extinction" purport to define impersonality, but really launch it on a metaphoric odyssey.

Though Eliot resists the implications of his argument, Wyndham Lewis senses that the concept of tradition puts the very notion of the individual in jeopardy.

> The past as *myth*—as history, that is, in the classical sense—a Past in which events and people stand in an imaginative perspective, a *dead* people we do not interfere with, but whose integrity we respect—that is a Past that any person who has a care for the principle of individual life will prefer to "history-as-evolution" or "history-as-communism" (*TWM* 238).

For Lewis, personal identity depends upon the deadness of the past. As Walter Benjamin has also pointed out, the *durée* does away with death, and thereby does away with history: for without death, time degenerates into "the miserable endlessness of a scroll."[41] Both critics believe that death engenders history, because it holds the present and the past apart, and separates one selfhood from another. Ironically, personality depends upon one's own capacity to die.

Though "Tradition and the Individual Talent" repeatedly returns to death, this is a very different kind of death from Lewis's or Benjamin's. If the most individual parts of a poet's work are those in which his ancestors resurge, *their* voices are more vigorous in death than *his* in life. Furthermore, the poet is most himself when he is least himself; most individual when he is most bespoken; most intimate when he is taking his dictation from the dead. "What is dead", says Eliot, is really "what is already living" (22); and by the same token, the living are already dying as they undergo continual extinction in the language of the past:

> What happens is a continual surrender of himself as he is at the moment to something which is more valuable. The progress of an artist is a continual self-sacrifice, a continual extinction of personality (17).[42]

In *Totem and Taboo* Freud argues that human beings first acknowledged death when they created ghosts, but this is also when they first defied it, by asserting that the dead return (SE XIII 61). In Eliot, the literary past is undead, too, and just as irrepressible. Since "Tradition and the Individual Talent" was published in 1919, its attitude to death may be seen as a reaction to the war just ended: as an attempt to come to terms with the immolation of the West by disavowing its finality.[43] At any rate, the dead in Eliot would not be dead enough for Lewis. And it is the loop in time which reawakens them in all their undiminished personality.

Undisciplined Squads of Emotion

There is also a loop in Eliot's own essay, and in the second half he rehabilitates the personality that he had humbled in the first. But this recovery is surreptitious, for he claims to be degrading authors into passive vehicles in which "emotions and feelings" may combine at will (19). However, feelings presuppose a feeler. Eliot is attacking expressivism with its own weapons, and he reinstates the feeling subject at the centre of the process of creation at the same time that he attempts to circumscribe his will. While Mallarmé believed that language necessarily entails impersonality, since it is always borrowed from the tribe, Eliot avoids this issue.[44] It is the poet's "nervous system" which perfects his poetry, rather than the words he uses to express those nerves.[45] The better the poetry, the more the author has reduced himself to "a finely perfected medium in which special, or very varied, feelings are at liberty to enter into new combinations" (18). This *diction* diminishes the author into a receptacle where "floating feelings" may be stored, but the *reasoning* restores his mastery. For Eliot never disputes the assumption that the work of art originates in an experiencing subject: "What every poet starts from is his own emotions." In fact, he seems to bait the icon of the author only so that it may prove its own resilience. Personality resurges, undefeated, because the concepts of emotion, communication, and expression ultimately guarantee its sway.

Caught in this contradiction, Eliot equivocates about the self's domain throughout his writings of this period. In "*Hamlet*" (1919), he criticises Shakespeare for showing too much of his personality; yet he criticises Massinger in 1920 because he has too little personality to show (*SE* 145, 217, 220). Marvell's wit is an impersonal virtue, while Tennyson's education is an impersonal defect.[46] In "Tradition and the Individual Talent" Eliot urges poets to escape their personalities; but in "Ben Jonson" (1919), he declares that the "creation of a work of art . . . consists in the transfusion of the personality . . ." (*SE* 157). In 1933 he describes the literary work as a "secretion" of the author's personality, and this term epitomises his ambivalence: for it could either mean exposed, secreting, or hidden in reserve, in secret (*UPUC* 145n.). It is as if the artist must be absent and present, Olympian and intimate at once.

In "The Method of Mr Pound" (1919), Eliot objects to poems that "make you conscious of having been written by somebody"—and it is the *writing*, as well as the *somebody*, that irritates him.[47] He implies that personality breaks forth when thought and writing break asunder, when language refuses to defer to what it means. Ideally, words efface themselves before their referents, as does the somebody who wrote them down. Eliot longs to write "poetry so transparent that we should not see the poetry, but that which we are meant to see through the poetry. . . . To get *beyond poetry*, as Beethoven, in his later works, strives to get *beyond music*."[48] He argues that in Dante's language there is no interruption between the surface and the core, between the words and the sensations they disclose.[49] It is only when a gap has opened in the language that the author needs to intervene, yet his intrusion exacerbates the fragmentation.

Even Shakespeare fails to overcome this gap. According to Eliot, Hamlet's feelings exceed their objects, just as Shakespeare's overshoot his power to embody them. It is this imbalance which engenders "personality", for the author and his problems re-emerge in his creation (*SE* 145–6). The antidote is the "objective correlative":

> The only way of expressing emotion in the form of art is by finding an "objective correlative"; in other words, a set of objects, a situation, a chain of events which shall be the formula of that *particular* emotion; such that when the external facts, which must terminate in sensory experience, are given, the emotion is immediately evoked. . . . Hamlet (the man) is dominated by an emotion which is inexpressible, because it is in *excess* of the facts as they appear. And the supposed identity of Hamlet with his author is genuine to this point: that Hamlet's bafflement at the absence of objective equivalent to his feelings is a prolongation of the bafflement of his creator in the face of his artistic problem (*SE* 145).

It is characteristic that language is omitted from this recipe: for Eliot assumes that literature is made of feelings, objects or events, not words. When the "formula" is right, the subject's feelings will transmit themselves intact, in spite of their translation into objects. Though he undergoes a temporary self-estrangement, the author's personality returns empowered, unadulterated by its sojourn with materiality. Once again, this regimen fortifies the very self it promised to restrain.

It is when mediation fails that personality obtrudes, when the *writtenness* of literature overwhelms its meaning. In fact, personality becomes the symptom of the failure of reference, when the sign mutinies against the sense. Eliot blames Milton for this catastrophe, which he calls the "dissociation of sensibility" (*SE* 288). For Milton wrenched the word and world apart, and bequeathed a broken language to posterity, where verse obeys the witchery of music rather than the laws of sense. The pleasure "arises from the *noise*", from a language which refuses to conceal itself, delighting in the "mazes" of its own sonority (*SP* 261–3). This reflexivity, moreover, draws attention to *person writing*, rather than the meanings that the writing should reveal. For this reason, Milton's "auditory imagination" is to blame for personality.

According to Eliot, Swinburne's ear was even more "abnormally sharpened" than Milton's, and his language still more radically split. In "Swinburne as Poet" (1920), Eliot writes: " 'The beauty of Swinburne's verse is the sound,' people say, explaining, 'he had little visual imagination' " (*SE* 324). Swinburne's poetry is even more diseased than Milton's because it imitates the unison of word and thing in a travesty of referentiality:

> Language in a healthy state presents the object, is so close to the object that the two are identified.
>
> They are identified in the verse of Swinburne solely because the object has ceased to exist, because the meaning is merely the hallucination of meaning, because the language, uprooted, has adapted itself to an independent life of atmospheric nourishment (*SE* 327).

While Milton divided sound from meaning, Swinburne overcomes the gap with a sham organic wholeness. In a perverse way, he follows Eliot's directives to the letter, but exaggerates them into caricatures of themselves. Though he fuses word and thing, as Eliot prescribes, he secretly abolishes the object, forsaking meaning for mellifluence. "It is, in fact, the word that gives him the thrill, not the object." Eliot complains that Milton writes English like a dead language, but Swinburne's verse is "very much alive", demonically vital. It mocks the animation the author should transfuse into his work with a perverse "life of its own" (*SP* 261; *SE* 327). In his verbal hothouse, Swinburne even cultivates an artificial species of impersonality:

> The world of Swinburne does not depend on some other world which it stimulates; it has the necessary completeness and self-sufficiency for justification and permanence. It is impersonal, and no one else could have made it (*SE* 327).

Swinburne unsettled Eliot's oppositions, for he is intrusive and impersonal at once. Moreover, he conceals the separation between sound and sense in an *ersatz*, but airtight, poetic unity. With its completeness, impersonality and self-sufficiency, his poetry becomes a parody of Eliot's aesthetics; and Eliot does not condemn him for his disobedience so much as for his uncanny simulation of his principles.

Displacement is the source of these poetic errors. For Swinburne lets the music of the language overwhelm its meaning until his words usurp the world they represent. In "Tradition and the Individual Talent", Eliot complains that modern writers seek novelty "in the wrong place", and that this displacement "discovers the perverse" (*SE* 21). The theory of impersonality sets out to put the author *in his place*, and to liberate the poem from his narcissism. Even subjectivism is acceptable within its bounds; and indeed the poet only tries to soar beyond his proper place when every place has grown improper to itself. For Eliot, the danger of displacement overshadows any of its side-effects, be they the auditory imagination or the cult of personality. Even verse itself becomes "perverse" if it attempts to take the place of something else. In his writings of the 1930s, Eliot renames displacement "heresy", and blacklists all its counterfeits and idols.

Coffee without Caffeine

> We returned to our places, these Kingdoms,
> But no longer at ease here, in the old dispensation,
> With an alien people clutching their gods.
>
> Eliot, "Journey of the Magi"

In 1933 Eliot revives the theory of impersonality, and Wyndham Lewis notes this "new dismemberment" with much amusement:

> Mr. Eliot's most recent critical book [*The Use of Poetry and the Use of Criticism*] is notable for one thing; and that is a new dismemberment of his much-discussed "personality". . . . For now he has disowned the Mr Eliot of 1923. . . . "In the course of time,"he tells us, "a poet may become merely a reader in respect of his own works." And Mr Eliot has become that. He reads *The Waste Land* with astonishment now. . . . It is not a question of Mr Eliot having *forgotton*, he assures us. He has "merely" *changed*.
>
> What all this means is that . . . he is driven to the expedient of announcing a further piecemealing of his personality (already one would have thought sufficiently cut up between the private self—the believer; the poet—the unbeliever; and the literary critic—not always very flattering to the poet, though of course not without a certain evident partiality for him all the same!). It is rather an extreme device—this disintegration into a multiplicity of chronologic selves.[50]

In *The Use of Poetry*, the work that Lewis is mocking, Eliot still argues that poems originate in personality, but that they change so radically in the execution "as to be hardly recognizable." In one sense, but a "very limited one", the author knows the meaning of his work better than anybody else; but what he knows is just its "embryology", rather than its final implications:[51]

> what a poem means is as much what it means to others as what it means to the author; and indeed, in the course of time a poet may become merely a reader in respect to his own work, forgetting his original meaning—or without forgetting, merely changing (*UPUC* 130).

In 1933 Eliot becomes the reader of "Tradition and the Individual Talent", and recreates impersonality as a political treatise. He begins *After Strange Gods* by saying: "Some years ago I wrote an essay entitled *Tradition and the Individual Talent*. . . . What I propose to attempt in these three lectures is to outline the matter as I now conceive it" (*ASG* 15). At this point his attack on personality joins forces with his battle against liberal individualism: his campaign "to renew our association with traditional wisdom; to re-establish a vital connection between the individual and the race; the struggle, in a word, against Liberalism . . ." (*ASG* 48). It is when tradition founders that the author's personality begins to take its place, and idiosyncracy becomes the touchstone of his greatness. This idolatry of novelty in art colludes with individualism in the political domain, and together they corrode the racial heritage:

> It is true that the existence of a right tradition, simply by its influence upon the environment in which a poet develops, will tend to restrict eccentricity to manageable limits: but it is not even by lack of this restraining influence that the absence of tradition is most deplorable. What is disastrous is that the writer should deliberately give rein to his individuality, that he should cultivate his differences from others; and that his readers should cherish the author of genius, not in spite of his deviations from the inherited wisdom of the race, but because of them (*ASG* 33).

This emergency demands a new critical administration. Tradition is too absorptive to counteract the spread of heresy. So Eliot demotes tradition, the secular worship of the dead, and instates a Christian "orthodoxy" in its stead. Tradition sinks to the unconscious.

> A *tradition* is rather a way of feeling and acting which characterises a group throughout generations; and . . . it must be, or . . . many of the elements in it must be, unconscious, whereas the maintenance of *orthodoxy* is a matter which calls for the exercise of all our conscious intelligence. . . . Tradition has not the means to criticise itself . . . (*ASG* 29).

While tradition must be lived and practised in a social group, orthodoxy "exists whether realized in anyone's thought or not" (*ASG* 30). In other words, the faith lives on, impersonal and imperturbable, in spite of human efforts to define it, deceive it, or deny it.[52]

To achieve impersonality in 1933, the artist must submit to orthodoxy and its absolute authority, rather than to the shifting values of tradition. For Eliot believes that liberalism has been in the offing for two centuries, attended by the cult of self in literature:

> it seems to me that the eminent novelists who are nearly contemporary to us, have been more concerned than their predecessors—consciously or not—to impose upon their readers their own *personal view of life*, and that this is merely part of the whole movement of several centuries towards the aggrandisement and exploitation of personality. . . . personality, with Jane Austen, with Dickens and with Thackeray, was more nearly in its proper place. The standards by which they judged

> their world, if not very lofty ones, were at least not of their own making (*ASG* 53).

Once again, the culprit in this passage is displacement, *misplacement*, rather than the personality *per se*. The secular values of Austen, Thackeray or Dickens grow dangerous only when they *take the place of* the eternal truths: and personality becomes the signature of this displacement. In "its proper place", personality may not be damnable; but the more the Church surrendered to the humanism of the nineteenth century, the more obstreperous the self became. Subjectivity expands as faith declines, for in Eliot's economy, the rise of one debilitates the other.

In *After Strange Gods*, Eliot opposes orthodoxy to heresy, but he introduces a third term which vacillates between the two antitheses (*ASG* 21). This is "Blasphemy", which he defines as a backhanded form of orthodoxy. He argues that "no one can possibly blaspheme . . . unless he profoundly believes in that which he profanes" (*ASG* 52). According to this definition, denial is the final mode of affirmation, for the blasphemer reasserts the power of the truths that he repudiates. He is like the psychoanalytic patient who unconsciously admits to the desires that he disavows. Heresy, by contrast, seeks truth *in the wrong place*, and fetishises substitutes and simulacra. Strange gods like Yeats's daimons, or Pound's Confucius, or Lawrence's dark deities of Mexico, dislodge the long-established icons of the West (*ASG* 41).

In his Harvard lectures of the spring, Eliot opposes Lawrence, a heretic, to Joyce, who blasphemes against the orthodoxy yet remains within its fold. "Joyce sees the particular from the general, the concrete from the abstract", he argues. "Lawrence *vice versa*."[53] By focussing on difference and plurality, Lawrence bolsters personality, and neglects the timeless principles uniting individuals together under an authority much greater than themselves. Because Joyce works the other way around, deducing the instance from its cause, his writing is a microcosm which propitiates its God.

> The relations of Paul Morel compared with the relations of Stephen Dedalus. Both wrong; but with Paul Morel you get individualism. . . .

> In Stephen, in spite of the greater sordidness, you get the Catholic idea: the sense that society is more important than the happiness of the individual, hence none of the sentimentality that you find in *Sons and Lovers*. In the latter you find only individuals, in the former you find society. To me *Sons and Lovers* is devoid of the moral sense, an evil book: and The Portrait is directed by the moral sense.[54]

In Lawrence, personality gets out of hand because he slights the typical for the eccentric, and forswears eternity for flux. It is this mode of thinking which dissociates his sensibility and mars his art: "in Lawrence you get the experience: then he theorises about it." In Joyce, on the other hand, "the idea and the sensation are one."[55] Lawrence fails to feel his thought as immediately as the odour of a rose, and this is why his personality intrudes, as the stigma of the rift within his art. Indeed, when such dissociation is in evidence, personality is never far behind: for the heresy that severs thought from feeling also alienates the self from its society and history. It is difficult to tell if personality perpetrated these divisions or if it represents the wreckage of their strife. Dissociation and the cult of self spring forth together, hatched in the same heresy like Sin and Death.

Eliot denounces Bergson and Matthew Arnold with equal vehemence for instigating modern heresy. Both supplanted true religion with a glittering sham, and the substitutes have pullulated ever since. "Literature, or Culture tended with Arnold to *usurp the place of* religion", Eliot writes.[56] All the heresies that plague the century may well derive from his first substitution.[57] Bergsonism, too, supplants devotion with the tawdry ornaments of piety. Just as Milton and Swinburne sever sound from sense, the Bergsonian divorces ritual from faith, preserving the emotions of the Mass "without the beliefs with which their history has been involved" (*UPUC* 135).[58] He substitutes this husk of meaning for the truth, and thence bows down to worship it. Similarly, readers who enjoy "scientific, or historical, or theological, or philosophic" writings "*solely* because of their literary merit are essentially parasites: and we know that parasites, when they become too numerous, are pests."[59] In Eliot, all heresies are parasitical in structure, for they rely on the traditions that they stimulate, as Spam depends on ham, or chicory on coffee. They are "transient stimulants", cheap thrills which drug the public with delusive sanctities (*ASG* 46). Arnold, for example, "discovered a new formula: poetry is not religion, but it is a capital substitute for religion—not invalid port, which may lend itself to hypocrisy, but coffee without caffeine, or tea without tannin" (*UPUC* 26). With so many phoney products on the spiritual market, it would be hard to tell the genuine from the heretical, were it not for the "smell of a 'personality' " which identifies a heretic as fingerprints identify a crook—or so Wyndham Lewis mocks.[60] For instance, Eliot detects "extreme self-consciousness" in Yeats's surrogate mythology, a "willed cultivation of imagery" in which his personality shows through (*ASG* 46). If he had chosen spirits who were well-established in the culture, rather than untimely interlopers, they could have helped to keep his personality in line. The poet who supplants the priest, the sound that overwhelms the sense, the art that feeds on the declining faith: these parasites eventually destroy the values that they poach upon.

If Eliot blames heresy on displacement, he blames displacement more and more insistently on *literature*. For heresy begins when literary pleasure overcomes the stern demands of sense. In Arnold, for example, poetry supplants belief: and just as Milton's verbal music stealthily destroys its sense, the parasitic reader neglects the *meaning* of the language for its *art*. Thus the fetishism of the signifier (the written or acoustic tissue of the word) becomes the archetype of modern heresies: for each of these replaces form for content, sound for meaning, rite for faith. In this logic, literature *necessarily* connives with heresy, because its form seduces attention from its sense; and furthermore because its tropes dramatise the very substitutions and displacements which engender idols and idolaters. Indeed, it begins to seem that Eliot will not get rid of heresy until he has abolished *rhetoric*.

The Revolution of the Word

Once these parasites have overrun tradition, only orthodoxy can contain the epidemic, and put the caffeine back into the coffee. Blasphemers like Joyce cannot stand alone against so many strange gods. From the 1930s onwards, Eliot reconstructs the body politic to strengthen it against the pestilence of heresy. At the same time he must reform the text, for his poetics reproduce his politics in what Gerontion calls a "wilderness of mirrors." It is displacement that Eliot condemns in both domains: for unless words and people remain in their appointed places, society and poetry must plummet to confusion. In "The Music of Poetry" (1942), he writes:

> ugly words are . . . words not fitted for the company in which they find themselves; there are words which are ugly because of rawness or because of antiquation; there are words which are ugly because of foreignness or ill-breeding (e.g. *television*): but I do not believe that any word well-established in its own language is either beautiful or ugly. . . . Not all words are equally rich and well-connected: it is part of the business of the poet to dispose the richer among the poorer, at the right points . . . (*PP* 32–3).

This conceit makes social and poetic harmony interchangeable. Just as a ruler legislates degree and precedence, the poet should enforce the pecking order of his words. He must also limit verbal immigrants and upstarts, for too much semantic mobility disturbs the traditions of the tongue. What goes for words goes for people too. In *After Strange Gods*, Eliot discourages "free-thinking Jews" from his utopia, partly because they threaten its homogeneity, but more importantly because they have no place, and they have come to stand for the porosity of boundaries (*ASG* 20). In *Notes towards the Definition of Culture*, he argues that "it would appear to be for the best that the great majority of human beings should go on living *in the place* in which they were born" (*NDC* 52: my emphasis). Though he permits some cultural diversity, he restricts it to satellite communities, which revolve around the central orthodoxy. Any restlessness within these regions jeopardises their integrity, unbalancing the delicate economy of difference. As Terry Eagleton remarks, "When the human beings begin to move, Eliot's structures begin to crumble."[61]

For Eliot identifies the bounds of *meaning* with the

boundaries of the community, so that the stability of one depends upon the other. In the epigraph to *Notes towards the Definition of Culture*, he cites the definition of definition from the *OED*, that paragon of verbal jurisdiction: "DEFINITION: 1. The setting of bounds; limitation (rare)—1483—*Oxford English Dictionary*." To define is to confine: to put things in their places and to keep them there. Displacement, on the other hand, erodes the very possibility of definition, for the boundaries that guard one tribe against another purify their dialects as well. In the same way, the poet must police his language to prevent his words from growing insubordinate. He must create a semantic world in which "every word is at home/*Taking its place* to support the others" (*LG* V 4–5 my emphases). So long as they remain at home, his words enforce the social equilibrium. When words "will *not stay in place*, / Will not stay still" (as Eliot puts it in "Burnt Norton"), they send convulsions through Christian society (*BN* V 16–17: my emphases).

Using the Globe Theatre as a paradigm, Eliot divides poetic language into echelons of meaning, reflecting the divisions of the body politic. Each reader's intellect becomes his inner aristocracy, while his ear becomes the groundling of his mind.[62] The highest level of the poem is its meaning, which intellect alone can apprehend; but the lower faculties enjoy the music long before they grasp the sense. These mental categories slip so smoothly into social ones that sometimes it is hard to tell which Eliot intends. For instance, he identifies the lower faculties with rhythm and tradition, but also with the lower orders of society, whom he romantically envisages as rustics:

> Round and round the fire
> Leaping through the flames, or joined in circles,
> Rustically solemn or in rustic laughter
> Lifting heavy feet in clumsy shoes,
> Earth feet, loam feet, lifted in country mirth
> Mirth of those long since under earth
> Nourishing the corn. Keeping time,
> Keeping the rhythm in their dancing
> As in their living in the living seasons. . . . (*EC* 33–41).

These peasants, "Keeping the rhythm in their dancing",

reanimate the past within the present, and thus unconsciously preserve the wisdom of their race. They live tradition as a rhythm rather than a thought. While the dancers change, their music rejuvenates itself perpetually:

> Tradition may be conceived as a by-product of right living, not to be aimed at directly. It is of the blood, so to speak, rather than of the brain: it is the means by which the vitality of the past enriches the life of the present (*ASG* 30).

In this passage (1934), tradition still resembles Bergson's notion of duration, but it has now become unconscious to orthodoxy, just as music is subliminal to meaning.

This unconsciousness is part of Eliot's new conception of impersonality. Yet although he has relented towards music, a certain anxiety remains, and rhythm in particular becomes a focus of ambivalence. On the one hand he ennobles it, for he insists that it is fundamental to poetry and to society—but only as the underside of both domains. He identifies sonority with yokels, savages, and instincts, while meaning is aristocratic, Apollonian. As he puts it, "Poetry begins, I dare say, with a savage beating a drum in a jungle, and it retains that essential of percussion and rhythm . . ." (*UPUC* 155). His views on rhythm reveal his foreign as well as his domestic policy, and in particular a nervous admiration for imperialism. He argues that the English language has absorbed the metres of its own invaders, so that its music functions as a "passport" into any foreign sensibility (*PP* 24, 37). Elsewhere, however, he implies that rhythm is more xenophobic than any other aspect of the language, for thought is general, while sound is racial: "a constant reminder of all the things that can only be said in one language, and are untranslatable" (*PP* 19, 23). This contradiction arises because regionalism is itself "a by-product of imperialism"—which implies that boundaries are the traces of their own transgression.[63] Rhythm institutes the sense of place, but it also undermines the very notion of locality, which is forever haunted by displacement from within. For if the region forges its identity in rhythm, this music also bears the traces of an infinite miscegenation, which mocks the purity of any race or any dialect.

Similarly, Eliot argues that the poet creates his personality in metre, more than any other aspect of his verse: yet his cadence is so fraught with echoes from the past that it condemns him to impersonality despite himself. This is because his precursors also left their signatures in rhythm: "a system of prosody is only a formulation of the identities in the rhythms of a succession of poets influenced by each other" (*PP* 37). Moreover, the music of poetry reaches back beyond recorded history to the first percussive orderings of time, so that the most rarefied of metres still murmurs with the savage drums. Eliot sees rhythm as the "frontier" to the unconscious, dividing nature from culture—but it is a pervious boundary which confounds the worlds it holds asunder (*PP* 30, 86–7). Sound, he says, is "like the jungle which, unless continually kept under control, is always ready to encroach and eventually obliterate the cultivated area."[64] The jungle is the source of poetry, but it also holds the seeds of its extinction, for its music could rise up to vanquish meaning and obliterate the poet's mark in time. Like Bergson, Eliot privileges rhythm as the temporal dimension of the poet's speech, where his true personality is to be found: but it is also in this music that identity dissolves, subverting nation, self, and racial purity at once.

Music is the inner life of language, because it activates the spirit of tradition. For this reason, the poet must attend to the sonorities of common speech, or "the poetic idiom goes out of date" (*PP* 31). Eliot's idea of speech corresponds to Bergson's view of time, where the past survives into the present because of its capacity to differ from itself. While the written language stultifies in space, Eliot believes "the spoken language goes on changing" (*PP* 31). Thus, "every revolution in poetry is apt to be, and often to announce itself to be a return to common speech" (*PP* 31). But this revolution turns backwards, not forwards, for the spoken tongue renews traditions rather than superseding them. For this reason, Eliot argues that the poet is the only "genuine and profound revolutionist"—not because he overturns the past, but because he summons back its living spirit.[65] To do so, he returns his words to their appointed places, and the critic's task is to enforce this dispensation:

> I conceive of literary criticism in the following way. The ideal critic should have both an intense concentration and an indefinite awareness. He should not be primarily concerned with sociology, or with politics, or with theology, or with any other ology; he should be primarily concerned with the word and its incantation; with the question whether the poet has used *the right word in the right place*, the rightness depending upon both the explicit intention and an indefinite radiation of sound and sense. He should differ from the practitioners of other sciences, not so much by what he needs to know and what he does not need to know—for indeed he needs to know everything—as by his centre of values; in the beginning was the word. In speech is both the highest level of consciousness, and the deepest level of unconsciousness. By speech false values are maintained, or real values are revealed.[66]

In this powerful defence of language Eliot seems to have overcome his earlier distrust of words: but it is important that he privileges "speech", not words *per se*. For his political motive is to purify the speech community, and to keep the members of the social group in earshot of each other. Because the *written* language overrides these boundaries, it resembles the nomadic Jews who threaten the cohesion of the group. But the worst offence of writing is the boost it gives to personality.

Speech restrains the speaker's egoism, because it necessarily involves "one person talking to another", and therefore presupposes a community. The speaker must address the understanding of his interlocutor, which keeps his hubris within bounds. On the other hand, we write, as we read, alone. Because "most poetry today is written to be read in solitude", tradition is anatomised among a thousand lonely chambers where readers mutely trace its runes (*PP* 31, 17). The writer is obliged to fumble towards an absent reader, while the reader deciphers his remains in silence. Eliot discourages "such individual benefit from poetry", advocating "something which it does collectively for us, as a society." An oral literature would help to nourish "that mysterious social personality which we call our 'culture' "; as opposed to the solipsism writing breeds (*PP* 18, 23). If the writer *spoke* directly to his audience, he would observe collective values instead of flattering his readers' egos and his own. Writing, on the other hand, encourages the dangerous privacy that nourishes the cult of self. Ironically, the *absence* of the writer is responsible for the inflation of his personality.

For Eliot, writing without speech is like coffee without caffeine. While the written word preserves the bare forms of tradition, the meaning ruins secretly within. Only voice reanimates the *history* which gives these forms their meaning and vitality. Moreover, Eliot speculates that "before the use of a written language a regular verse form must have been extremely helpful to the memory—and the memory of the primitive bards, story-tellers and scholars must have been prodigious" (*PP* 16). Like Plato, he believes that memory deteriorates as writing takes its place, because the community alienates its power to preserve the past into an exterior mnemonic aid. History fades into forgetfulness, leaving only verbal detritus behind: "a chronicle, an accumulation of manuscripts and writings of this kind and that" (*PP* 56). In Eliot's logic, writing incites heresy because it separates the spirit from the letter, and thus commences an illimitable series of displacements. Sooner or later, any written marks desert the place of their origination. As we shall see, *The Waste Land* dramatises this diaspora, for here the writings of the past deracinate themselves and drift among the withered stumps of time. Their meaning fluctuates depending on the company they keep, and the poem hints that it is helpless to control their prodigality. Only in a written culture can the ritual divest itself of history, or the alphabet supplant the voice, the incantation of the word. In Eliot, it takes a revolution to overthrow the letter and to turn the course of history back to the "reality of speech."[67]

It was in poetic drama that he hoped to bring about this revolution. A public art, the theatre subordinates the written word to its enunciation, for the play exists in the performance, rather than between the covers of a book. "The dependence of verse upon speech is much more direct in dramatic poetry than in any other" (*PP* 33). Furthermore, the theatre summons its spectators from their solitude, and reassembles the community. The author, too, submits his ego to the exigencies of the dramatic form, which compels him to introduce "a more impersonal point of view", because "his idiom must be comprehensive of all the voices" (*SE* 321; *PP* 33). In this way, his poetry knits him into the social fabric, and he becomes the spokesman of his people rather than a hidden idol, exiled by his own creation. By discarding "personality", he forfeits nothing but the phantom of his writing and his fading actuality.

In Eliot, writing typifies the parasitic stratagems of heresy, because it copies speech but takes its place. In fact, it *institutes* the possibility of the displacements that heresy depends upon. Moreover, writing is itself a heresy, perhaps the first and certainly the most redoubtable: and heresy could also be regarded as a form of writing, as Eliot conceives these terms. It was to shun them both that he resorted to dramatic poetry, and to loosen writing's stranglehold on speech. Even so, he glimpses that his discourse harbours the very heresies it strives to purge:

> both the view which I have taken in this essay, and the view which contradicts it, are, if pushed to the end, what I call heresies (not, of course, in the theological, but in a more general sense). Each is true only within a limited field of discourse, but unless you limit fields of discourse, you can have no discourse at all.[68]

According to this argument, limits engender heresies, but the intelligibility of discourse depends upon these limits, too. This implies that even the most orthodox pronouncement must be haunted by its own interior perversion. For heresy is no longer an outside, a shadow or negation of the truth, but the intimate condition of its utterance.

This is not the only opposition that collapses here, for Eliot's terms relentlessly contaminate their own antitheses. For instance, he invokes the theatre as his paradigm of oral culture, but drama is really the vocal repetition of a writing, rather than originary speech. Similarly, he honours rhythm as the most distinctive property of speech: yet rhythm is a kind of writing in the voice, scored in the flux of time. In Eliot's criticism, writing *inhabits* speech just as the dead invade the living voice, and just as heresy encroaches on the discourse of its exorcism. To resist his *own* displacements, he imposes bound after bound, definition after definition, patiently defending oppositions as they crumble. In fact, his theory operates like an obsessional catharsis, as Freud describes this structure. For the obsessive invents a ritual to punish his forbidden wishes, but the ceremonial itself becomes forbidden by contagion, "till at last the whole world lies under an embargo" (SE XIII 27). When Eliot becomes his own inquisitor and excommunicates his diatribes against the heretics, it is as if his discourse had itself become the crime it strove to scourge.

An End and a Beginning

This chapter has shown how Eliot attacked Bergson's cult of subjectivity, first through philosophical critique and later through the evolution of the doctrine of impersonality. For the problem of personality haunts each of Eliot's aesthetic categories, and it pervades his politics as well. In his early work he blames the dissociation of sensibility for the rise of personality, because the author's self intrudes when thought and feeling split apart. A universal topsy-turviness ensues, where ritual displaces meaning as poetry displaces faith, and the written chronicle supplants the living past. Furthermore, the worship of the author endangers all religions, and Eliot blames writing for concocting this anathema. In the privacy of writing, the author and the reader nurture one another's solipsism, and the individual takes centre stage in both domains. Only a return to speech can save tradition from the counterforces which corrode it from within, be they writing, silence, heresy, displacement, privacy. But speech itself is tainted by the writing it excludes, just as discourse is imbrued with heresy. It seems that every true god brings a strange god in his wake, even one as strange as personality.

* * *

Eliot's early verse unfolds as a serial of fictive selves, each more lonely and sequestered than the last. Indeed, they personify the solitude of reading and writing that he deplores in prose. Yet the more hermetic subjectivity becomes, the more it seems to lose its anchorage. For this reason, personality and impersonality begin to interpenetrate; and the next chapter explores the early poetry in order to detect their hidden intimacy.

Notes

1. Cited by Greene, *op.cit.*, p. 10.
2. Cited by Hugh Kenner, *The Invisible Poet: T. S. Eliot* (New York: MacDowell, Obolensky, 1959; repr. London: Methuen, 1965), pp. 40, 59.
3. The draft of this paper, together with his lecture notes, are now lodged in the Houghton Library at Harvard.
4. See A. E. Pilkington, *Bergson and his Influence: A Reassessment* (Cambridge: CUP, 1976), Ch. 1, for a brief and lucid exposition of Bergson's philosophy.
5. A good discussion of Bergson's transition from the dualism of the *Essai* to the "middle ground" of *Matière et mémoire* may be found in Milič Capek, *Bergson and Modern Physics* (New York: Humanities Press; Dordrecht, Holland: Reidel, 1971), pp. 189–222.
6. See Kant, *Critique of Pure Reason*, trans. Norman Kemp Smith (1929; repr. London: Macmillan, 1978), pp. 157–75.
7. See also Henri Bergson, "Histoire des théories de la mémoire", in *Mélanges*, ed. André Robinet (Paris: Presses universitaires de France, 1972), p. 623.
8. *A Treatise of Human Nature*, ed. L. A. Selby-Bigge, 1888; rev. edn P. H. Nidditch (Oxford: Clarendon, 1978), pp. 251–63.
9. Hume, *Treatise*, pp. 251–3: discussed by Eliot in Notes 13.
10. *Treatise*, p. 635.
11. *Ibid.*, p. 634.
12. See also *CE* 322–3: "Instead of attaching ourselves to the inner becoming of things. . . . We take snapshots, as it were. . . . the mechanism of our ordinary knowlege is of a cinematographical kind."
13. Bergson, "Conférence de Madrid", *Mélanges*, p. 1220.
14. Virginia Woolf, *To the Lighthouse* (1927; Harmondsworth: Penguin, 1964), p. 202.
15. Bergson, "Conférence de Madrid", *Mélanges*, p. 1224.
16. Bergson, *La pensée et le mouvant*, cited by Romeo Arbour, *Henri Bergson et les lettres françaises* (Paris: Librairie José Corti, 1955), p. 118.
17. Cited by Arbour, p. 112.
18. For this use of "spacing" see Jacques Derrida, "The Double Session", in *Dissemination* (Chicago: University of Chicago Press; London: Athlone, 1981), pp. 173–285. See also Derrida, *Positions*, trans. Alan Bass (Chicago: University of Chicago Press, 1981), p. 81; and Gayatri Chakravorty Spivak, Introduction to Derrida, *Of Grammatology* (Baltimore and London: Johns Hopkins University Press, 1976), p. 69.
19. Bergson speaks of the "trespassing of the idea of space upon the field of pure consciousness. . . . conceived under the form of an unbounded and homogeneous medium, [time] is nothing but the ghost of space haunting the reflective consciousness" (*TFW* 98–9).
20. Bergson, "The Problem of Personality", The Gifford Lectures, 1914,

at the University of Edinburgh (21 April–22 May), in *Mélanges*, p. 1060. These lectures closely resemble those that Eliot heard in Paris in 1910–11.

21. The main focus of Eliot's attack is the first few pages of Bergson's *Essai*, where he argues that pure "intensities" or passions are described in the quantitative categories of "extension" (Draft 1–2). See *TFW* 1–10.
22. Eliot, "A Prediction in Regard to Three English Authors, Writers Who, Though Masters of Thought, are Likewise Masters of Art", *Vanity Fair*, 21, no. 6 (1924), p. 29; Eliot, review of *Three Reformers: Luther, Descartes, Rousseau* by Jacques Maritain, *TLS*, 1397 (27 September 1928), p. 818. See also Eliot, "London Letter", *Dial*, 71 (1921), 216; and *SW* 66.
23. This is one of Eliot's earliest letters to Pound from Merton College: MS, 2 February, [1915], Pound Archive, Beinecke.
24. See Le Brun, "T. S. Eliot and Henri Bergson", pp. 149–61; 274–86.
25. *Essai*, p. 92.
26. *CE* 214: Eliot discusses this passage in Draft 11.
27. See also Gilles Deleuze, "La conception de la différence chez Bergson", *Les études bergsoniennes*, 4 (1956), 88: "La durée, *c'est ce qui diffère avec soi*."
28. See Gilles Deleuze, *Le Bergsonisme* (1966; Paris: Presses universitaires de France, 1968), p. 50.
29. See *SW* 45–6.
30. See Bloom, *Poetry and Repression* (New Haven and London: Yale University Press, 1976), pp. 2–3.
31. The essay was first published in the September/October and the November/December issues of *The Egoist*, 1919.
32. "The Varieties of Metaphysical Poetry", three lectures delivered at Johns Hopkins University, January 1933 (The Turnbull Lectures), MS, T. S. Eliot Collection, Houghton Library, bMS Am 1261 Restricted; Undergraduate Lectures: English 26: "English Literature from 1890 to the Present Day", MS (Spring 1933), Houghton (henceforth English 26).
33. Letter to William Carlos Williams, TS, 18 December [1931], in Pound Archive, Beinecke.
34. See Preface to 1964 edn of *UPUC*, pp. 9–10.
35. Letter from Eliot to Pound, TS, 28 December 1959, in Pound Archive, Beinecke. See also *CC* 24–5.
36. See Bateson, " 'Impersonality' Fifty Years After", *Essays in Critical Dissent* (London: Longman, 1972), pp. 153–62.
37. See Le Brun, "T. S. Eliot and Henri Bergson", p. 155.
38. My argument here is indebted to an essay by my student Ira Paneth at Amherst College, 1985.
39. *Criticism and Ideology* (London: New Left Books, 1976), p. 147.
40. John Chalker, "Authority and Personality in Eliot's Criticism", in *Eliot in Perspective: A Symposium*, ed. Graham Martin (London: Macmillan, 1970), p. 206.
41. See Walter Benjamin, *Charles Baudelaire: A Lyric Poet in the Age of*

High Capitalism, trans. H. Zohn (London: New Left Books, 1973), pp. 144–5.

42. Lewis would probably detect the influence of Bergson in this reversal of the living and the dead. For Bergson may abolish death, but he reanimates dead matter in return, in a restless and indiscriminate apostrophe. As Lewis says: "Dead, physical, nature comes to life." Man, on the other hand, has become a " 'physical thing' ", and personality is nothing more than " 'the continuous transition of one physical event into another' " (*TWM* 450, 458).
43. Peter Middleton puts forward this idea in "The Academic Development of *The Waste Land*", forthcoming in *Glyph*. He also points out that in the same year Freud wrote *Beyond the Pleasure Principle*, and it is startling that both these works concern themselves with the compulsion to repeat, which both regard as the irruption of death in life. These themes will return in the context of *The Waste Land*, which will be discussed in Chapter IV.
44. See, for instance, Mallarmé, *Oeuvres complètes*, ed. Henri Mondor and G. Jean-Aubry (Paris: Gallimard, 1945), pp. 366, 372, 851.
45. See Eliot, "Philip Massinger" (1920), *SE* 211.
46. "Andrew Marvell" (1921), *SE* 304; "William Blake" (1920), *SE* 319.
47. *Athenaeum*, no. 4669 (1919), p. 1065.
48. From an unpublished lecture on Yeats and Lawrence, delivered in New Haven, Conn.; cited by F. O. Matthiessen, *The Achievement of T. S. Eliot* (Boston: Houghton-Mifflin, 1935), p. 90.
49. See "Milton [I]" (1936), *SP* 263; "The Metaphysical Poets" (1921), *SE* 288.
50. *Men Without Art* (London: Cassell, 1934), pp. 95–7. See also *PP* 133. Actually, Eliot had suspected that Richards was "wrong" about *The Waste Land* some six years earlier, in Lewis's own journal, *The Enemy*: see Eliot, "A Note on Poetry and Belief", *Enemy* 1 (1927), 16.
51. See *UPUC* 126, 138, 130; *PP* 30.
52. See William Chase, *The Political Identities of Ezra Pound and T. S. Eliot* (Stanford, California: Stanford University Press, 1973), p. 161.
53. Joyce and Lawrence I, English 26.
54. Joyce and Lawrence I, English 26.
55. Joyce and Lawrence II, English 26.
56. "Arnold and Pater" (1930), *SE* 424: my emphasis.
57. Eliot had been alarmed about this particular heresy since 1924, when he warned that of all "tendencies towards obliteration of distinctions, the most dangerous is the tendency to confuse literature with religion—a tendency which can only have the effect of degrading literature and annihilating religion" ["Commentary", *Criterion*, 2 (1924), 373. See also *NDC* 28]. This displacement sets off an epidemic, which gradually corrodes the very possibility of definition.
58. In Eliot's "Dialogue on Dramatic Poetry" (1928), the Bergsonian neglects "the meaning of the Mass" to revel in its *art* (*SE* 48).
59. "Religion and Literature" (1935), *SE* 389–90.
60. See *Men Without Art*, p. 79.

61. "Eliot and a Common Culture", in Graham Martin, ed., *Eliot in Perspective*, p. 281.
62. See *UPUC* 153; and Eagleton, "Eliot and a Common Culture", p. 281.
63. Lecture I, English 26.
64. Eliot, "That Poetry is Made with Words", *New English Weekly*, 15, no. 2 (1939), cited by Gertrude Patterson, *T. S. Eliot: Poems in the Making* (Manchester: Manchester University Press, 1973), p. 10.
65. "The Varieties of Metaphysical Poetry", III.
66. "The Varieties of Metaphysical Poetry", III.
67. "The Varieties of Metaphysical Poetry", III.
68. "Dante" (1929), *SE* 270.

CHAPTER II

The Spider and the Weevil: Self and Writing in Eliot's Early Poetry

In Ovid's *Metamorphoses*, the river-god Cephisus rapes Liriope the nymph, and she gives birth to a child of unearthly beauty named Narcissus.[1] But Tiresias, the prophet, warns her that the child will only live to a ripe age "If he ne'er know himself" (III 348). Narcissus grows more beautiful with every year, and as a youth he captivates young women and young men alike, but he spurns all their loves. One day, when he is hunting in the woods, Echo the nymph catches sight of him and is instantly inflamed with love. Doomed by Juno never to originate but only to repeat the words of others, she tempts Narcissus by returning his own speech, as if she knew that he could only love the echo of his own desire. When she reveals herself to him, he recognises her as other and repulses her. Consumed with love, her flesh decays until there is nothing left but voice and bones, and as her bones return to rock she dwindles to a desolate refrain.

At last, taking pity on his disappointed lovers, the goddess Nemesis draws Narcissus to a hidden pool, which seduces him with his own shimmering reflection. This spatial, visionary double now avenges Echo, the dilatory double of his speech. Just as Echo's bones had turned to rock, he stares in wonder at his beauty, "like a statue carved from Parian marble" (III 419). In a capture too complete, a reciprocity too perfect, his image woos him, smiles with him, weeps with him. "What I desire I have", he moans, in the anguish of his own satiety: "strange prayer for a lover, I would that my love were absent from me" (III 466–8). And just as Echo is unselved by her own voice, so Narcissus dies into the image that he worships, a shadow transfixed by his own shadow in the Stygian flood (III 504–5).

Narcissus rejects Echo because repetition undermines subjectivity, when his own voice returns to him as other: but he escapes the temporal difference in the voice to be trapped into the spatial repetition of the gaze. Since he only knows himself through doubling, selfhood originates in rupture. But John Brenkman has pointed out that it is when the silent image mimes his *speech*, as the dead letter mocks the living voice, that Narcissus can misrecognise the shadow as himself, and die. For this reason, the mirror image is a kind of writing, "a non-living representation of the voice", and the "drama of Narcissus . . . read as a drama of the self—puts the self in primordial relation to its other, to spatiality, to death, to 'writing.' "[2] In Ovid, Narcissus can accede to selfhood only in the face of writing, where death solicits him in mute ventriloquy.

When Eliot completed "The Death of Saint Narcissus" in 1915, it is as if he canonised Narcissus as the patron saint of autobiographers, and prefaced all his future speculations on himself with Ovid's fable.[3] The autobiographer pursues his images in language as Narcissus woos his image in the pool, and yet the search for self conceals a wish for self-perdition: "I would that my love were absent from me . . .". To write is to inscribe one's absence from oneself: temporal division, for the self that was eludes the self that is, while the written and the writing selves can never coincide; spatial division, for writing externalises memory and halts the flux of subjectivity. This is why Narcissus turns to Parian marble when he is confronted with the writing of himself, transformed into the tomb of his own image. This chapter will explore three early works of Eliot, three different kinds of failure of identity. Serial and aleatory, Saint Narcissus drifts from form to form, in the dreamy devolution of his images. On the other hand, Prufrock's subjectivity is all too fixed, "pinned and wriggling" in a paranoic opposition to the other. Finally, "Gerontion" breaks Narcissus's looking-glass into a "wilderness of mirrors", and the mansion of the self is blasted by the winds of otherness.

Diabolical Mysticism

"The Death of Saint Narcissus" had a hard time being born. Pound submitted the poem to Harriet Monroe's magazine, *Poetry*, in 1915, but Eliot promptly withdrew the text from publication. The surviving galley proof is "scored through by hand with the manuscript directive 'Kill' (i.e. suppress) in the margin of each section", as if to emulate its suicidal hero.[4] Lyndall Gordon speculates that Eliot may have thought the poem too personal.[5] Indeed, it would be fitting if the text were put to death for its self-revelations, since it is such a failure to extinguish personality that condemns Narcissus to embrace his death. Furthermore, the poem is still dying in the silence of its critics. Hived off into the *Poems Written in Early Youth*, "Narcissus" has fallen to the ranks of juvenilia, and both its author and its readers treat the poem as a "quarry" for *The Waste Land*.[6] Slightly altered, the first stanza reappears in "The Burial of the Dead"; and Phlebas the Phoenician supersedes Narcissus, who also "passed the stages of his age and youth" in fluid metamorphoses.[7] Yet "The Death of Saint Narcissus" deserves an independent reading, as Eliot's most fierce yet most ambivalent attack on personality.

Its ambiguities begin with its title, and particularly with the name of its protagonist. Narcissus, Bishop of Jerusalem, escaped into the desert in the second century A.D., falsely accused of "a certain grave slander to his hurt."[8] Eliot's Narcissus flees into the desert, too, but his name conflates this hounded bishop with Narcissus of the pagan legend, and also with the persecuted Saint Sebastian. During his travels through Belgium and Italy in the summer of 1914, Eliot saw three paintings of St Sebastian, by Mantegna, Hans Memling, and Antonello da Messina, and was struck by the eroticism of the images—though he was hasty to insist that a female saint would be more titillating.[9] Bound and helpless, his firm flesh flayed with arrows, it is his terrible beauty that unites Sebastian with Narcissus. Both these allusions suggest that the poem is exploring the perversions of mysticism, which had intrigued Eliot since 1907. In his notes on philosophy at Harvard, he describes delusional insanity as "a diabolical mysticism, mys. upside down"; and he also observes that the sexual element is "very prominent" in religious disorders.[10] Indeed, it is erotism which perverts the martyrdom of Saint Narcissus, for he immolates himself in onanistic ecstasy: "Because his flesh was in love with the burning arrows . . ." (34). The poem also seems to mock its author's future doctrine of impersonality, by hinting at a masochistic pay-off in the regimen of self-surrender. In "Narcissus", self-punishment and self-delight enmesh each other like the tree: "Twisting its branches among each other / And tangling its roots among each other" (22–3).

The hero and narrator interpenetrate. The narrator begins his tale outside the cave, and he seems to stand outside Narcissus's mind. But he gradually merges with the hero's consciousness, as if Narcissus were divulging his own secrets in the third person. What is more, the "death" of Saint Narcissus turns out to be the story of his lives, or of his lives and deaths in love with one another. The text begins and ends with an invocation of the tomb; between, he glides through metamorphoses. Each stanza, almost every line, creates the self anew, like a phenomenological assembly-line. The moment he beholds himself, Narcissus slips out of his own clutches, only to take form again in some new beauty radically other than the old. As a tree, he is twisted in his own branches; as a fish he writhes in his own grasp: "his ancient beauty / Caught fast in the pink tips of his new beauty' (26–7). He becomes a young girl, violated by a drunken old man, who is just another incarnation of himself: "he felt drunken and old" (32). It is as if self-consciousness entailed the rape of self by self: for Narcissus can only know himself by being someone other, and that otherness returns to him as violence. The arrows which assail him are the piercing corners of his flesh, and his body is itself the wound that goads him into exile:

> By the river
> His eyes were aware of the pointed corners of his eyes
> And his hands aware of the pointed tips of his fingers.
>
> Struck down by such knowledge
> He could not live men's ways, but became a dancer before God.
> (13–17)

Man or woman, fish or tree, each death of self engenders a new life, and personality unravels through the chain of being. In a mockery of Genesis, Narcissus populates the world with phantoms made in his own image.[11]

In this protean world, there is no memory but frantic clutching, as each embodiment dissolves, followed by a stranger beauty and a crueller obsolescence. Consciousness "watches its successive modes of existence pass, one after another, and escape it", as Georges Poulet has written in another context. "To feel oneself live is to feel oneself leave behind, in every instant, an instant which *was* the very self."[12] The poem is exploring time—autobiographical time—in which the present folds back narcissistically upon the past, to seize the fading image of the self. Like the autobiographer, the narcissist longs to defeat the temporal and spatial difference that separates him from his image—yet he can only love himself because that self is severed from within. Time frustrates narcissism but sustains it, too, for the time in which the narcissist eludes his own embrace is the time which perpetuates desire. It is this delay that Eliot calls "the shadow" in "The Hollow Men":

> Between the idea
> And the reality
> Between the motion
> And the act
> Falls the Shadow
>
> (V, 5–9)

"The Death of Saint Narcissus" is a maze of shadows, too: dark mementoes of the interval between the author and the act. They return as the shadows of the morning and the evening in *The Waste Land*: the time before and after which overshadows the present, taunting the subject with his difference from himself. Indeed, all these shadows pose a threat to *presence*, and for this reason they foreshadow death. "Narcissus", like *The Waste Land*, lures the reader to the shadows—"(Come in under the shadow of this red rock)."[13] It is as if to come into the poem is to come into the darkness, and watch the shadows play upon the tomb as they played upon the walls of Plato's cave (another fable of the love of sunless simulacra).[14] In Ovid, the tale of Echo frames Narcissus's tragedy; and Eliot frames his own "Narcissus" in the tomb where it began, to make the text itself an echo-chamber.

For narcissism is not only the hero's malady, but a diagnosis of the *text*, its own perverse self-referentiality. Mallarmé imagined the poem as a grotto where language narcissistically reflects itself; and "The Death of Saint Narcissus" has encrypted reference, so that its words can only echo themselves.[15] Claustral, circular, the poem's repetitions gesture backwards to enfold its own ancient beauty in its new. The "convulsive thighs and knees" (19) of the third stanza are remembered in the sixth, when the old man assaults the young girl: and the victim and the violator oscillate in pseudo-symmetry, as if brutality and suffering were mirror-images of one another. As motifs repeat themselves, they alter, for it is difference that elicits repetition: and nothing can be doubled unless it has already double-crossed its self-identity. Within the first stanza, the rock changes from grey to red, because the day has worn its course from dawn to dusk, and time is the accomplice to alterity. The colour of Narcissus turns from grey to green (7, 38). The last line of the poem echoes the last line of the first stanza, but the shadow that was "on his lips" (7) has entered "in his mouth" (39). This change from "on" to "in" summarises the interiorising movement of the poem as a whole, for in the last line the text embraces its own image in a final circularity in which it, too, falls silent in its self-satiety.

Lyndall Gordon argues that "where Narcissus differs from *The Waste Land* pilgrim is in his failure to receive a sign."[16] But his beauty is itself a sign that marks him off: "he could not live men's ways . . ."[17]. To be a dancer before God is to make oneself into a sign, directed by the most inscrutable of choreographers. And, in the end, Narcissus dies into a trace, forfeiting his being to the "sign of blood":[17]

> He danced on the hot sand
> Until the arrows came.

As he embraced them his white skin surrendered itself
to the redness of blood, and satisfied him.
Now he is green, dry and stained
With the shadow in his mouth.

(35–9)

Here, the body of Narcissus turns from grey to green as if his own unliving image had begun to stir, and the whole cycle of self-love and self-oblivion had recommenced.[18] While the shadow in his mouth suggests his guilty pleasures, it could also represent the "stain" of speech: like writing, it traces a lost voice. If the text invites the reader to the grave, it is to reactivate this corpse of speech, a sign from which all selfhood has departed.

In Ovid, Narcissus confronts the silent traces of his living voice, and knows himself as relic, simulacrum. Being written, he is already mostly dead. His death is implicated in his doubling, as Freud links death to the compulsion to repeat, and as the tomb, in Eliot, reverberates with doubles, shadows, repetitions.[19] Like Narcissús, the autobiographer sacrifices self to writing, in his compulsion to repeat his life; but Eliot's laconic allegory implicates the reader, too. To seek one's image in the play of its reflections is to face one's death foreshadowed in the sepulchre of textuality.

Prufrock's Fixation

Freud argues that a narcissist may love:

(*a*) what he himself is (i.e. himself),
(*b*) what he himself was,
(*c*) what he himself would like to be,
(*d*) someone who was once part of himself.[20]

This list reveals that narcissism is an epistemological position, as well as an erotic one, because the self can only love the self by disavowing time. The narcissist denies the difference between what he was, what he is, and what he might have come to be, coercing all his past and future selves into the delusion of the present. Even in Ovid, Narcissus never "is", for his presence is founded on its representation, and his identity is just the phantom of his own imago. Likewise, Eliot's Narcissus can only love a self that has already slipped away, because there is no present tense in narcissistic time. His world consists of his discarded incarnations, too alien to be integrated in the self, and yet too similar to break his solipsism.

"The Love Song of J. Alfred Prufrock" was written earlier than "Saint Narcissus", but the crypt of narcissism has already been shattered. For the subject is patrolled at every moment, positioned by a gaze he cannot tame.[21] While Narcissus sees himself and makes himself his object, Prufrock sees himself *being seen*. He no longer loves himself but the look that constitutes his being from beyond. "The eyes that fix you in a formulated phrase" (56) fix the self in language and in space, estranging it to two exteriorities: and Prufrock owes his selfhood to the other as he owes his face to the faces that he meets. The rhythm of the poem is convulsive, for the other always takes the subject by surprise, and the moment of subjection is abrupt and ineluctable.

The title, "Love Song", appeals to someone else, but instead of a specific being, a general unease of otherness surrounds the speaker like the yellow fog, remorseless and impersonal. Often Prufrock acts as his own voyeur, pinned and wriggling under his own pitiless eye. For if he sees himself being seen, this is rather how he would be seen—were anybody really looking. We are not in Merleau-Ponty's world, which reciprocates the gaze of its spectator, but in the realm of Lacan's "*regard*", which *overlooks* the subject, penetrating to the death that founds his being: "as if a magic lantern threw the nerves in patterns on a screen" (105).[22] Here paranoia is the least of all delusions, much less deceitful than the ego that fancies itself master of the visible. The spectator is neither an external presence nor a mere projection of the self, for the gaze transpierces the interiority on which the very fiction of the self depends. Maurice Blanchot captures this sense of otherness in his essay "The Solitude of Writing":

> When I am alone . . . I am not alone, but am already returning to myself in the form of Someone. Someone is there, where I am alone. The fact of

> being alone is that I belong to this dead time that is not my time, nor yours, nor common time, but the time of Someone. Someone is what is still present when no one is there. In the place where I am alone, I am not there, there is no one there, but the impersonal is there: the outside as that which anticipates, precedes, dissolves all possibility of personal relationship. . . . Then fascination reigns.[23]

It is a coincidence that Blanchot is speaking of the solitude of *writing*: for Prufrock, too, renounces voice for letter, pleading aphasia as Hamlet pleads apraxia. This adulterated solitude could also set the scene for psychoanalytic transference. Because of the silence of the analyst, the analysand is constantly returning to himself as someone else, subjected to his own silent scrutiny. Indeed, Lacan would argue that "The Love Song" belongs to the same tradition as the transference, because they both derive from courtly love: a refined way of "making up for the absence of sexual relation by pretending that it is we who put an obstacle to it."[24] Like the forbidden mistress, the analyst calls forth the patient's love precisely by refusing to requite it. Moreover, Lacan insists that love is all that analytic discourse ever really speaks about: "Speaking of love, in analytic discourse, basically one does nothing else."[25] Here he may be recalling Freud, who in his essay on "A Special Type of Choice of Object Made by Men" suggests that analysis and literature are rivals for the same elusive object: the power to give speech to love.

> Up till now we have left it to the creative writer to depict for us the "necessary conditions for loving" which govern people's choice of an object. . . . But there is one circumstance which lessens the evidential value of what he has to say. Writers are under the necessity to produce intellectual and aesthetic pleasure, as well as certain emotional effects. . . . In consequence it becomes inevitable that science should concern herself with the same materials whose treatment by artists has given enjoyment to mankind for thousands of years, though her touch must be clumsier and the yield of pleasure less. These observations will, it may be hoped, serve to justify us in extending a strictly scientific treatment to the field of human love. Science is, after all, the most complete renunciation of the pleasure principle of which our mental activity is capable (SE XI 165).

According to Freud, psychoanalysis—the science of love—transcends its fumblings and convulsions. The scientist defeats the poet and his formerly exclusive rights to love: for scientific discourse overcomes the flesh with words, while poets are condemned to grope for both eternally. However, Lacan argues that far from a renunciation of the pleasure principle, "speaking of love is in itself a *jouissance*": and even Freud hints that science is not so much a non-lover as a bad lover.[26] Science suddenly becomes a "she", and we learn that her touch is clumsier than the poet's and her yield of pleasure less. Science may be wiser than poetry, but there is little doubt which Freud would rather spend the night with. The following pages will compare two discourses of love, one "scientific", one "poetic"—not to arbitrate their claims to love but to reveal their secret intimacy with each other. For psychoanalysis is in love with literature: its passion is betrayed in the insistence of the literary in its own procedures, and the uncanny reappearance, in the purest moments of its theory, of a scene of writing or a scene of reading. As we shall see, "The Love-Song of J. Alfred Prufrock" and Freud's papers on transference-love both complicate the question of impersonality, by submitting self and other to the vagaries of "love."

* * *

The word "transference" has two meanings in Freud, and both these meanings find a role in "Prufrock". Transference, in the singular, refers to the romance of therapy, where the patient weaves the analyst into the script of an archaic love. As in *Hamlet*, each must stage a "mousetrap" for the other, and both compulsively repeat another scene, with ghosts for audience. But Freud first used "transference" to mean displacement, as in the chimeras of a dream, where wishes glide from sign to sign. François Roustang has pointed out that these two meanings are continuous, because the transference in treatment is the detour through which love must lose its way, as wishes err through the displacements of the dream, or death divaricates through life.[27] On the rare occasions when Freud speaks of transferences in the plural, he usually means displacements, but gradually the singular form absorbs the plural. In this way, the fortunes of the *word* repeat the course of the analysis, in which the circulation of desire congeals into a single love, a stark subjection (SE XII 104).

These two meanings also correspond to two forms of magic which Freud discusses in *Totem and Taboo*. Contagious magic operates through contiguity, and thus compares to metonymy and synecdoche, while imitative magic works through similarity, like metaphor.[28] To cast a spell on someone through contagious magic, the witch must steal his hair, his garments, or his name, and this part then yields the power of the whole. Imitative magic, on the other hand, demands the manufacture of an effigy. "Whatever is then done to the effigy", writes Freud, "the same thing happens to the detested original . . ." (SE XIII 79). In treatment, the analyst plays effigy in order to ensnare the patient's love and conjure up the spirits of the dead, to whom all love in Freud eventually returns. To urge the patient to suppress her transference-love, he argues, "would be just as though, after summoning up a spirit from the underworld by cunning spells, one were to send him down again without having asked him a single question"—overwhelming or otherwise (SE XII 164). Clearly it is perilous to raise the demons of the transference, in spite of all the wonders that they tell: yet Freud assures us that "when all is said and done, it is impossible to destroy anyone *in absentia* or *in effigie*" (SE XII 108). Why "destroy"? It seems that the transference has now become the scene of death, rather than the theatre of desire. Lawrence once wrote that "It takes two people to make a murder: a murderer and a murderee"—but in the transference it is impossible to tell the difference, for both are spectres of each other's love.[29]

Because the effigy stands in for someone who is absent, usually for somebody already dead, death and absence are the intimate conditions of its masquerade. Death, indeed, can only manifest itself through simulacra. It necessitates the spectacle "without the repetition of which we could remain foreign to and ignorant of . . . the fiction, more or less removed from reality, of death", in Bataille's words.[30] Death *is* theatre, for it is always represented, never lived: and the theatre, in its turn, could be regarded as the art of vicarious unbeing. Similarly, Freud argues that primitive man first acknowledged death when he staged it in the form of ghosts; but this is also when he first defied it, by asserting that the dead return.[31] This equivocality extends to gods and demons, effigies and fetishes: for all these representations deny the truancy of their originals, as ghosts deny the very death they figure forth. Freud's argument implies that even the belief in other people originates in the belief in ghosts, so that the "other" is merely the phantom of a phantom, a demon in ruins. In the transference, the analyst, as effigy, must occupy the place of death, while the patient, like the primitive, submits to the supremacy of death in the same gesture with which he seems to be denying it (SE XIII, p. 93). For death indwells in the effigy itself, in the very act of theatralisation.

This may be the reason why Hamlet so exults in the success of the play within the play, as if he had already murdered Claudius by staging it.[32] And psychoanalysis confounds the world and stage as much as Hamlet does. For instance, when the transference first makes itself felt, Freud says there is "a complete *change of scene*":

> it is as though some piece of make-believe had been stopped by the sudden irruption of reality—as when, for instance, a cry of fire is raised during a theatrical performance. No doctor who experiences this for the first time will find it easy to retain his grasp on the analytic situation and to keep clear of the illusion that the treatment is really at an end (SE XII 162: my emphases).

It is only later that he finds that the fire and the cry are just the greatest masquerade of all. For the drama of analysis is a struggle to the death, where no one can be finally killed, because nothing real *takes place*. Even the transference fizzles into silence. For it is when the patient does *not* speak that Freud detects the signs of transference-love, and contends that every thought connected to the analyst has been replaced by nothing (SE XII 138). The theory of the transference is therefore the nothing that comes of nothing, a romance to dispel the silence that unnames the nothing of desire. Perhaps this is why Freud finds the transference *funny*—where love no longer touches and death no longer kills, and neither actor knows his lines, since both are dummies of a blind ventriloquism.[33] To extend Freud's metaphor, transference is all smoke and no fire; or better, a fire drill, rehearsing a catastrophe which has always already occurred and yet could never come to pass.

Though the patient has forgotten the love that he repeats, it is his desire which remembers *him* and seizes him in its automatism. This love adulterates the present with the past, because the "now" is nothing but the repetition of a past which can neither be remembered nor be stilled. The transference creates the simulacrum of a present in which no presence can be realised. As Freud writes, "the patient does not *remember* anything of what he has forgotten or repressed, but *acts* it out. . . . He *repeats* it, without . . . knowing that he is repeating it" (SE XII 150). Thus memory no longer guarantees the continuity of personality in Freud, for it eludes the governance of consciousness. But it is love which compels the patient to repeat, and to create the theatre of his own malaise, a love which Freud repeatedly identifies with writing. To the well-educated layman, he suggests, "things that have to do with love are incommensurable with everything else; they are, as it were, written on a special page on which no other writing is tolerated" (SE XII 160). For Freud, however, the page of love is never clean, and every passion superscribes a palimpsest. The accidents of early years predetermine one's capacity to love, and they produce "what might be described as a stereotype plate (or several such), which is constantly repeated—constantly reprinted afresh—in the course of the person's life . . ." (SE XII 99–100). Two years later, in 1914, he reiterates that love consists of "new editions of old traits" (SE XII 168). The reprints and the re-editions of this very metaphor suggest a kind of printerly tic in Freud, compelling him to reinscribe the theme of reinscription. It is this tic which persuades Derrida that psychoanalysis is a "writing-machine."[34] But it is a love-machine by the same token, for love and writing both dissolve into the tragicomic drama of revision.

Like transference, revision has no present tense, for it can either mean a second, after vision, or a preparation endlessly prolonged. It means "the waste sad time / Stretching before and after", in Eliot's words (*BN* V 38–9). Like Harold Bloom's "revisionary poet", the patient must overcome the writing of the dead if he is to alter the script of his desire. J. Alfred Prufrock is a revisionary, too, much as he would like to be a visionary, and it is the impossibility of sexual relation that enables him to stage his love: a staging which in Freud becomes another kind of writing. Yeats suggests that "the passions, when . . . they cannot find fulfillment, become vision"; but in "Prufrock" they become *re*vision, re-enactment, epilogue.[35] The integrity of subjectivity dissolves, because the love that brings the subject into being is always second-hand, twice-sung. As we shall see, the "Love Song" is structured like the transference, much as the transference is fraught with poetry in Freud.

* * *

Hugh Kenner says that "J. Alfred Prufrock is a name plus a voice."[36] This is a useful formula, for it insists that Prufrock is an artifact of language, rather than a person in the common sense: but it fails to register the tension between the name and the voices of the text. There is a sharp disjunction between the poem and its title; between the love song we expect, and the monologue we hear; between the speaker and his name. Like a letter without an address, Prufrock's love song returns to sender. As early as the first line, when Prufrock beckons to a nameless other, the poem puts its persons and positions into jeopardy: "Let us go then, you and I". Is the you, here, male or female, dead or alive? A lover or a friend? An alter ego or an effigy? Most critics think that Prufrock is addressing his divided self, and Robert Langbaum even argues that "we all" agree upon this reading.[37] Eliot himself suggested that the "you" stood for an "unidentified male companion", but most readers have ignored the hint, perhaps because it whispers of a homosexual attachment: though Eliot protested that it had "no emotional content whatever."[38] If the "you" is part of Prufrock, even an estranged, dissociated part, it does not threaten the decorum of the text nor endanger the monopoly of subjectivity. When the critics sense a split in Prufrock's *personality*, however, they have really made a diagnosis of the text itself, because its broken idioms belie the singularity of voice and proper name. Traces of a prolonged incubation, these incongruities have disconcerted many readers. Ezra

Pound urged Eliot to cut the Hamlet passage, which he had composed in 1910 at Harvard; C. K. Stead could have wished he had removed the fog.[39] But the meaning of the text depends upon the fissures of its discourse, for they dramatise the speaker's dislocation from himself, misfitted in the language which bespeaks him.

Kristian Smidt argues that the "you" invokes the reader—perhaps unwittingly suggesting that the poem is a love song to its own interpreter.[40] This is less improbable than it might seem, for Prufrock seeks a lover's understanding from the reader, and it is impossible to separate the sexual from the textual flirtation. "Speaking of love is in itself a *jouissance*", as Lacan says: and in "Prufrock" the act of speech *becomes* the act of love, in the moment that they both become impossible.[41] As its title intimates, "Prufrock" is exploring love *and* song, the articulation of language and desire, and the digressions that divert them both from satisfaction. The speaker never makes his declaration, any more than he consummates his love, but the ruses which defer his union with the object of his ardour serve the purpose of sustaining the desire of desire. For Prufrock is in love with language, with fetishes and decoys and deflections, with all the signs that separate him from his dream of total revelation, yet also keep that dream tormentingly alive. It is unclear from the title whether Prufrock writes the love song or the song writes him, whether it is *by* him or *about* him. But the rhetorical obsessiveness suggests that the subject is entrammelled in his discourse like an actor imprisoned in a script, or an analyst conscripted in the transference. His poem is in love with the process of its composition, even as it courts the other in its longing for a reference beyond itself. Though it may address a lover, the reader, or the self, it is primarily a love song to a love song: a song of longing for the power, shared by all the greatest bards, to sing of love.[42] Moreover, it is a song-in-progress, beset by all the wishes and frustrations that attend upon the act of writing as they dog the enterprises of desire. Prufrock despairs of his prowess in the language, even more than in the act, of love, deprived of both performance and performative: "And how should I begin?" "So how should I presume?" (69, 54).

All Prufrock's actions can be understood in terms of language *or* desire, and his whole universe trembles between word and flesh. He cruises language much as he noctambulates among the streets, which represent his own discursive strategems: "a tedious argument / Of insidious intent" (8-9). The steps he climbs are "stops and steps of the mind", and of the poem's own decisions and revisions (48).[43] The constant repetitions—"There will be time, there will be time"—do not mean that there is time for everything, but that the poem is beginning and beginning, unable to decide on one line and discard another (29). It is writing as it might be raining, and the subject is enslaved to an autonomous compulsion to revise:

> There will be time to murder and create . . .
> And time yet for a hundred indecisions,
> And for a hundred visions and revisions,
> Before the taking of a toast and tea.
>
> (28–34)

Hands "lift and drop a *question* on your plate" (30); eyes "fix you in a formulated *phrase*" (56) (my emphases); and the sea is where we drown in *voices* rather than in foam:

> We have lingered in the chambers of the sea
> By sea-girls wreathed with seaweed red and brown
> Till human voices wake us, and we drown.
>
> (129–31)

Prufrock hesitates, digresses, deferring both his amorous and his discursive realisations. Like the act of love, the act of writing is continually suspended in a kind of *scriptum interruptum*.

If he could confess his love, Prufrock dreams that he would know himself. "I shall tell you all"! he cries (95). But the very processes of narrative reduce his history to synecdochic smithereens: "Then how should I begin / To spit out all the butt-ends of my days and ways?" (59-60). Remembering becomes dismembering, as all his memories and dreams disintegrate into the butt-ends of impossible totalities. Prufrock is himself a moving fragmentation: a bald spot, a morning coat, a simple pin, some arms and legs, all casually thrown together. When he says, "I should have been a pair of ragged claws" (73), even the claws are decomposing, let alone the lobster. He sees his "head (grown slightly bald) brought in upon a platter" (82), decapitated before he ever had a chance to sing from empty cisterns or exhausted wells, like the visionary that he hoped to be.[44] The city, too, dissolves into the refuse of the lives that have passed by, leaving nothing but the sawdust of their trodden dreams. Its hotels are reduced to oyster-shells: and the fog licks its synecdochic tongue into the corners of the evening like an abject Cheshire cat.

Meanwhile, the female body unravels into an inventory of its parts and its associated bric-à-brac: hands, faces, voices, eyes, arms, teacups, and the skirts that trail across the floor. Prufrock never speaks *about* his love, for he is subjected to his own desire, which circulates through objects and part-objects: "Arms that are braceleted and white and bare / (But in the lamplight, downed with light brown hair!). . . . Arms that lie along a table, or wrap about a shawl" (64–7). Dismembered, fetishised, these lovely arms reveal that it is the phantasmal amputations of synecdoche that liberate the body for desire.[45] Desire circumambulates through orts and fragments, eroding any bodily *Gestalt*: and Love is the unfamiliar name that "Prufrock" gives this skittish deconstruction.

One of Eliot's first readers, the anonymous reviewer for *The Times Literary Supplement*, glimpsed these rhetorical disintegrations more clearly than his later, friendlier critics:

> Mr. Eliot's notion of poetry—he calls the "observations" poems—seems to be a purely analytical treatment, verging sometimes on the catalogue, of personal relations and environments, uninspired by any glimpse beyond them and untouched by any genuine rush of feeling. . . . Among other reminiscences which pass through the rhapsodist's mind and which he thinks the public should know about are dust in crevices, smells of chestnuts in the streets, and female smells in cluttered rooms, and cigarettes in corridors, and cocktail smells in bars.
>
> The fact that these things occurred to the mind of Mr. Eliot is surely of the smallest importance to any one—even to himself. They certainly have no relation to "poetry". . . .[46]

As far as this critic is concerned, everything that poetry had formerly excluded as eccentric now returns impertinently to the light. In "Prufrock", these fragments form a kind of switchboard for the transmigrations of desire, subversive of the very notion of totality. Through their sheer itemisation, the objects in the poem overwhelm the self, and do Prufrock's experiencing for him. For example, the evening etherised upon a table transfers the speaker's anaesthesia to the atmosphere. But the image seems to etherise—or otherise—the subject in return, to bleed him of his body and his consciousness. Indeed, the ether is the least fragmented body in the poem, and the only body that enjoys its sensuality. It is the fog that "licks" and "rubs", the air that indulges in caresses:

> And the afternoon, the evening, sleeps so peacefully!
> Smoothed by long fingers,
> Asleep . . . tired . . . or it malingers,
> Stretched on the floor, here beside you and me.
>
> (75–7)

Here, Prufrock's love is staged "beside" him, in the empty air. But it is important that the air is associated with the afternoon or evening, for Prufrock is etherised by *time*. This is the time that separates desire from fulfillment, motive from execution, thought from speech: in Eliot's words, "the awful separation between potential passion and any actualization possible in life."[47] Time defers.

The way that time defers is through revision. Time itself becomes the object of revision, for the whole poem agonises over writing time. The incessant repetition of "There will be time" is itself a way of losing time, as Nancy K. Gish suggests;[48] but also a way of gaining it, to prolong the re-editions of desire. "Stretched . . . beside you and me", time deflects Prufrock's ardour from his lover. But in this process time itself becomes the object of desire, in the form of the voluptuary sweetness of the evening. Indeed, Prufrock addresses time so constantly, in every tone of envy, rage, pain, impatience, longing, humour, flattery, seduction, that he can only really be in love with time.

Revisionary time: because revision has no present tense, and neither does "The Love Song". Instead, the poem hesitates between anticipation and regret for missed appointments with the self, the other or the muse. It begins in the future tense ("there will be time . . ." [23ff]); shifts into the perfect ("For I have known . . ." [50ff]); and finally subsides into the past conditional, the tense of wishful thinking: "I should have been . . ." (73). Because presence would mean speech, apocalypse, Prufrock only pauses in the present tense to say what he is not—"No! I am not Prince Hamlet" (a disavowal that conjures up the effigy that it denies, since Hamlet is the very spirit of theatricality). The poem concludes dreaming the future, faithful if only to its hopeless passion for postponement: "Till human voices wake us, and we drown." Prufrock feels the need to speak as a proof of his identity and as a rock to give him anchorage: yet speech would also mean his end, for voices are waters in which Prufrocks drown.

Through time, all Prufrock's aims have turned awry. His passion and his speech have lost themselves in detours, never to achieve satiety. Love becomes desire—tormenting, inexhaustible—while speech and revelation have surrendered to writing and revision, to the digressions which prolong his dalliance with time. Time is the greatest fetish of them all, the mother of all fetishes, since it is through time that all aims turn aside to revel in rehearsals, detours, transferences. What Prufrock longs for is a talking cure because, like Freud, he thinks that speech alone can transform repetition into memory. What talking remedies is *writing*: for his illness lies in his obsessive re-editions of the text of love.[49] But Prufrock's very histrionics show he is condemned to re-enactment, to forget what he repeats in a script that restlessly obliterates its history. It is by remembering the past that the subject can establish his identity, but only by forgetting it can he accede to his desire. Refusing to declare his love, or pop the overwhelming question, Prufrock renounces the position of the speaking subject, but he instigates the drama of revision in its stead. And it is by refusing sexual relation that he conjures up the theatre of desire. The love song Prufrock could not *sing* has been *writing* itself all the time, and the love that could not speak its name has been roving among all the fetishes his rhetoric has liberated to desire. We had the love song, even if we missed the meaning.

Gull against the Wind

> It was not, we remember, the "immense spaces" themselves but their *eternal silence* that terrified Pascal.
>
> T. S. Eliot (*UPUC* 133)

Here I am.

So speaks Gerontion—or the voice suspended from his title—or the writings that his name does not entitle us to read as his. Does "Gerontion" designate the speaker? Or does it name the house he does not own? The battle he did not fight? The thoughts he cannot choose but think? As soon as speech begins, the "I" begins to lose itself in the giddy nowness of a discourse without a source, the abyss of a "here" without a name. The gap between Gerontion's name and his "I am" is the first of many "windy spaces" in the text (16): *brisures* where the bond between the speaker and his voice is welded in its own dissolve, immuring him into a prisonhouse of language.[50] For the house in which the speaker stiffens is built out of the words he frames around his own vacuity. "Being read to by a boy" (2), Gerontion's meditation is encrypted in another text, and it is impossible to tell his voice from this reiteration of another's. Here I am, in a language which I only rent and do not own, a house whose fissures threaten all propriety of discourse.

All is "hidden when we would backward see from what region of remoteness the whatness of our whoness hath fetched its whenceness," writes Joyce in The Oxen of the Sun (*U* 391). Identity, or "whoness", depends upon whenceness, upon a date of birth, a locus of origination. But Gerontion has no origin. All he has is the "dead present" of his house, whose landlord is a parody of whenceness:[51]

> And the Jew squats on the window sill, the owner.
> Spawned in some estaminet of Antwerp,
> Blistered in Brussels, patched and peeled in London.
>
> (8–10).

In this fascistic image, the Jew reduces history to vagrancy, contagion, and miscegenation rather than the revelation of the spirit. Under his dominion, Gerontion forfeits his own past:

> I was neither at the hot gates
> Nor fought in the warm rain
> Nor knee deep in the salt marsh, heaving a cutlass,
> Bitten by flies, fought.
>
> (3–6)

"Gerontion" figures history as a bad investment, a pointless avarice. "Since what is kept must be adulterated" (58), to preserve the past is merely to corrupt it. This is why the withered stumps of time lie strewn about, sterile and illegible: "Rocks, moss, stonecrop, iron, merds" (12). Here the very words have been reduced to entropy, verbless and immemorious.

Thus it is no accident that critics restore meaning to the poem by restoring history to its words. In the face of Gerontion's oblivion, or history's vicious coquetry (33–43), Frye speaks of the "mnemonic adhesiveness" of the language, Pearson of "association", and Kenner (after Empson) of the "echoes and recesses" of the words.[52] These readings reverse the poem's strategies, replenishing its broken images with memory and sense; they shut away, as best they can, the infinite spaces and their eternal silence which terrify Gerontion as they terrified Pascal. For the text has less to do with time than space, less to do with history than amnesia. Evolution gives way to repetition, and Gerontion's monologue retraces its own steps, as if enunciation were itself a science of forgetting.

For example, the second half of the poem resumes most of the motifs of the first, except that the devouring are now to be devoured. Mr. Silvero, Madame de Tornquist, Fräulein von Kulp, who partook of their unspeakable communion in the juvescence of the text, are now to be consumed, as the poem and the year turn back again, and the tiger resurges like a scar: "The tiger springs in the new year" (48). Indeed, the text itself unravels like a spring: a spring about to snap and break into a demonic repetition of the *cogito*. "I am a thing that thinks", writes Descartes, like Gerontion entombed in his own thoughts. "I shall now close my eyes, I shall stop my ears, I shall call away all my senses, I shall efface even from my thoughts all the images of corporeal things . . .".[53] "I have lost my sight, smell, hearing, taste and touch", Gerontion echoes (59). The trouble with the *cogito*, however, is that the self confirms its own existence only in the instant of self-consciousness, and therefore to stop thinking is to cease to be. This is why Gerontion obsessively repeats, "Think now. . . . Think now. . . . Think. . . . Think at last. . . . Think at last . . ." (33, 36, 43, 48, 50).

The poem begins with Gerontion thinking in his house, but ends with his dry thoughts rattling in his brain, after the Jew and all the other "squatters" are evicted. These inmates were themselves the figments of his reverie, and the house the image of his consciousness. Rather than the master of its mansion, the ego has become the tenant of a rented house: and the very spatiality of this motif casts suspicion on Descartes's belief in unextended mind. The "windy spaces" are the index of an irreducible extension: they mean that identity can never close upon itself, on the inside of its own interiority.[54] They designate a *movement*, a spacing rather than a space, for every effort to subdue the wind displaces it, and opens up another hole, another draught. Space is not a place but a contagion, that rushes through the corridors of history, whistles through the cracks under the door, and blows through every fissure of the house, the brain, the text, into the cunning passages between the words. It even insinuates itself into the sneeze. This wind no longer breathes divine afflatus—there is no blessing in this breeze—for it was woven in the "vacant shuttles" of a writing that is the forgetting of the spirit, a writing that is spacing (29).[55]

Mallarmé imagined writing as a sky turned inside out: the white stars on the night sky form an inverted image of the words swaddled in their darkness on the page. "Tu remarquas on n'écrit pas, lumineusement, sur champ obscur, l'alphabet des astres . . . l'homme poursuit noir sur blanc."[56] *L'alphabet des astres*—astral and disastrous—both senses of "des astres" suit Gerontion's alphabet. The poem ends in disaster: for the tenants of the house are disengorged and whirled among the interstellar winds. In "Gerontion", however, "noir sur blanc" surrenders in the end to "blanc sur blanc". Discourse perishes beneath the blizzard of its blanks, as the "Gull against the wind" dissolves into white feathers on a whiter snow:

> De Bailhache, Fresca, Mrs. Cammel, whirled
> Beyond the circuit of the shuddering Bear
> In fractured atoms. Gull against the wind, in the windy straits
> Of Belle Isle, or running on the Horn.
> White feathers in the snow, the Gulf claims,
> And an old man driven by the Trades
> To a sleepy corner.
>
> (67–73)

The windy spacing that inhabits writing takes command, as if the Trades had swept away the last saving darkness of the word. The whole text stutters on the *cogito*, to intimate that Descartes could not shut extension out: interiority is howling with the winds of space, the chilled delirium of exteriority (62). This violence is reinscribed in windstorms, windy spaces, vacant shuttles, snow, the whitenesses bespattered through the text; together with the mazy vacancies of history, the spider's web and the corrosive writings of the weevil—all those figures with which the poem meditates its own spacing, its own exploding interior.[57] Household pests, the spider and the weevil sculpture space into the very architecture of interiority. It is impossible to fumigate the prisonhouse of language, to rid it of these stealthy artisans of negativity. The poem ends in fractured atoms, because its thoughts no longer have an I to think them, nor a house to shelter them against the blasts of space, the storms of snow.

The Backward Devils

In "Saint Narcissus", "Prufrock", and "Gerontion", Eliot creates three paradigms of subjectivity, all of which confound the notion of a unified integral self. The series opens ominously with Saint Narcissus, who courts his death in his infatuation with his image. The world of "Narcissus" is a world in flux, where the hero slips through his own fingers, driven as relentlessly through incarnations as the poem drives the reader through non sequiturs. It is such a world that Eliot repudiates in 1927, complaining that "if there is no fixed truth, there is no fixed object for the will to tend to. If truth is always changing, there is nothing to do but sit down and watch the pictures."[58] On the other hand, Prufrock longs to fix himself, but instead he is fixated in and by the other, and he dwells in a revisionary time, trapped between nostalgia and suspense for a self-coincidence which never can occur. While Kant determines time to be the "inner sense", and Heidegger perceives it as "the essence of all autosolicitation", Prufrock's time consists in the delay which separates the subject from himself.[59] Gerontion, too, complains that history "gives too late" or "gives too soon", eroding the presence of the self (39, 41). Inside and outside, self and other, time and space contaminate each other—as if the weevil, in its restless deconstruction, had consumed the walls that hold antitheses apart.

Framed within the repetition of another text, Gerontion turns into the reader of his own discourse, a fate which Eliot foretells for every poet. In a lecture on "The Varieties of Metaphysical Poetry", he declares that the poet "is not necessarily aware of all the implications of his own work. Indeed he had better not be occupied with general questions at all. He is an accident, & should behave as such."[60] (Since writing is disaster in "Gerontion", the writer is as accidental as could be, the helpless agent of his own dissemination.) If the writer cannot *own* his work, all he can do is *read* it: "in the course of time a poet may become merely a reader in respect of his own works, forgetting his original meaning . . .". At this stage, "what a poem means is as much what it means to others as what it means to the author . . .".[61] But now the author is an other too, and he has as much or little right as any *hypocrite lecteur* to shrug aside the poem's embryology. However, if Gerontion is the paradigm, reading must imply the loss of self, rather than the mastery of meaning. The reader is "fundamentally anonymous", as Blanchot writes: "he is any reader, unique but transparent. Instead of adding his name to the book . . . he rather erases all names by his nameless presence . . .".[62] The act of reading is an act of dispossession, as violent as the explosion of Gerontion's house, and the reading subject is a roving cancellation, driven by his own forgetfulness.

In his book *On Poetry and Poets*, Eliot argues that speech, at its most fundamental level, means "one person talking to another", and therefore presupposes a community. On the other hand, we read and write alone: and Eliot laments that "most poetry today is written to be read in solitude."[63] What unites Narcissus, Prufrock and Gerontion is their solitude, which is beyond bereavement, eviction or senility, beyond the pain and the absurdity of sex: theirs is that solitude beyond the very possibility of integration that Eliot associates with reading and with writing (*PP* 31, 17). Saint Narcissus never speaks at all, but retreats into the desert of his self-delight, leaving nothing but a shadow where his voice should be. Prufrock only writes because he is convinced that he cannot be heard: like Guido in the poem's epigraph, who speaks because he knows that he is dead. Gerontion is not a "character", but a dull head among windy spaces, a space where reading and rewriting recommence, evacuating every interlocutor. These names are not confessing their life-stories, nor divulging the labyrinths of their psychologies. They are telling us that they cannot be told. They exist in the paralysis between the need and the impossibility of speech: "And how should I begin?"

In *Four Quartets*, Eliot attempts to rescue history, and to restore the self through the circumnavigations of the memory. But he did not arrive at "Little Gidding" until he had traversed *The Waste Land*.

Notes

1. Ovid, *Metamorphoses*, trans. Frank Justus Miller (London: Heinemann; Loeb Classical Library, 1936), Vol. I, Bk. III, pp. 148–61, lines 339–510. Book and line numbers henceforth given in text.
2. John Brenkman, "Narcissus in the Text", *Georgia Review*, 30 (1976), 320. Compare Plato, who argues that painted images resemble writing in that both maintain a "most majestic silence": *Phaedrus*, trans. R. Hackforth, in *Collected Dialogues*, p. 521.

3. Eliot, *Poems Written in Early Youth* (London: Faber and Faber, 1967), pp. 34–5; all quotations from the poem come from *CPP* 605–6. Line numbers to Eliot's poems henceforth given in text.
4. See *Poems Written in Early Youth*, p. 42.
5. *Eliot's Early Years*, p. 94.
6. See, *inter alia*, Marianne Thormählen, *The Waste Land: A Fragmentary Wholeness* (Lund: CWK Gleerup, 1978), p. 11. Recently, some readings of the poem have at last appeared: e.g. Vicki Mahaffey, " 'The Death of Saint Narcissus' and 'Ode': Two Suppressed Poems by T. S. Eliot", *American Literature*, 50 (1979), 604–12; Nancy R. Canley, "From Narcissus to Tiresias: T. S. Eliot's Use of Metamorphosis", *Modern Language Review*, 74 (1979), 281–6; Gregory S. Jay, *T. S. Eliot and the Poetics of Literary History* (Baton Rouge and London: Louisiana State University Press, 1983), pp. 101–8.
7. *The Waste Land*, 25–9; 318.
8. See Eusebius, *The Ecclesiastical History and the Martyrs of Palestine*, trans. Lawlor and Oulton (London: Macmillan, 1927), Vol. I, Bk. VI, Section 9, pp. 184–5; see also Peter F. Anson, *The Call of the Desert: The Solitary Life in the Christian Church* (London: SPCK, 1964), p. 9; Gordon, *Eliot's Early Years*, pp. 91, 58; and Nancy K. Gish, *Time in the Poetry of T. S. Eliot* (London: Macmillan, 1981), pp. 51–2.
9. See Gordon, *Eliot's Early Years*, pp. 61–2; 61n.
10. Eliot, Notes on Philosophy, Ms., Houghton Library, Cambridge, Mass., b.MS Am 1691 (130). See also Gordon, *Eliot's Early Years*, p. 70; and pp. 141–2, for a bibliography of Eliot's reading in mysticism, 1908–14.
11. The dancer and the tree are also favoured Romantic images, and the corpse which withers in the tomb may represent the undead narcissism of Romanticism, which Eliot will never quite succeed in burying. A further possibility is that Eliot borrowed the transformations of Narcissus from the fragments of Empedocles, which he would have read in John Burnet's *Early Greek Philosophy* at Harvard. Empedocles claims to be an exiled divinity, condemned by a decree of Necessity to "wander thrice ten thousand years from the abodes of the blessed, being born throughout the time in all manners of mortal forms. . . . I have been ere now a boy and a girl, a bush and a bird and a dumb fish in the sea", he laments. And now that these wandering spirits are encased in flesh, he mourns that "We have come under this roofed-in cave" [Empedocles, *Purifications*, in John Burnet, *Early Greek Philosophy* (London: A. and C. Black, 1908), Fragments 115, 117, 120, pp. 256–7]. The transmigrations and the cave resemble Eliot's; but they prove that the poem is polymorphously allusive, rather than exhausting its prefigurements.
12. Georges Poulet, *Studies in Human Time*, trans. Elliot Coleman (Baltimore: Johns Hopkins University Press, 1956), p. 16.
13. *The Waste Land*, 26.
14. See Plato, *The Republic*, trans. Paul Shorey, Bk. VII, in *Collected*

Dialogues, p. 747ff.

15. See Mallarmé, *Oeuvres complètes*, p. 851; and Jacques Derrida, "The Double Session", in *Dissemination*, p. 210ff.
16. *Eliot's Early Years*, p. 91.
17. See *Murder in the Cathedral*, *CPP* 11, lines 274–5.
18. Eusebius writes, "Narcissus appeared from somewhere, as if come to life again", after his exile among the rocks (Eusebius, *Ecclesiastical History*, Vol. I, Bk. VI, Section 9, p. 185).
19. See Freud, *Beyond the Pleasure Principle*, SE XVIII 1–64.
20. Freud, "On Narcissism: An Introduction", SE XIV 90.
21. Gordon says that "Prufrock" was completed in July-August, 1911 (*Eliot's Early Years*, p. 45); and Eliot, in a letter to John C. Pope, stated that the poem was conceived in 1910. See Pope, "Prufrock and Raskolnikov Again: A Letter from Eliot", *American Literature*, 18 (1947), 319–21. "Prufrock" was first published in *Poetry*, 6 (1915), 130–5.
22. See Maurice Merleau-Ponty, *The Visible and the Invisible*, trans. Alphonso Lingis (Evanston: Northwestern University Press, 1968), p. 139; Jacques Lacan, "Of the Gaze as Objet Petit a", in *The Four Fundamental Concepts of Psycho-Analysis* (London: Hogarth, 1977), pp. 65–119.
23. *The Gaze of Orpheus and Other Literary Essays*, trans. Lydia Davis (Barrytown, New York: Station Hill, 1981), p. 74.
24. See *Feminine Sexuality: Jacques Lacan and the Ecole Freudienne*, ed. Juliet Mitchell and Jacqueline Rose (New York: Norton, 1982), p. 141.
25. *Ibid.*, p. 154.
26. *Ibid.*, p. 144.
27. See Roustang, *Psychoanalysis Never Lets Go*, trans. Ned Lukacher (Baltimore: Johns Hopkins University Press, 1980), pp. 66–7; see also SE XVIII 1–64.
28. Freud, *Totem and Taboo*, SE XIII 81. See also Roman Jakobson, "Two Aspects of Language and Two Types of Aphasic Disturbances", in Jakobson and Halle, *Fundamentals of Language* (The Hague: Mouton, 1956), p. 81.
29. See Lawrence, *Women in Love* (1921; New York: Random, 1950), p. 36.
30. Quoted in Jacques Derrida, "From Restricted to General Economy: A Hegelianism without Reserve", in *Writing and Difference* (Chicago: University of Chicago Press, 1978), p. 258.
31. See Ch. I: see also "The 'Uncanny' ", where Freud speaks of the double as at once the "assurance of immortality" and the "uncanny harbinger of death" (SE XVII 235).
32. See Ernest Jones, *Hamlet and Oedipus* (1949; New York: Norton, 1976), p. 89: the idea is Otto Rank's.
33. See SE XII 159.
34. See Derrida, "Freud and the Scene of Writing", in *Writing and Difference*, p. 227ff.
35. Yeats, *Per Amica Silentia Lunae* (1917), in *Mythologies* (1959; New

York: Macmillan, 1969), p. 341.

36. *The Invisible Poet: T. S. Eliot*, p. 35. On p. 3, Kenner argues that the name was an unconscious reminiscence of "Prufrock-Littau, furniture wholesalers."

37. See Langbaum, "New Modes of Characterization in *The Waste Land*", in *T. S. Eliot in his Time: Essays on the Occasion of the Fiftieth Anniversary of The Waste Land*, ed. A. Walton Litz (Princeton: Princeton University Press, 1973), p. 98. For critics who agree with Langbaum, see, for instance, George Williamson, *A Reader's Guide to T. S. Eliot: A Poem-by-Poem Analysis* (New York: H. Woolf, 1953), pp. 59, 65; Elizabeth Schneider, "Prufrock and After: The Theme of Change", *PMLA*, 87 (1972), 1104 C. K. Stead, *The New Poetic: Yeats to Eliot* (London: Hutchinson, 1964), pp. 149, 152, 154; see also Langbaum, *The Poetry of Experience: The Dramatic Monologue in Modern Literary Tradition* (New York: Norton, 1957), p. 190. My own view is closer to Robert M. Adams, who sees Prufrock as "a set of quasi-persons", in "Precipitating Eliot", in Litz, ed., *Eliot in his Time*, p. 148.

38. Quoted from a letter to Kristian Smidt in his *Poetry and Belief in the Work of T. S. Eliot* (1949; repr. London: Routledge and Kegan Paul, 1961), p. 85.

39. *L* 153; Stead, *The New Poetic*, p. 153.

40. Smidt, *Poetry and Belief*, p. 85.

41. *Feminine Sexuality*, ed. Mitchell and Rose, p. 154.

42. This is John E. Jackson's idea, in *La Question du moi: Un aspect de la modernité poétique européenne: T. S. Eliot—Paul Célan—Yves Bonnefoy* (Neuchâtel: Editions de la Baconnière, 1978), p. 50.

43. See "Ash Wednesday", line 114: *CPP* 93.

44. See *The Waste Land*, V, 385, *CPP* 73.

45. See Freud, "On Fetishism", SE XXI 149–57. In "The 'Uncanny' " (1919), Freud compares the double, which represents the "energetic denial of the power of death", to the multiplication of phallic symbols in dreams, which represent the denial of castration (SE XVIII 235). Structurally, the fetish and the ghost have many similarities.

46. Anon., review of *Prufrock and Other Observations*, *TLS*, 805 (1917), 299. For a similar view in an early reviewer see Anon., review of *Ara Vos Prec*, *TLS*, 948 (1920), 184. Terry Eagleton also mentions the fetishistic aspect of "Prufrock" in *Exiles and Emigrés* (London: Chatto and Windus, 1970), p. 143.

47. Eliot, "Beyle and Balzac", review of *A History of the French Novel, to the Close of the Nineteenth Century*, Vol. II, by George Saintsbury, *Athenaeum*, 464 (1919), 392–3.

48. Gish, *Time in the Poetry of T. S. Eliot*, pp. 15–16.

49. It was Josef Breuer's patient "Anna O." who coined the phrase "the talking cure" for psychoanalysis: see Breuer and Freud, *Studies on Hysteria*, SE II 30.

50. See Jacques Derrida, *Of Grammatology*, p. 65. See also Friedrich Nietzsche, *Der Wille Zur Macht*, in *Gesammelte Werke* (München:

Musarion Verlag, 1922), Vol. XIX, no. 522, p. 34.
51. See Blanchot, *The Gaze of Orpheus*, p. 74.
52. Northrop Frye, *T. S. Eliot* (Edinburgh and London: Oliver and Boyd, 1963), p. 84; Gabriel Pearson, "Eliot: An American Use of Symbolism", in *Eliot in Perspective*, ed. Graham Martin, pp. 85–6; Hugh Kenner, *The Invisible Poet*, p. 116. For speculations on the influence of Henry Adams on Eliot's view of history, see Harvey Gross, " 'Gerontion' and the Meaning of History", *PMLA*, 73 (1958), 299–304.
53. René Descartes, *Philosophical Works*, trans. Elizabeth S. Haldane and G. R. T. Ross (1911); repr. New York: Dover, 1931), p. 157.
54. See Derrida, *Positions*, pp. 81, 94.
55. See Derrida, *Of Grammatology*, p. 24. In *Positions*, Derrida stresses that spacing is a *movement*, an activity (p. 81).
56. Mallarmé, "Quant au livre", in *Oeuvres complètes*, p. 370.
57. See Derrida, "The Double Session", in *Dissemination*, pp. 175–286, for a similar analysis of the play of "les blancs" in Mallarmé.
58. See Bonamy Dobrée, "T. S. Eliot: A Personal Reminiscence", in *T. S. Eliot: The Man and his Work*, ed. Allen Tate (New York: Dell, 1966), p. 78.
59. See Kant, *Critique of Pure Reason*, pp. 65–6; Heidegger, *Kant and the Problem of Metaphysics* (Bloomington: Indiana University Press, 1962), p. 194. See also John Brenkman's fuller discussion of these passages in "Narcissus in the Text", p. 314.
60. Eliot, "The Varieties of Metaphysical Poetry" III, MS., Houghton Library, Cambridge, Mass.
61. *UPUC* 130: see the discussion of these passages in Chapter II.
62. Blanchot, *The Gaze of Orpheus*, p. 93.
63. See Chapter II.

CHAPTER III

The Waste Land: A Sphinx without a Secret

In a fable of Oscar Wilde's, Gerald, the narrator, finds his old companion Lord Murchison so puzzled and anxious that he urges him to unburden his mind. Murchison confides that he fell in love some time ago with the mysterious Lady Alroy, whose life was so entrenched in secrecy that every move she made was surreptitious, every word she spoke conspiratorial. Fascinated, he resolved to marry her. But on the day he planned for his proposal, he caught sight of her on the street, "deeply veiled", and walking swiftly towards a lodging house, where she let herself in with her own key. Suspecting a secret lover, he abandoned her in rage and stormed off to the Continent to forget her. Soon afterwards, however, he learnt that she was dead, having caught pneumonia in the theatre. Still tormented by her mystery, he returned to London to continue his investigations. He cross-examined the landlady of the lodging house, but she insisted that Lady Alroy always visited her rooms alone, took tea, and left as blamelessly as she had come. " 'Now, what do you think it all meant?' " Murchison demands. For Gerald, the answer is quite simple: the lady was " 'a sphinx without a secret.' "[1]

Now, *The Waste Land* is a sphinx without a secret, too, and to force it to confession may also be a way of killing it. This poem, which has been so thoroughly *explained*, is rarely *read* at all, and one can scarcely see the "waste" beneath the redevelopments. Most commentators have been so busy tracking its allusions down and patching up its tattered memories that they have overlooked its broken images in search of the totality it might have been. Whether they envisage the poem as a pilgrimage, a quest for the Holy Grail, an elegy to Europe or to Jean Verdenal, these readings treat the text as if it were a photographic negative, tracing the shadows of a lost or forbidden body.[2]

This is how Freud first undertook interpretation, too, but his patients forced him to revise his method, and his experience may shed a different kind of light upon *The Waste Land*. In *Studies on Hysteria*, Freud and Breuer argue that "hysterics suffer mainly from reminiscences" (and by this definition, *The Waste Land* is the most hysterical of texts).[3] Since the hysteric somatises her desire, enciphering her memories upon her flesh, Freud imagined that he could alleviate her suffering by salvaging the painful recollections. However, these archaeologies would leave her cold. For this reason, he shifted his attention from the past to the present, from reminiscence to resistance, from the secrets to the silences themselves (SE XVIII 18).

Now, *The Waste Land*, like any good sphinx, lures the reader into hermeneutics, too: but there is no secret underneath its hugger-muggery. Indeed, Hegel saw the Sphinx as the symbol of the symbolic itself, because it did not know the answer to its own question: and *The Waste Land*, too, is a riddle to *itself*.[4] Here it is more instructive to be scrupulously superficial than to dig beneath the surface for the poem's buried skeletons or sources. For it is in the silences *between* the words that meaning flickers, local, evanescent—in the very "wastes" that stretch across the page. These silences curtail the powers of the author, for they invite the *hypocrite lecteur* to reconstruct their broken sense. Moreover, the speaker cannot be identified with his creator, not because he has a *different* personality, like Prufrock, but because he has no stable identity at all. The disembodied "I" glides in and out of stolen texts, as if the speaking subject were merely the quotation of its antecedents. Indeed, this subject is the victim of a general collapse of boundaries. This chapter examines *The Waste Land* in the light of Freud—and ultimately in the darkness of *Beyond the Pleasure Principle*—to trace the poem's suicidal logic.

Throbbing between Two Lives

Let us assume, first of all, that *The Waste Land* is about what it declares—waste. A ceremonial purgation, it inventories all the "stony rubbish" that it strives to exorcise (20).[5] The "waste *land*" could be seen as the thunderous desert where the hooded hordes are swarming towards apocalypse. But it also means "waste ground", bomb sites or vacant lots, like those in "Rhapsody on a Windy Night", where ancient women gather the wreckage of Europe.[6] It means Jerusalem or Alexandria or London—any ravaged centre of a dying world—and it foreshadows the dilapidation of centricity itself. The poem teems with urban waste, butt-ends of the city's days and ways: "empty bottles, sandwich papers, / Silk handkerchiefs, cardboard boxes, cigarette ends" (177–8). However, it is difficult to draw taxomomies of waste, because the text conflates the city with the body and, by analogy, the social with the personal. Abortions, broken fingernails, carious teeth, and "female smells" signify the culture's decadence, as well as bodily decrepitude. The self is implicated in the degradation of the race, because the filth without insinuates defilement within.[7]

It is waste *paper*, however, which appals and fascinates the poem, the written detritus which drifts into the text as randomly as picnics sink into the Thames (177–8). Many modernist writers comb the past in order to recycle its remains, and Joyce is the master of the scavengers: "Nothing but old fags and cabbage-stumps of quotations", in D. H. Lawrence's words.[8] Joyce treats the rubbish heap of literature as a fund of creativity ("The letter! The litter!"), disseminating writings as Eliot strews bones.[9] A funeral rather than a wake, *The Waste Land* is a lugubrious version of Joyce's jubilant "recirculation"of the past, in which all waste becomes unbiodegradable: "Men and bits of paper, whirled by the cold wind . . ." (*BN* III 15).[10] Indeed, *The Waste Land* is one of the most abject texts in English literature, in every sense: for abjection, according to Bataille, "is merely the inability to assume with sufficient strength the imperative act of excluding abject things", an act that "establishes the foundations of collective existence."[11] Waste is what a culture casts away in order to determine what is not itself, and thus to establish its own limits. In the same way, the subject defines the limits of his body through the violent expulsion of its own excess: and ironically, this catharsis *institutes* the excremental. Similarly, Paul Ricoeur has pointed out that social rituals of "burning, removing, chasing, throwing, spitting out, covering up, burying" continuously *reinvent* the waste they exorcise.[12]

The word "abject" literally means "cast out", though commonly it means downcast in spirits: but "abjection" may refer to the waste itself, together with the violence of casting it abroad. It is the ambiguity of the "abject" that distinguishes it from the "object", which the subject rigorously jettisons (ob-jects). According to Julia Kristeva, the abject emerges when exclusions fail, in the sickening collapse of limits. Rather than disease or filth or putrefaction, the abject is that which "disturbs identity, system, order": it is the "in-between, the ambiguous, the composite."[13] In the "brown fog" of *The Waste Land*, for example, or the yellow fog of "Prufrock", the in-between grows animate: and Madame Sosostris warns us to fear death by water, for sinking banks betoken glutinous distinctions.[14] In fact, the "horror" of *The Waste Land* lurks in the osmoses, exhalations and porosities, in the dread of *epidemic* rather than the filth itself, for it is this miasma that bespeaks dissolving limits.[15] The corpses signify the "utmost of abjection", in Kristeva's phrase, because they represent "a border that has encroached upon everything": an outside that irrupts into the inside, and erodes the parameters of life.[16] It is impossible to keep them underground: Stetson's garden is an ossuary, and the dull canals, the garrets, and the alleys are littered with unburied bones. "Tumbled graves" (387) have overrun the city, for the living have changed places with the dead: "A crowd flowed over London Bridge, so many, / I had not thought death had undone so many" (62–3). *The Waste Land* does not fear the dead themselves so much as their invasion of the living; for it is the collapse of boundaries that centrally disturbs the text, be they sexual, national, linguistic, or authorial.

Kristeva derives her notion of abjection from Freud's *Totem and Taboo*, which was written ten years before the publication of *The Waste Land* and anticipates its itch for anthropology.[17] Like Eliot, Freud draws analogies between the psychic and the cultural, linking "civilised" obsessionality to "savage" rites. In both cases the ritual "is ostensibly a protection against the prohibited act; but *actually* . . . a repetition of it" (SE XII 50). *The Waste Land* resembles this obsessive rite, because it surreptitiously repeats the horror that it tries to expiate. In particular, it desecrates tradition. The poem may be seen as an extended "blasphemy", in Eliot's conception of the term, an affirmation masked as a denial. For the text dismantles Western culture as if destruction were the final mode of veneration. As Terry Eagleton argues:

> behind the back of this ruptured, radically decentred poem runs an alternative text which is nothing less than the closed, coherent, authoritative discourse of the mythologies which frame it. The phenomenal text, to use one of Eliot's own metaphors,is merely the meat with which the burglar distracts the guard-dog while he proceeds with his stealthy business.[18]

However, Eagleton omits a further ruse: for the poem uses its nostalgia to conceal its vandalism, its pastiche of the tradition that it mourns. Indeed, a double consciousness pervades the text, as if it had been written by a vicar and an infidel. The speaker is divided from himself, unable to resist the imp within who cynically subverts his pieties. Thus, Cleopatra's burnished throne becomes a dressing table, time's wingèd chariot a grinning skull (77, 186): but there are many subtler deformations.

Take, for instance, the opening words. The line "April is the cruellest month" blasphemes (in Eliot's sense) against the first lines of *The Canterbury Tales*, which presented April's showers as so sweet. At once a nod to origins and a flagrant declaration of beginninglessness, this allusion grafts the poem to another text, vaunting its parasitic in-betweenness. Only the misquotation marks the change of ownership, but the author's personality dissolves in the citational abyss. This is why Conrad Aiken once complained that Eliot had created " 'a literature of literature' . . . a kind of parasitic growth on literature, a sort of mistletoe . . .".[19] As blasphemy, *The Waste Land* is obliged to poach upon the past, caught in a perpetual allusion to the texts that it denies.[20] For it is only by corrupting Chaucer's language that Eliot can grieve the passing of his world:

April is the cruellest month, breeding
Lilacs out of the dead land, mixing
Memory and desire, stirring
Dull roots with spring rain.
Winter kept us warm, covering
Earth in forgetful snow, feeding
A little life with dried tubers.

(1–7)

Because these lines allude to Chaucer, they invoke the origin of the tradition as well as the juvescence of the year.[21] But words like "stirring", "mixing", and "feeding" profane beginnings, be they literary or organic, provoking us to ask what "cruelty" has exchanged them for uniting, engendering, or nourishing. Thus the passage whispers of the words *its* words deny, and sorrows for the things it cannot say. Most of the lines stretch beyond the comma where the cadence falls, as if the words themselves had overflown their bounds, straining towards a future state of being like the dull roots that they describe. They typify the way *The Waste Land* differs from itself, forever trembling towards another poem which has already been written, or else has yet to be composed.

This betweenness also overtakes the speaking subject, for the first-person pronoun roams from voice to voice.[22] The "us" in "Winter kept us warm" glides into the "us" of "Summer surprised us," without alerting "us", the readers, of any change of name or locus. At last, the "us" contracts into the couple in the Hofgarten, after having spoken for the human, animal and vegetable worlds. What begins as an editorial "we" becomes the mark of a migration, which restlessly displaces voice and origin. Throughout the poem, the "I" slips from persona to persona, weaves in and out of quoted speech, and creeps like a contagion through the

Prothalamion or Pope or the debased grammar of a London pub, sweeping history into a heap of broken images.

However, Eliot insisted in the Notes to *The Waste Land* that Tiresias should stabilise this drifting subject, and rally the nomadic voices of the text:[23]

> 218. Tiresias, although a mere spectator and not indeed a "character", is yet the most important personage in the poem, uniting all the rest. Just as the one-eyed merchant, seller of currants, *melts into* the Phoenician Sailor, and the latter is *not wholly distinct* from Ferdinand Prince of Naples, so all the women are one woman, and the *two sexes meet* in Tiresias. What Tiresias *sees*, in fact, is the substance of the poem.[24]

But what *does* Tiresias see? Blind as he is, the prophet has a single walk-on part, when he spies on the typist and her lover indulging in carbuncular caresses.[25] In this Note, moreover, Eliot emphasises the *osmosis* of identities more than their reunion in a central consciousness. For Tiresias's role within the poem is to "melt" distinctions and confuse personae:

> I Tiresias, though blind, throbbing between two lives,
> Old man with wrinkled female breasts, can see
> At the violet hour, the evening hour that strives
> Homeward, and brings the sailor home from sea,
> The typist home at teatime, clears her breakfast, lights
> Her stove, and lays out food in tins.
> Out of the window perilously spread
> Her drying combinations touched by the sun's last rays,
> On the divan are piled (at night her bed)
> Stockings, slippers, camisoles, and stays.
> I Tiresias, old man with wrinkled dugs
> Perceived the scene, and foretold the rest—
> I too awaited the expected guest.
> He, the young man carbuncular, arrives. . . .
>
> (218–31)

Here the seer turns into a peeping Tom, the most ambiguous of spectators. "Throbbing between two lives", Tiresias could be seen as the very prophet of abjection, personifying all the poem's porous membranes. A revisionary, he foresees what he has already foresuffered, mixing memory and desire, self and other, man and woman, pollution and catharsis. The

Notes which exalt him are "abject" themselves, for they represent a kind of supplement or discharge of the text that Eliot could never get "unstuck", though he later wished the poem might stand alone.[26] Now that the manuscript has been released (1971), the poem throbs between two authors and three texts—the Notes, the published poem, and the drafts that Pound pruned so cunningly. The text's integrity dissolves under the invasion of its own disjecta. Just as its quotations confuse the past and present, parasite and poet, the poem leaks in supplements and prolegomena.

The typist symptomises this betweenness, too. Her profession parodies the poet's, demoted as he is to the typist or amanuensis of the dead. Too untidy to acknowledge boundaries, she strews her bed with stockings, slippers, camisoles, and stays, and even the bed is a divan by day, in a petit bourgeois disrespect for definition. She resembles the neurotic woman in "A Game of Chess", who cannot decide to go out or to stay in, as if she were at enmity with their distinction. Eliot himself declares that all the women in *The Waste Land* are one woman, and this is because they represent the very principle of unguency. "Pneumatic bliss" entails emulsive demarcations.[27] Yet the misogyny is so ferocious, particularly in the manuscript, that it begins to turn into a blasphemy against itself. For the poem is enthralled by the femininity that it reviles, bewitched by this odorous and shoreless flesh. In fact, woman is the spirit of its own construction, the phantom of its own betweennesses. In "The Fire Sermon", Eliot personifies his broken images in a woman's bruised, defiled flesh; and it is as if the damsel Donne once greeted as his new found land had reverted to the old world and an urban wilderness:

> "Trams and dusty trees.
> Highbury bore me. Richmond and Kew
> Undid me. By Richmond I raised my knees
> Supine on the floor of a narrow canoe."
>
> "My feet are at Moorgate, and my heart
> Under my feet. After the event
> He wept. He promised 'a new start'.
> I made no comment. What should I resent?"

"On Margate Sands.
I can connect
Nothing with nothing.
The broken fingernails of dirty hands.
My people humble people who expect
Nothing."
        la la

To Carthage then I came

Burning burning burning burning
O Lord Thou pluckest me out
O Lord Thou pluckest

burning

(292–311)

The body and the city melt together, no longer themselves but not yet other. It is as if the metaphor were stuck between the tenor and the vehicle, transfixed in an eternal hesitation. Both the woman and the city have been raped, but the "he" seems passive in his violence, weeping at his own barbarity. The victim, too, consents to degradation as if it were foredoomed: "I raised my knees / Supine. . . . What should I resent?" (As Ian Hamilton observes, "no one in *The Waste Land* raises her knees in any other spirit than that of dumb complaisance."[28]) "Undone", the woman's body crumbles in a synecdochic heap of knees, heart, feet, weirdly disorganised: "My feet are at Moorgate, and my heart / Under my feet." But the city which undid her decomposes, too, in a random concatenation of its parts—Highbury, Richmond, Kew, Moorgate—and ends in broken fingernails on Margate Sands.

Itinerant and indeterminate, the "I" slips from the woman to the city, and then assumes the voice of Conrad's Harlequin in *Heart of Darkness*, who apologises for a humble and exploited race. At last it merges with the "I" who came to Carthage in St Augustine's *Confessions*. As the last faltering words suggest, it is impossible to "pluck" the speaking subject out of the conflagration of the poem's idioms. The I cannot preserve its own identity intact against the shrieking voices which assail it, "Scolding, mocking, or merely chattering" according to their whim (*BN* V 18). In *The Waste*

Land, the only voice which *is* "inviolable" is the voice that does not speak, but only sings that phatic, faint "la la."

These notes allude to the warblings of the nightingale, who fills the desert "with inviolable voice" (101). In Ovid, however, the nightingale was born in violation. Tereus, "the barbarous king" (99) raped his wife's sister Philomela, and cut out her tongue so that she could not even name her own defiler ("Tereu . . ." [206]). But Philomela weaves a picture of his crime into her loom so that her sister, Procne, can decode her wrongs.[29] In this way, her web becomes a kind of writing, a dossier to defend her speechless flesh. After reading it, Procne avenges Philomela by feeding Tereus the flesh of his own son. In *The Waste Land*, Eliot omits the web, and he ignores this violent retaliation, too. He alludes only to the ending of the myth, when the gods give both the sisters wings to flee from Tereus's wrath. They change Philomela into a nightingale to compensate her loss of speech with wordless song.[30] By invoking this story, Eliot suggests that woman is excluded from language through the sexual violence of a man. As Peter Middleton has pointed out, she is awarded for her pains with a pure art which is powerless and desolate—"la, la."[31]

In *The Waste Land* as in Ovid, writing provides the only refuge from aphasia, but it is a weapon that turns against its own possessor. Rather than the record of the victim's wrongs, writing has become the very instrument of violation: and it invades the male narrator's speech as irresistably as the "female stench" with which it comes to be associated (*WL Fac* [39]). Although Eliot quotes Bradley to the effect that "my experience falls within my own circle, a circle closed on the outside", this circle has been broken in *The Waste Land* (412n.). Here no experience is proper or exclusive to the subject. Moreover, the speaker is possessed by the writings of the dead, and seized in a cacophony beyond control.

Prince of Morticians

> Curious, is it not, that Mr. Eliot
> Has not given more time to Mr. Beddoes
> (T. L.) prince of morticians
>
> Pound, Canto LXXX

In "Tradition and the Individual Talent" Eliot celebrates the voices of the dead, but he comes to dread their verbal ambush in *The Waste Land*.[32] In the essay, he claimed that "not only the best, but the most individual poetry" is that which is most haunted by its own precursors. Only thieves can truly be original. For any new creation gains its meaning in relation to the poems of the past, and writing is a voyage to the underworld, to commune with the phantasmal voices of the dead. Eliot published this essay immediately after World War I, in 1919, the same year that Freud was writing *Beyond the Pleasure Principle*. As Middleton has pointed out, they both confront the same material: the unprecedented death toll of the First World War. Like Freud's theory of repetition, Eliot's account of influence attempts to salvage something of a past that had never been so ruthlessly annihilated—however fearsome its reanimation from the grave. Whereas Freud discovers the death drive in the compulsion to repeat, *The Waste Land* stages it in the compulsion to citation.

In 1919 Freud also wrote his famous essay on the "uncanny", which he defines as "whatever reminds us of this inner compulsion to repeat."[33] *The Waste Land* is uncanny in a double sense, for it is haunted by the repetition of the dead—in the form of mimicry, quotation and pastiche—but also by a kind of Hammer horror: bats with baby faces, whisper music, violet light, hooded hordes, witches, death's heads, bones, and zombies (378–81). According to Freud, "heimlich" literally means "homely" or familiar, but it develops in the direction of ambivalence until it converges with its opposite, *unheimlich* or uncanny.[34] Thus the very word has grown unhomely and improper to itself. The passage Eliot misquotes from *The White Devil* provides a good example of the double meaning of uncanniness:

> O keep the Dog far hence, that's friend to men,
> Or with his nails he'll dig it up again!
>
> (74–5)

Since the passage is purloined from Webster, the very words are ghostly revenants, returning as extravagant and erring spirits. This kind of verbal kleptomania subverts the myth that literary texts are private property, or that the author can enjoy the sole possession of his words. But Eliot writes Dog where Webster wrote Wolf, and friend where Webster wrote foe. Thus he tames the hellhound in the same misprision that domesticates the discourse of the past. Friendly pet and wild beast, the Dog becomes the emblem of the poem's literary necrophilia, and the familiar strangeness of the past that Eliot himself has disinterred.[35]

Quotation means that words cannot be anchored to their authors, and the fortune-tellers in the text personify this loss of origin. For prophecy means that we hear about a thing before it happens. The report precedes the event. The bell echoes before it rings. Tiresias, for instance, has not only foreseen but actually "foresuffered all", as if he were a living misquotation.[36] A fake herself, Madame Sosostris lives in fear of imitators ("Tell her I bring the horoscope myself"), nervous that her words may go astray ("One must be so careful these days"). This anxiety about originality and theft resurges in the form of Mr Eugenides. A Turkish merchant in London, he also speaks demotic French: and the word "demotic", Greek in etymology, alludes to Egyptian hieroglyphics. Being a merchant, he is not only the product but the sinister conductor of miscegenation, intermingling verbal, sexual and monetary currencies. Even his pocketful of currants could be heard as "currents", which dissolve identities and definitions, like the "current under sea" that picks the bones of Phlebas, his Phoenician alter ego.[37] His reappearances suggest that repetition has become an virus, unwholesome as the personages who recur. Indeed, the poem hints that literature is nothing but a plague of echoes: that writing necessarily deserts its author, spreading like an epidemic into other texts. Any set of written signs can fall into bad company, into contexts which pervert their meaning and their genealogy.

The worst company in *The Waste Land*, both socially and rhetorically, is the London pub where Lil is tortured by her crony for her bad teeth and her abortion. Here, the publican's cry, "HURRY UP PLEASE ITS TIME", becomes as vagrant as a written sign, orphaned from its author. Any British drinker knows its origin, of course, so Eliot does not identify the speaker, but sets the phrase adrift on a semantic odyssey. When it interrupts the dialogue, the two discursive sites contaminate each other.

> You ought to be ashamed, I said, to look so antique.
> (And her only thirty-one.)
> I can't help it, she said, pulling a long face,
> It's them pills I took, to bring it off, she said.
> (She's had five already, and nearly died of young George.)
> The chemist said it would be all right, but I've never been the same.
> You *are* a proper fool, I said.
> Well, if Albert won't leave you alone, there it is, I said,
> What you get married for if you don't want children?
> HURRY UP PLEASE ITS TIME
> Well, that Sunday Albert was home, they had a hot gammon,
> And they asked me in to dinner, to get the beauty of it hot—
> HURRY UP PLEASE ITS TIME
> HURRY UP PLEASE ITS TIME
> Goonight Bill. Goonight Lou. Goonight May. Goonight.
> Ta ta. Goonight. Goonight.
> Good night, ladies, good night, sweet ladies, good
> night, good night.
>
> (156–72)

This is the same technique that Flaubert uses in the fair in *Madame Bovary*, where Emma and Rodolph wallow in romance, while the voice of the Minister of Agriculture splices their sentiment with swine. In *The Waste Land*, the more the publican repeats his cry, the more its meaning strays from his intentions. Instead of closing time, it now connotes perfunctory and brutal sexuality: it means that time is catching up with Lil, in the form of dentures and decay, and rushing her culture to apocalypse. There is no omniscient speaker here to monitor these meanings, no "pill" to control their pullulation. It is as if the words themselves had been demobbed and grown adulterous. When Ophelia's good-byes creep in, just as the dialogue is closing, the allusion dignifies Lil's slower suicide: "Good night, ladies, good night, sweet ladies, good night, good night." Yet at the same time, the text degrades Ophelia by suturing her words to Lil's, reducing Shakespeare to graffiti.[38]

In general, the poem's attitude towards Shakespeare and the canon resembles taboos against the dead, with their mixture of veneration and horror (SE XIII 25). As Freud says, "they are expressions of mourning; but on the other hand they clearly betray—what they seek to conceal—hostility against the dead . . ." (SE XIII 61). But he stresses that it is not the dead themselves so much as their "infection" which is feared, for they are charged with a kind of "electricity" (SE XIII 20–2, 41). The taboo arises to defend the living subject from their sly invasions. But strangely enough, the taboo eventually becomes prohibited itself, as if the ban were as infectious as the horrors it forbids. Prohibition spreads like a disease, tainting everything that touches it, "till at last the whole world lies under an embargo" (SE XIII 27). A similar reversal takes place in *The Waste Land*, where the rituals of purity are perverted into *ersatz* desecrations of themselves. When Mrs. Porter and her daughter wash their feet in soda water, the ceremony of innocence is drowned, and the baptismal rite becomes its own defilement.

According to Freud, there are two ways in which taboo can spread, through contact and through mimesis. To touch a sacred object is to fall under its interdict. But the offender must also be tabooed because of "the risk of imitation", for others may follow his example (SE XIII 33). These two forms of "transference" work like tropes, since the first, like metonymy, depends on contiguity, the second on similitude like metaphor (SE XIII 27).[39] Freud adds that taboo usages resemble obsessional symptoms in that "the prohibitions lack any assignable motive", and they are "easily displaceable". It is as if the spread of the taboo depended on the power of rhetorical displacement: and underneath the fear of the contagion is the fear of tropes, the death-dealing power of figuration (SE XIII 28).

Displacement is indeed the malady the poem strives to cure, but its own figures are the source of the disorder. Though Eliot condemns Milton for dividing sound from sense, it is precisely this dissociation which produces the semantic epidemic of *The Waste Land*. It is the rats, appropriately, who carry the infection. They make their first appearance in "rats' alley"; but here a note refers us mischievously to Part III, where another rat peeks out again, like a further outbreak of the verbal plague:

White bodies naked on the low damp ground
And bones cast in a little low dry garret,
Rattled by the rat's foot only, year to year.

However, Eliot seems to have forgotten one rodential apparition in between:

But at my back in a cold blast I hear
The *rattle* of the bones, and chuckle spread from ear to ear.

A *rat* crept softly through the vegetation
Dragging its slimy belly on the bank
While I was fishing in the dull canal
On a winter evening round behind the gashouse
Musing upon the king my brother's wreck
And on the king my father's death before him.
White bodies naked on the low damp ground
And bones cast in a little low dry garret,
Rattled by the *rat's* foot only, year to year.

(III 185–95: my emphases)

It is the sound, here, which connects the rattle to the rat, as opposed to a semantic link between them. And it is the rattle of the words,rather than their meaning, that propels the poem forward. Indeed, the sound preempts the sense and spreads like an infection.

Notice that the text associates the rattle of the rats with "the king my brother's wreck" and "the king my father's death before him." For the contiguity suggests that it is these calamities that taint these signs, causing them to fester and grow verminous. Wrenched from their context in *The Tempest*, these deaths suggest the downfall of the father, as do the oblique allusions to the Fisher King, a figure Eliot derives from Jessie Weston's study of the Grail romance.[40] According to this legend, the King has lost his manhood, and his impotence has brought a blight over his lands. Eliot connects the Fisher King to "the man with three staves" in the Tarot pack, as if to hint that both have failed to fecundate the waste land, to fish the sense out of its floating signifiers. Their emasculation corresponds to other injuries, particularly to the mutilation of the voice: as if the phallus were complicit with the Logos. Lacking both, language has become a "waste of breath", a barren dissemination: "Sighs, short and infrequent, were exhaled . . .".

In the *Waste Land* manuscript, this anxiety about the Logos remains explicit. For here the pilgrim is searching for the "one essential word that frees", entrammelled in his own "concatenated words from which the sense seemed gone."[41] In the finished poem, all that remains of the lightning of the Word is the belated *rattle* of the sign, the "dry sterile thunder" of the desert (342). And this is why the poem is for ever grieving its belatedness: for not only does it come too late to establish an originary voice, but after the nymphs, after the messiah, after the tradition:

> After the torchlight red on sweaty faces
> After the frosty silence in the gardens
> After the agony in stony places. . . .
>
> (322–4)

The manuscript goes on at this point to lament the lateness of its own inditing: "After the ending of this inspiration."[42] For writing, in the waste land, is the "wake" of voice—at once the after-image of the author and his obsequies.

If writing is in league with death, however, it is also in cahoots with femininity. In *The Waste Land*, the "hearty female stench" converges with the odour of mortality—and both exude from *writing*, from the violated and putrescent corpse of speech. To use the text's sexology, writing and the stink of femininity have overpowered the priapic realm of voice. Eliot to some extent repressed this hearty female stench when he excised it from the manuscript: but it survives in the strange synthetic perfumes of the lady in "A Game of Chess", which "troubled, confused / And drowned the sense in odours". ("Sense", here, may be understood as both semantic and olfactory: as if, under the power of the feminine, the sense of words becomes as "unguent . . . or liquid" as her scents.) Now, the strange thing about smell, as opposed to vision for example, is that the subject smelling actually imbibes the object smelt, endangering their separation and integrity. And it is the fear of such *displacements* that Eliot's misogyny reveals, a terror deeper even than the dread of incest, which is merely the most scandalous offence to place. In *The Waste Land*, the fall of the father unleashes infinite displacements, be they sexual, linguistic or territorial. Even personal identity dissolves into the babble of miscegenated tongues.[43] As effluvia, the feminine dissolves the limits of the private body, and the boundaries of the self subside into pneumatic anarchy. It is as if the father's impotence entailed the dissolution of identity, imaged as asphyxiation in the body of the feminine.

At the end of the poem, Eliot demolishes the discourse of the West, petitioning the East for solace and recovery.

> London Bridge is falling down falling down falling down
> *Poi s'ascose nel foco che gli affina*
> *Quando fiam uti chelidon*—O swallow swallow
> *Le Prince d'Aquitaine à la tour abolie*
> These fragments I have shored against my ruins
> Why then Ile fit you. Hieronymo's mad againe.
> Datta. Dayadhvam. Damyata.
> Shantih shantih shantih
>
> (426–33)

Here at last the poem silences its Western noise with Eastern blessings. But ironically, the effort to defeat its own "concatenated words" has only made the text more polyglot, stammering its orisons in Babel. It is as if the speaking subject had been "ruined" by the very fragments he had shored. " 'Words, words, words' might be his motto", one of Eliot's earliest reviewers once exclaimed, " 'for in his verse he seems to hate them and to be always expressing his hatred of them, in words.' "[44] Because the poem can only abject writing with more writing, it catches the infection that it tries to purge, and implodes like an obsessive ceremonial under the pressure of its own contradictions.

The Violet Hour

It is in another ceremonial that Freud discovers the compulsion to repeat, in the child's game he analyses in

Beyond the Pleasure Principle. Here, his grandchild flings a cotton-reel into the abyss beyond his cot, and retrieves it with an "aaaa" of satisfaction, only to cast it out again, uttering a forlorn "oooo." Freud interprets these two syllables as primitive versions of the German words "fort" (gone) and "da" (here), and he argues that the child is mastering his mother's absences by "staging" them in the manipulation of a sign (SE XVIII 28). Indeed, Freud compares this theatre of abjection to the catharses of Greek tragedy, and he sees the child's pantomime renunciation as his first "great cultural achievement."

It is important, however, that the *drama* fascinates the child rather than the toy itself, for the bobbin belongs to a series of objects which he substitutes indifferently for one another.[45] While the cotton-reel stands for the mother, rehearsing her intermittencies, it also represents the child himself, who sends it forth like an ambassador. As if to emphasise this point, he tops his first act by staging his own disappearance. Crouching underneath a mirror, he lisps, "Baby o-o-o-o!" [Baby gone!], in a kind of abject inversion of Narcissus. By casting *himself* out, the child founds his subjectivity in a game that can only end in death. As Kristeva writes: "I expel *myself*, I spit *myself* out, I *abject* myself within the same motion through which 'I' claim to establish *myself*."[46] By attempting to control his world with signs, the subject has himself become a function of the sign, *subjected to* its own demonic repetition.

In this scenario, Freud intervenes between the mother and the child, bearing the law of language. For it is he who transforms the oscillation of the child's vowels into intelligible speech. But he neglects the vengeful pleasure that the infant takes in their vibratory suspense and in the *rattle* of their sounds. It is significant, moreover, that the little boy never changed his "o-o-o-o" into the neutral "fort" when he acquired the command of language. Instead, he sent his bobbin to the trenches. "A year later", Freud writes:

> the same boy whom I had observed at his first game used to take a toy, if he was angry with it, and throw it on the floor, exclaiming: "Go to the fwont!" He had heard at that time that his absent father was "at the front," and was far from regretting his absence . . . (SE XVIII, p. 16).

Like this child, *The Waste Land* is confronting the specific absence that succeeded World War I, and it evinces both the dread and the desire to hear the voices at the "fwont" again.[47] In fact, the poem can be read as a seance, and its speaker as the medium who tries to raise the dead by quoting them. Its ruling logic is "prosopopeia", as Paul De Man defines the trope:

> the fiction of an apostrophe to an absent, deceased, or voiceless entity, which posits the possiblity of the latter's reply and confers upon it the power of speech. Voice assumes mouth, eye and finally face, a chain that is manifest in the etymology of the trope's name, *prosopon poien*, to confer a mask or face (*prosopon*).[48]

With the dead souls flowing over London Bridge, the corpses in the garden and the hooded hordes, *The Waste Land* strives to give a face to death. But it is significant that these figures have no faces, or else that they are hidden and unrecognisable:

> Who is the third who walks always beside you?
> When I count, there are only you and I together
> But when I look ahead up the white road
> There is always another one walking beside you
> Gliding wrapt in a brown mantle, hooded
> I do not know whether a man or a woman
> —But who is that on the other side of you?
>
> (360–6)

Here, these nervous efforts to reconstitute the face only drive it to its disappearance. Neither absent nor present, this nameless third bodies forth a rhetoric of disembodiment, and figures the "continual extinction" of the self. For the speaker rehearses his own death as he conjures up the writings of the dead, sacrificing voice and personality to their ventriloquy. Freud compares his grandchild to victims of shell-shock, who hallucinate their traumas in their dreams, repeating death as if it were desire. This is the game *The Waste Land* plays, and the nightmare that it cannot lay to rest, for it stages the ritual of its own destruction.

Notes

1. Oscar Wilde, "A Sphinx without a Secret", *Complete Writings*, Vol. VIII, pp. 121–32.
2. In fact the criticism reads more like a quest for the Holy Grail than the poem does. For the Holy Grail interpretation, see Grover Smith, *T. S. Eliot's Poetry and Plays: A Study in Sources and Meaning* (Chicago: University of Chicago Press, 1956), pp. 69–70, 74–7; and Edmund Wilson, *Axel's Castle: A Study in the Imaginative Literature of 1870–1930* (New York and London: Scribner's, 1931), pp. 104–5. Helen Gardner subscribes to this position with some qualifications in *The Art of T. S. Eliot* (London: Cresset Press, 1949), p. 87. George Williamson reconstructs *The Waste Land* ingeniously in *A Reader's Guide*, esp. pp. 129–30. For Jean Verdenal see John Peter, "A New Interpretation of *The Waste Land*", in *Essays in Criticism*, 2 (1952), esp. p. 245; and James E. Miller, *T. S. Eliot's Personal Waste Land: Exorcism of the Demons* (University Park, Pennsylvania: Pennsylvania State University Press, 1977), *passim*.
3. Freud revises this formula, however, in *The Interpretation of Dreams*, where he states that "Hysterical symptoms are not attached to actual memories, but to phantasies erected on the basis of memories." The editor notes that in a letter to Fliess Freud explained that "Phantasies are psychical facades constructed in order to bar the way to these memories" (SE V 491, 491n.). These facades both bar the way to memory and screen it as one screens a film: they *enact* what cannot be remembered. (Freud also uses the term "facade" to describe the work of "secondary revision" in the dream, which is discussed at further length in Chapter V.)
4. See *Hegel's Aesthetics: Lectures on Fine Art*, trans. T. M. Knox (Oxford: Clarendon, 1975), pp. 360–1.
5. Just as "Ash-Wednesday" strives to be a prayer, *The Waste Land* aspires to the condition of ritual. This fascination with cathartic rites drew Eliot towards the theatre in his later work, but his poems also crave performance, incantation.
6. Suggested by Peter Middleton in "The Academic Development of *The Waste Land*", forthcoming in *Glyph*.
7. Paul Ricoeur has pointed out that "impurity was never literally filthiness" and "defilement was never literally a stain", for the notion of impurity is "primordially symbolic". See Ricoeur, *The Symbolism of Evil*, trans. Emerson Buchanan (Boston: Beacon Press, 1967), pp. 35, 39.
8. Quoted by Jennifer Schiffer Levine in "Originality and Repetition in *Finnegans Wake* and *Ulysses*", *PMLA*, 94 (1979), 108.
9. James Joyce, *Finnegans Wake*, p. 93, line 24.
10. *Ibid.*, p. 3, line 2.
11. Quoted in Kristeva, *Powers of Horror: An Essay on Abjection*, trans. Leon S. Roudiez (New York: Columbia University Press, 1982), p. 56.
12. Ricoeur, *Symbolism of Evil*, p. 35.

13. Julia Kristeva, *Powers of Horror*, p. 4; see also p. 9.
14. See *Waste Land*, 61, 208, etc.
15. Eliot originally quoted Kurtz's last words "The horror! the horror!" from Conrad's *Heart of Darkness* as the epigraph to *The Waste Land*: see *WL Fac*, p. 3.
16. *Powers of Horror*, pp. 4, 3.
17. For contemporary interest in anthropology, see Kern, *The Culture of Time and Space*, pp. 19–20, 32, 34.
18. Terry Eagleton, *Criticism and Ideology*, pp. 149–50.
19. See Conrad Aiken, "An Anatomy of Melancholy" (1923); repr. in *A Collection of Critical Essays on The Waste Land*, ed. J. Martin (Englewood Cliffs, New Jersey: Prentice Hall, 1968), p. 54.
20. Thus it could be said that writing *engenders* blasphemy, just as law is the prerequisite to crime.
21. See Chaucer, General Prologue to the *Canterbury Tales*, lines 1–4.
22. Alick West pointed this out long ago: see *Crisis and Criticism* (London: Lawrence and Wishart, 1937), pp. 5–6, 28.
23. For critics who see Tiresias as an omniscient narrator, see *inter alia* Grover Smith, *Eliot's Poetry and Plays*, pp. 72–6; F. O. Matthiessen, *The Achievement*, p. 60. For critics more sceptical of Tiresias's role, see Graham Hough, *Image and Experience: Studies in a Literary Revolution* (London: Duckworth, 1960), p. 25; Juliet McLaughlin, "Allusion in *The Waste Land*", *Essays in Criticism*, 19 (1969), 456; Paul LaChance, "The Function of Voice in *The Waste Land*", *Style*, 5, no. 2 (1971), 107ff.
24. *CPP* 52: my emphases, except for "*sees*."
25. Genevieve W. Forster takes the extraordinary view that the scene with the typist is therefore the "substance of the poem": in "The Archetypal Imagery Of T. S. Eliot", *PMLA*, 60 (1945), 573.
26. See *PP* 110. For a summary of critical responses to the Notes, see Thormählen, *A Fragmentary Wholeness*, pp. 61–8. See also Eliot's own comments in "The Art of Poetry I: T. S. Eliot, An Interview", *Paris Review*, no. 21 (1959); repr. in Donald Hall, ed., *Remembering Poets: Reminiscences and Opinions* (New York: Harper, 1978), p. 207. In *PP* 109, Eliot admits to including the Notes "with a view to spiking the guns of those critics of my earlier poems who had accused me of plagiarism."
27. See Eliot, "Whispers of Immortality":

    Grishkin is nice: her Russian eye
    Is underlined for emphasis;
    Uncorseted, her friendly bust
    Gives promise of pneumatic bliss. (17–20)

28. Ian Hamilton, "*The Waste Land*", in *Eliot in Perspective*, ed. Martin, p. 109.
29. While Freud once said that weaving was woman's only contribution to civilisation, and that it originates in the "concealment of genital

deficiency" (SE XXII 132), Ovid makes women's weaving into the invention of the *text*.

30. See Ovid, *Metamorphoses*, VI, 412–674. Ovid juxtaposes her story to Arachne's, another weaving tattle-tale, who fraught her web with "heavenly crimes", depicting Zeus in all the shapes he took to ravish nymphs and mortal women: *Metamorphoses*, VI, 103–33.
31. Peter Middleton, "The Academic Development of *The Waste Land*", forthcoming in *Glyph*.
32. Helen Gardner argues that *The Waste Land* is an "exercise in ventriloquism", but she makes the dead the dummies, Eliot the ventriloquist. I suggest that the poem works the other way around. See Gardner, "*The Waste Land*: Paris 1922", in *Eliot in his Time*, ed. Litz, p. 78.
33. "The 'Uncanny' ", SE XVII 238.
34. *Ibid.*, 222–6.
35. Curiously, Freud's word "unheimlich" also alludes to property: for *heimlich* literally means "homely", but it develops in the direction of ambivalence until it converges with its opposite, "unhomely" (see SE XVII 222–6).
36. Even in *The Odyssey*, his prophecies make action a redundancy, for the deed becomes the mere mimesis of the word.
37. I owe this pun and some of the preceding formulations to my student John Reid at Amherst College, 1986.
38. Andrew Parker pointed out to me in conversation that "degradation" in the poem always occurs through the association with the lower classes.
39. See "Prufrock's Fixation", Chapter III.
40. See Jessie Weston, *From Ritual to Romance* (1920; Garden City, New York: Doubleday, 1957), Ch. 9, pp. 113–36.
41. *WL Fac* 109, 113.
42. *WL Fac* 109.
43. Lacan claims that the paternal law is "identical to an order of Language. For without kinship nominations, no power is capable of instituting the order of preferences and taboos which bind and weave the yarn of lineage down through succeeding generations." ("The Function of Language in Psychoanalysis", in *The Language of the Self*, ed. Anthony Wilden [New York: Dell, 1968], p. 40.) In *The Waste Land*, the phallus stands for these discriminations, but all three staves have detumesced, and the father has been shipwrecked on the ruins of his own distinctions.
44. Anon., review of *Ara Vos Prec*, *TLS*, no. 948 (1920), 184. See also Gabriel Pearson, "Eliot: An American Use of Symbolism", in Martin, ed., *Eliot in Perspective*, pp. 83–7, for an illuminating discussion of "the social as well as verbal logic" of "the conversion of words into the Word."
45. In the same way, Ricoeur argues that defilement is acted out through "partial, substitutive and abbreviated signs" which "mutually symbolise one another": *Symbolism of Evil*, p. 35.

46. Kristeva, *Powers of Horror*, p. 3.
47. See Middleton, "The Academic Development of *The Waste Land*".
48. Paul De Man, "Autobiography as De-facement", *Modern Language Notes*, 94 (1979), 926: repr. as Ch. 4 in *The Rhetoric of Romanticism* (New York: Columbia University Press, 1984).

CHAPTER IV

The Figure in the *Four Quartets*

> Dawn points, and another day
> Prepares for heat and silence. Out at sea the dawn wind
> Wrinkles and slides. I am here
> Or there, or elsewhere. In my beginning.
>
> (*EC* I 47–50)

In *Four Quartets*, the speaker seems to be the master of his utterance, if not quite easy in his new domain. More cautious and more cunning than Gerontion, he does not even try to utter, "Here I am". Instead, he only claims that "I am here / or there, or elsewhere. In my beginning". But his voices harmonise enough for critics to agree with Kristian Smidt that the "*Quartets* are personal and emotional." Helen Gardner, too, insists that "there is no attempt to disguise the personal and confessional nature of the poems."[1] Though she claims to be investigating the *composition* of the *Four Quartets*, she treats the poem as a window to the poet, so that the words evanesce into the life:

> Just as, when asked for the significance of "autumn", Eliot replied simply "it *was* autumn," so here [in the fourth section of "Burnt Norton"] he might answer those who look for mystical meanings in the sunflower, clematis, and Kingfisher: "There *was* a clematis; There *was* a kingfisher."[2]

The poem itself replies: "Other echoes / Inhabit the garden"—though Gardner refuses to acknowledge them. Leavis, on the other hand, thinks the poem would be better off without the poet, who infects it with a "very personal" revulsion against life. C. K. Stead agrees that the poem is "dangerously" subjective.[3]

Despite their different verdicts, these critics all conflate the poet with the speaker, and in so doing disregard the counsel of the text itself, which pedagogically insists upon their non-coincidence: "where you are is where you are not" (*EC* III 46). In the *Quartets*, the self slips out of its own grasp, because its past and future incarnations never coalesce:

> You are not the same people who left that station
> Or who will arrive at any terminus . . .
>
> (*DS* III 16–17)

> time is no healer: the patient is no longer here.
>
> (*DS* III 8)

In fact, the whole poem muses on the breach between the written and the writing selves, never answering the questions that it has to pose. How can I write when I have died in every moment that it took my words to reach the page? How can I remember what never happened? How can I desire what flesh cannot endure, its apocalyptic presence to itself? In the *Quartets*, it is the knowledge of the failure of his own discourse that goads the poet into speech, the absurdity of autobiography: "Because one has only learnt to get the better of words / For the thing one no longer has to say . . ." (*EC* V 5–6).

However, one could argue that Eliot protests authorial humility too much, for the manuscripts reveal an urge to hush, if not to banish, unintended echoes. Like *The Waste Land*, the *Quartets* raid the work of others and incorporate much flotsam from the past. But they homogenise these voices into their own "dignified and commodious" sonorities.[4] "To devise a measure is to devise a voice", as Kenner says: and it is the poem's rhythm that creates the phantom of a single speaker.[5] While the misquotations in *The Waste Land* draw attention to their own displacement, they melt into the music of the *Four Quartets*, which alternates from voice to voice uninterruptedly. The most emphatic borrowing occurs in the "daunsinge" passage of "East Coker" (I 24–46), where the archaic spelling marks the intervention of another voice—but this voice belongs to Thomas Elyot! No relation, but a reinscription of the poet's name. Grover Smith has pointed out that each of the *Quartets* "took its name from a place having for Eliot some personal or family association"; and Gardner also notices that William Eliot and Andrew Eliot have a minor part to play.[6] Surreptitiously, the dominion of the name expands with every movement of the text, as if to mime the poet's literary territorialism.

It is in the service of his revolution that Eliot devises his new cadence, for "Every revolution in poetry is apt to be, and sometimes to announce itself to be, a return to . . . speech" (*PP* 31). More precisely, the *Quartets* could be understood as a "secondary revision" of *The Waste Land*, in Freud's sense of the term. According to Freud, the dream consists of "disconnected fragments of visual images, speeches and even bits of unmodified thoughts", assembled into a "disordered heap": like *The Waste Land* and its heap of broken images. Through secondary revision, the dream dissembles these lacunae to pass itself off as a " 'well-constructed' " narrative.[7] In *Four Quartets*, this editing occurs through voice and temporality. The rhythm of the poem overcomes its spatial interruptions, thus redeeming time in formal terms. Thematically, revision takes the form of history—a Bergsonian history in which the past is constantly rejuvenated by the present: "History is now and England. / . . . Quick, now, here, now, always—" (*LG* V 24, 39). In form and content, therefore, it is time which must regenerate the wastes of space, and speech which must restore traditions atomised by writing. To use Eliot's idiom, the *Quartets* must release the "unheard music" hidden in the letter, and conciliate "the ear, / The murmuring shell of time" (*DS* III 24–5). Even the way the poem brims the page reoccupies the space that gapes around *The Waste Land*'s verbal ruins. While *The Waste Land* resists voicing, the music of the *Quartets* urges us to read aloud, so that the reading act becomes the revolution that restores the spirit to the letter, voice to history.

To globalise his revolution, Eliot endows each of the four elements with speech. The "Earth feet" and the "loam feet" of *East Coker* incarnate the poetic "feet" that regulate the measure: as if the element of earth were the embodiment of rhythm (*EC* I 37). In "Burnt Norton" it is the air which fills with laughter, with the voices of the children in the leaves (*BN* I 40–1). In the "Dry Salvages", articulated voice breaks forth out of the uproar of the sea: "The sea has many voices,/ Many gods and many voices" (*DS* I 24–5). In "Little Gidding" the dead give speech to fire: "the communication / Of the dead is tongued with fire beyond the language of the living" (*LG* I 50–1). A Chorus from *The Rock* elaborates this alchemy:

> Out of the sea of sound the life of music,
> Out of the slimy mud of words, out of the sleet and
> hail of verbal imprecisions,
> Approximate thoughts and feelings, words that have
> taken the place of thoughts and feelings,
> There spring the perfect order of speech, and the beauty of
> incantation.
>
> (*CPP* 164)

Here Eliot suggests that speech emerges out of the decay of speech: the "sea of sound" or the primeval slime of sheer sonority. In the *Quartets*, the lyric voice forever threatens to relapse into this groundswell. This chapter will explore how Eliot opposes voice to this "white noise", just as he shores the proper name against the tumbled graves which haunt the text with their illegible inscriptions.[8] Yet strangely, the patterns he imposes conjure forth the tumult that they struggle to control.

Before proceeding, however, it is important to acknowledge how stubbornly the text resists this reading. In many ways, the *Four Quartets* set out to justify the ways of English vicars: a task which only an American, perhaps, could execute with such conviction. At moments, Eliot seems to be determined to turn poetry into one of the caring professions. His critics, for the most part, follow suit. Yet in spite of all the reverence for God, England, and the Past, there is another impulse in the *Four Quartets* to smash these shibboleths: a scepticism which challenges the self, its history, and the whole epistemology which has confected them. This reading concentrates upon the moments when the text escapes its complacencies, for these are where its terror and its beauty re-emerge.

Disfiguration

In *Four Quartets*, it is the dance which patterns chaos, weaving continuity through space and time. In the body politic, for instance, the "daunsinge" of the peasants consecrates the rhythm of tradition; while "the dance along the artery" duplicates the dancing of the stars.[9] But Eliot creates a dance of language, too, in which the different modes of discourse interpass and alternate. Each becomes "a way of putting it", rather than the refuge of a final truth. For the "point" does not reside in any single voice but in its friction with its own antithesis:

> at the still point, there the dance is,
> But neither arrest nor movement. And do not call it fixity,
> Where past and future are gathered. Neither movement
> from nor towards,
> Neither ascent nor decline. Except for the point, the
> still point,
> There would be no dance, and there is only the dance.
> (*BN* II 17–21)

Each statement here confutes itself, and the use of paradox unsettles the fixity of sense. Even the syntax enhances the suspense of categories: for the "still points" of punctuation fall in the middle of the lines, instead of sealing off their edges and their meanings. Each line hesitates between two sentences, as "the soul's sap quivers" between two worlds. Words waver too: "still", for instance, implies both stasis and perpetuity. The dance itself becomes an image of the pivots of the sentence and the poem's disputations with itself.

In the previous section, however, Eliot suggests that the dance controls the circulation of the lymph together with the syntax of the sky. His diction here is crucial:

> The dance along the artery
> The circulation of the lymph
> Are *figured* in the drift of stars
> Ascend to summer in the tree

We move above the moving tree
In light upon the *figured* leaf. . . .
(*BN* II, 6–11: my emphases)

Eliot is probably borrowing these cosmic correspondences from Plato's *Timaeus*, which argues that the world takes its pattern from the triangle. This eternal image "circulates" throughout the elements, and multiplies itself in "compound figures"—like the figures in Eliot that decorate the leaf and orchestrate the stars.[10] However, Timaeus perceives the lower world as a facsimile of a celestial original: and Eliot disturbs this hierarchy. In the lyric from "Burnt Norton", the "figure" oversteps the bound between above and below built into the structure of mimetic thought. For it embodies a principle of repetition, *acts it out*, xeroxes itself throughout the chain of being. Indelible yet indeterminate, it resurges like an algebraic figure in each of the equations of the cosmos.

Eliot may have borrowed the term "figure" from Plato (or rather from his translator, Jowett, who uses it so lavishly); but he invests it with an even wider range of meanings.[11] According to his friend John Hayward, Eliot exploited the *OED* as he was writing *Four Quartets*, and he eagerly incorporated "rich and well-connected" words.[12] The word "figure" appears twice in this passage and frequently reverberates throughout the poem. Since he was on the look-out for verbal repetitions, he must have meant to weave it through the text, gathering associations as it moved. He must also have been intrigued that its meanings cram four pages of the dictionary. To begin with, "figure" may refer to choreography or to the figure who performs it, confounding the dancer with the dance. A figure in music means " 'any short succession of notes, either as a melody or a group of chords, which produces a single, complete, and distinct impression' (Grove)" (*OED*). Thus the figure hesitates between the realms of space and time, at the crux of all the text's dubieties. "Figured" can mean traced or ornamented, but Eliot also uses it to mean predicted or foredoomed:

Either you had no purpose
Or the purpose is beyond the end you figured
And is altered in fulfilment. (*LG* I 33–5)

In the *Quartets*, every figure is necessarily *pre*figured. For if the stars initiate the dance along the bloodstream or the gyrations of the boarhound and the boar, the constellations are themselves bright shadows of the patterns that they motivate. Moreover, since the "figured leaf" could also mean a written page, it implicates the poem's own calligraphy, and the "figures" of its rhetoric as well.[13]

So much for the definitions of the figure; but what about its movements, its logistics? The first section of "Little Gidding" uses the term "figured", the second "disfigured" (*LG* I 34, II 94). But the third movement completes the sequence with "transfigured", as if to supersede its predecessors:

> See, now they vanish,
> The faces and places, with the self which, as it could,
> loved them,
> To become renewed, *transfigured*, in another pattern.
> (*LG* III 14–16: my emphasis)

This triad suggests the dialectic, where thesis is disfigured by antithesis, so that both can be transfigured in a synthesis. For it is only through this death and this erasure—"See, now they vanish"—that the reconciliation may occur. This sublation enables the *Quartets* to overcome erasure and to reappropriate the "wastage" of the past (*DS* II 22). The legal and financial terms that swarm the text seem to reassert its husbandry, in metaphors of gifts, bequests, covenants, values, payments, additions, debts, receipts. Nonetheless, the notion of "disfiguration" marks a punctual amnesia in the order of remembrance, an unavoidable expense the dialectic can scarcely budget for. To glimpse these losses it is necessary to pursue the whole economy of memory.

The Floors of Memory

> We had the experience but missed the meaning,
> And approach to the meaning restores the experience
> In a different form, beyond any meaning
> We can assign to happiness.
> (*DS* II 45–8)

In this system, to miss the meaning is the premium one pays in order to insure the past against oblivion. After the event, the meaning recreates the past, and restores it dialectically in a different form. The verse itself enacts this movement, reincorporating its own past, as the words "experience" and "meaning" rhythmically return, the syntax swelling to defeat the very commas which might interrupt its fluid continuity. Like the sentence, meaning moves "beyond" each point of rest, pressing relentlessly into another intensity.

That was a way of putting it. But one could also say that it is meaning which *effaces* the experience, for the one condemns the other to forgetfulness. "The pattern is new in every moment", because it has disfigured the experience it supersedes (*EC* II 35). We *think* we can remember that we have forgotten, and therefore we devise a "meaning" to cover—and recover—our amnesia. But this meaning constitutes a new experience of doubtful pedigree. And this experience in turn effaces meaning, moves "beyond" it, and beyond the "happiness" of any simple satiety of sense. Rather than a dialectical progression, each experience undoes another, and the self becomes a crucible of decomposing memories.

This structure resembles Bergson's model of remembrance. He too argues that experience is always fringed with memories, because the mind submerges each perception into the welter of the past. "Reflective perception is a *circuit*", he contends, in which each new perception has to circumnavigate the old. The diagram which illustrates this theory could also illustrate the structure of the *Four Quartets*, with their spirals of experience and retrospection (*M&M* 128). Here the circuit A nearly coincides with the object O, and with the instant of its apprehension. But even A denotes an after-image, which ripples through the circuits of the mind. The schema implies that we "rebuild" the object as we apprehend it, but this also means we must initially *forget* it so that we can recompose it out of ghosts. Bergson goes on to argue that each perception is "repeated an endless number of times on the different storeys of memory" (*M&M* 129). In fact, it is impossible to constitute an object without invoking these galleries of recollection. This means that endless

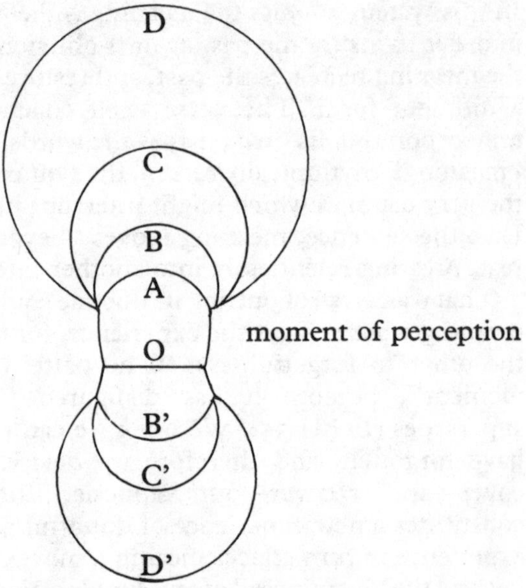

repetitions must already have occurred before the subject even "sees" the thing. The mind is thus marooned between a present steeped in recollection and a past adulterated by its own futurity.[14]

The "still point" in the *Four Quartets* compares to the O in Bergson's diagram: for the poem's voices circulate around this point like the memories that cling around the object, cushioning the mind against the shock of apprehension like a pearl around a grain of sand (*M&M* 112n.). Eliot grants the still point ontological priority—it represents the Word, and he constantly laments the failure of his words to do it justice. In this way he *re-invents* the metaphysical, patiently manufacturing the inexpressible. In fact, the whole poem is a kind of industry for processing forgetfulness into a theology of meaning. For the still point may also designate the blank amnesia that institutes the knowable, and which can only retrospectively be understood as God. This struggle between recollection and oblivion reveals itself most vividly in the first movement of "Burnt Norton" and the return of the familiar compound ghost in "Little Gidding".

* * *

"Burnt Norton" begins by disrupting the complacency of memory, and the inveterate belief that time advances in a line, straight or circular. Memory dissolves into "a world of speculation": a specular world of echoes and reflections. Even a forgetting may never have occurred, since there is no guarantee that the past ever existed. The footfalls that echo in the memory are echoes of the words which posit them: "My words echo / Thus, in your mind" (I 14–15). They also echo Augustine's *Confessions*:

> Although past things are related as true, they are drawn out from the memory,—not the things themselves, which have passed, but the words conceived from the images of the things which they have formed in the mind as footprints in their passage through the senses.[15]

Here the words reflect the images, which mirror the footprints, which trace the disappearance of the apparition of the thing. But Eliot even doubts that there is an original to recollect: for the passage was never taken, nor did it issue in the rose garden.

Yet it is this garden that we are invited to enter: the "first world" where memory is already mixing with desire. The deception of the thrush conducts us to the pool, which fills with "water out of sunlight" and turns into a mirror (I 35): the very image of a world of "speculation". Here it is that "they", "dignified, invisible", achieve a figure and a face: "And they were behind us, reflected in the pool" (I 38). In temporal terms, "behind" could mean before or after, as if the figures were mirages of the future and the past, abolishing the present. In spatial terms, the image appears before us, its source behind us: yet it is only through the image that They become visible at all. In fact, They take shape in the very moment that we turn our back on them and blot them out. Transfixed by the image, we renounce the "reality" it bodies forth ("human kind / Cannot bear very much reality" [42–3]). With its ripples of fantasy and recollection, the pool reflects the act of seeing, rather than the thing beheld. For in a garden where "the roses / Had the look of flowers that are looked at", the gaze can only speculate upon itself, and the pool can only be the mirror of Narcissus, where shape materialises at the cost of its possession (I 28–9). What is more, the figures are composed of water and of sunlight, which diffuse the very images they shape.[16] Presently, "they" vanish, as if the power of prosopopeia had unleashed a counter-spirit of disfiguration: "Then a cloud passed, and the pool was empty" (I 39). To posit figure is to posit ground—but "Burnt Norton" grounds the figure in its own dissolve.

This duplicity returns in other episodes of imaging: for instance, in the voices of the sea.

> The sea howl
> And the sea yelp, are different voices
> Often together heard: the whine in the rigging,
> The menace and caress of wave that breaks on water,
> The distant rote in the granite teeth,
> And the wailing warning from the approaching headland
> Are all sea voices. . . .
>
> (*DS* I 26–32)

Like the waves, the voices here dissolve into the sea of sound, as momentary apparitions cast out of the torrent. For water "generates the very possibility of structure, pattern, form, or shape by way of the disappearance of shape into shapelessness", in De Man's words.[17] Here Eliot's fable of the origin of voice harks back to the myth of Proteus, in which the sea becomes a paradigm of figuration, too: and Proteus is shapeless because he has too many shapes, effervescing in their own exuberance. In this strange logic, form unforms, shape unshapes, and every poem is an epitaph—its own.

Fire, like water, destroys the shapes that it creates, and this may be the reason that Heraclitus sees it as the figure of figures: "*pyros tropai*".[18] Eliot probably knew this formula, since he cites Heraclitus in the epigraph: and the phrase anticipates his own poetic conflagrations. In "Little Gidding" the dead return as the masters of the lyric utterance, and for this reason they are "tongued with fire", lyric arsonists. The trope itself becomes a pyre, consumed in the violence of its own constitution. As Eliot says:

> The only hope, or else despair
> Lies in the choice of pyre or pyre—
> To be redeemed from fire by fire.
>
> (*LG* IV, 5–7)

This is a rhetorical, as well as a religious, ultimatum, for the pyrotechnics of the text imply that every trope or figure immolates another. It is in this sense that the only hope, or else despair, lies in another figure and another fire.

It is when the speaker summons his dead master that the incendiary logic of the figure is fulfilled. Like "Burnt Norton", "Little Gidding" begins by sweeping time away, and by creating "its own season", its "Midwinter spring" (I 1). In the second movement, night and day give way to the poem's own "uncertain hour", purged of antecedents and futurity (II 25). The ghost appears in all the "glimmering ambivalence" of the figures of the pool, the sea, the sunlight, or the garden.[19] He stands for memory but also for oblivion, forgotten in the moment that he is recalled. " 'I may not comprehend, may not remember' ", cries the speaker, as the ghost refuses to remind him of the theories he has already forgotten. But the speaker fears he will forget the ghost's new figures in the very shock of their enunciation:

> I said: "The wonder that I feel is easy,
> Yet ease is cause of wonder. Therefore speak:
> I may not comprehend, may not remember."
> And he: "I am not eager to rehearse
> My thought and theory which you have forgotten. . . .
> For last year's words belong to last year's language
> And next year's words await another voice. (II 55–66)

Caught between the discourse of the future and the past, the spectre marks a rift in memory where speech dissolves into amnesia. He, too, is "known, forgotten, half recalled", obsolescing as he shapes his face: "And he a face still forming . . ." (II 40, 48). In fact, the manuscripts reveal that Eliot systematically defaced the ghost to render him "Both intimate and unidentifiable" (II 43).[20]

However, the narrator also loses face, as if the ghost could only rise by reducing his ephebe to a phantom:

> So I assumed a double part, and cried
> And heard another's voice cry: "What! Are *you* here?"
> Although we were not. I was still the same,
> Knowing myself yet being someone other—
> And he a face still forming. . . . (II 44–8)

In a contest for self-destruction or self-invention, each figure hovers between life and death, struggling to save his features from oblivion. This violence belies the "easy wonder" that the speaker vaunts towards his precursor, as if he had eluded the agony of influence. But in his master's eyes he also sees his own estranged, uncanny gaze, transfixing him like the Medusa. "Knowing myself yet being someone other", he plays a "double part", staging his own death and watching his identity disfeaturing. The struggle ends in the evacuation of the street, banishing the figure from the text:

> The day was breaking. In the disfigured street
> He left me, with a kind of valediction,
> And faded on the blowing of the horn.
>
> (*LG* II 94–6)

When Eliot changed the "dismantled street" (already an ingenious pun) to the "disfigured street" in his revisions, he introduced a subtle resonance.[21] The word "disfigured" commonly means "mutilated", and it implies unfaced, unrecognisable. But in this context it literally means *figureless*—emptied of persona, phantom, shape, face, rhetoric. It is also important that this meeting has transpired "nowhere", with "no before and after"; for in the poetics of this text the figure is unmade in the very instant of its incarnation. Yet this timeless moment when unbeing becomes being and defacement fact has to be presented as an allegory, because words move "only in time" (*BN* V 2). And only when the figure splits into the speaker and the ghost can it be and not be at the same time. The figure does not *take place*, and more important, it does not *take time*, for it is not an historical event, but a lesion in temporality, which brings forth all the *business* of a history.

Jean-François Lyotard argues that "language, at least in its poetic usage, is possessed, haunted by the figure": and it is telling that the *Quartets* picture figuration in the form of phantoms.[22] For these chimeras mark the moments when the figure glints in speech, deranging discourse as a dream disturbs the night. Less than a picture, other than a word, the figure marks the spatiality that glimmers in and out of language, petulant and irreducible. According to Freud, the unconscious is the kingdom of the figure, and conscious discourse is forever vexed by the convulsions when the figure irrupts into the word. Moreover, Freud associates the figure with desire, in the sense that the dream is the figuration of a wish. What is it that the *Quartets* desire? "Little Gidding" hints that all poetic speech is haunted by the wish to give a face to death. "Costing not less than everything" (*LG* V 41): for to figure death is to disfigure self, and to abolish discourse in hallucination.

Disease in Signatures

Wavering "between two worlds", the ghost of "Little Gidding" represents the hesitation of the *Quartets* as a whole, caught between antinomies that often look alike (*LG* II 141; III 1). Eliot insisted that "there really isn't any heart of the matter": for the poem's oppositions face each other like the speaker and the ghost, in mutual interdestruction.[23] As we have seen, the poem hovers between the belief in the redemption of the past and the darker knowledge of its loss. This dubiety in turn suspends the self between identity and an impersonality of violent forgetfulness.

At the same time, however, Eliot insists upon a *nostos*, "A condition of complete simplicity", when this ambivalence will come to rest (*LG* V 40). "Home is where one starts from", he muses:

> As we grow older
> The world becomes stranger, the pattern more complicated
> Of dead and living. Not the intense moment
> Isolated, with no before and after,
> But a lifetime burning in every moment
> And not the lifetime of one man only
> But of old stones that cannot be deciphered.
>
> (*EC* V 19–25)

It is these old stones that complicate the pattern, forcing their illegibility into the living voice. The poem insinuates that the home one starts from is the stone which will obliterate one's name:

And any action
Is a step to the block, to the fire, down the sea's throat
Or to an illegible stone: and that is where we start.

(*LG* V 12–14)

This passage implicates the tombstone in the fire and the sea, those emblems of destruction and creation. For articulated speech begins in the "sea's throat", and dissolves in the tumult of its waves: while the fire—*pyros tropai*—destroys the very tropes it summons from its flames. And this is where we start from: the stone which unnames what it names, the wordless thunder of the sea. In the beginning was disfiguration, hints the poem: and it is to this still point of illegibility that all its explorations must return. "Unappeased and peregrine", the *Quartets* strive to reassert the name, and to recuperate identity through memory. But the tombstones, the fire and the sea, the dry pool and the disfigured street bespeak the punctual extinction of the self. If the poem is an epitaph, the figures on its stone no longer even spell a name.

Into Another Intensity

Eliot's early criticism shows how slippery the term impersonality becomes because it serves so many contradictory demands. Does the poet choose to be impersonal, or is the very act of writing suicidal? Eliot never quite resolves the question. He uses the doctrine to promote reserve, humility and self-effacement, but also to suggest the transcendence or apotheosis of the self. The doctrine implicates other fields of knowledge, too: for it attacks the politics of individualism and even the metaphysics of the soul. The first chapter of this book traced the instabilities that turn the doctrine of impersonality against itself, till it converges with its own antithesis. The next three chapters analysed the poetry to see how Eliot composes fictive personalities. In each case a double logic has emerged, in which the more the poet struggles to suppress subjectivity, the more it reappears in other forms and disguises. But the reverse is also true: "Little

Gidding" hints that self-engendering necessarily implies a self-erasure, and that the written I is necessarily a ghost.

Pound, too, demands impersonality and yet remains addicted to its contrary. On the one hand, he argues that poets should efface themselves before their objects, in a stark laconic registration of reality; but on the other hand, he clings to the belief that poetry originates in self-expression. Like Eliot, he asserts the value of tradition, and argues that the poet is the product of his history, rather than a godlike and autonomous creator. Yet he never overcomes a sneaking admiration for the egoist. Vestiges of his suppressed delight in individualism and originality creep into his sternest circumscriptions of the self. Less guarded and inhibited than Eliot, Pound was unable to espouse the poetics of repression so whole-heartedly. He remains ambivalent about impersonality throughout his work, and the next two chapters examine his dubieties.

Many similarities emerge. Both poets use the doctrine of impersonality to attack their own infatuation with its opposite. Both conscript the doctrine into their political campaigns, exposing its reactionary implications. Both employ personae in their early poetry in order to conceal their subjectivity, and both perceive the limitations of this practice, too. Later their epic verse becomes impersonal and autobiographical at once. But Eliot promotes the doctrine more enthusiastically than Pound, who grows increasingly obsessed with self-creation. *The Cantos* are his private diary, where he telescopes the Western and the Eastern worlds into the store-room of his subjectivity. Far from impersonal, this project is megalomaniacal. Yet in the text itself his personality disbands among the *bricolage* like the fallout after an explosion (or a "BLAST", if we are to preserve his idiom). What *The Cantos* show is that the author is neither absent nor present in the ordinary senses of those words. They show that *the subject is never where he thinks he is.* It is not through memory or self-reflection that Pound inscribes himself within the text, but in the very schisms of his tortured thought. He is written through his whole epistemology. In particular, his economic theory serves to hide him from himself while it surreptitiously disseminates his signature.

The last chapter of this book will show how the flight from the name determines the shape of Pound's creative enterprise.

Notes

1. Smidt, *Poetry and Belief*, p. 213; Gardner, *The Composition of Four Quartets* (London: Faber, 1978), p. 29. For a similar view, see Gish, p. 92. For an opposite view, see Kenner, *The Invisible Poet: T. S. Eliot* (New York: Macdowell, Obolensky, 1959), p. 293, who describes the *Quartets* as "Old Possum's last disappearing trick".
2. *Composition*, p. 39; see p. 29 for the letter to which Gardner is referring.
3. F. R. Leavis, *The Living Principle* (London: Chatto and Windus, 1975), p. 243; C. K. Stead, *The Imposed Structure of the Four Quartets*, in *T. S. Eliot: Four Quartets: A Casebook*, ed. Bernard Bergonzi (London: Macmillan, 1969), p. 211.
4. For the suppression of Sir Thomas Browne, for instance, see Gardner, *Composition*, pp. 99, 42–3, 46–8, 52–3.
5. Kenner, *The Invisible Poet*, p. 250.
6. Grover Smith, *T. S. Eliot's Poetry and Plays*, p. 251.
7. *On Dreams* (1901), SE V 660, 667.
8. I take the term "white noise" from Lawrence R. Schehr's translation of Michel Serres's term "bruit de fond": see Serres, "Noise", trans. Schehr, *Sub Stance*, 40 (1983), 50–1.
9. It is likely that Eliot took the image of the dance from Plato's *Timaeus*, for it is from this text and from St Augustine's *Confessions* that the poem borrows its philosophy of time. See *The Confessions of St. Augustine*, trans. J. G. Pilkington (New York: Horace Liveright, 1927), Ch. II, esp. pp. 283–304. St Augustine himself was following Plato; see the *Timaeus*, in *The Dialogues of Plato*, trans. B. Jowett (Oxford: Clarendon, 1875), Vol. III, pp. 619–23. For a detailed study of these sources, see Staffan Bergsten, *Time and Eternity: A Study of the Structure and Symbolism of T. S. Eliot's Four Quartets*, Studia Litterarum Upsaliensia, no. 1 (Stockholm: Bonniers, 1960), pp. 55–112. Yet although Plato is his earliest source, Eliot could scarcely speak of dancing without remembering Yeats, whose ghost haunts "Little Gidding".
10. *Timaeus*, pp. 636ff., 632. According to Timaeus, these figures imprint themselves in matter, which he calls "the natural recipient of all impressions". He compares it variously to a writing surface; to a mother who receives the imprint of the father's seed; and finally to molten gold, which can be struck into an infinite variety of forms: "Suppose a person to make all kinds of *figures* of gold and never to cease

transforming them out of one form into all the others . . ." (*Timaeus*, p. 632: my emphasis.) In fact, these metaphors themselves enact what they depict, the proliferation of the figures of the universe.

11. See *Timaeus*, pp. 623, 627, 632, 633, 636, 639, 642, for various uses of the term "figure".
12. See Gardner, *Composition*, p. 120.
13. Christopher Tucker pointed out to me that "figured leaf" occurs in Tennyson's *In Memoriam*, xliii.ll.
14. Bergson distinguishes between two forms of memory, one of which "imagines", while the other "repeats". The first he calls the "spontaneous" or voluntary memory, for it is here that he believes that freedom lies. To call up the past in the form of an image, he explains, "we must be able to withdraw ourselves from the action of the moment", for we are "always situated at the point where [our] past expires in a deed". Therefore, it is only in a "rift" in the present, when the exigencies of action are suspended, that these phantoms of the past may surge into the mind. But the other form of memory, the motor memory, is geared to action. Bergson thinks it is misnamed, for it consists of "*habit interpreted by memory* rather than memory itself." When we *memorise* a poem, for example, we repeat the text without recalling the history of its mastery. What is more, Bergson argues that the very repetition drives us to *forget* the past. "Spontaneous recollection is perfect from the outset", he claims: "it retains in memory its place and date" (*M&M* 88–101). But the motor memory *un*dates and deracinates these images, for repetition "can add nothing to [the] image without *disfiguring* it . . ." (*M&M* 95: my emphasis).

    Rather than a separate counterforce, however, the motor memory perverts the faculty of recollection from *within*. This means that repetition and forgetting are native to the principle that they transgress. Indeed, each memory subverts the other in perpetual attrition. While it is usually the motor habits which deface the images of voluntary retrospection, the reverse can also come to pass. Sometimes, Bergson argues, spontaneous memory remains intact while the capacity for motor action is destroyed. For instance, certain patients can call to mind the image of a place they know, but cannot find their way around it in reality (*M&M* 108–9). Apraxia in this case, amnesia in the other, this double-sided memory offers only an impracticable image or obliterating act.
15. *Confessions*, Bk. XI, Ch. 18, p. 289.
16. See De Man, "Shelley Disfigured", p. 55.
17. Ibid., p. 53.
18. Marc Shell, *The Economy of Literature* (Baltimore and London: Johns Hopkins University Press, 1978), p. 52.
19. See De Man, "Shelley Disfigured", p. 53.
20. See Gardner, *Composition*, pp. 174–6. Other critics have gone to some lengths to restore the spectre's undisfigured face: Aldritt, for instance, identifies him with Mallarmé [*Eliot's "Four Quartets": Poetry as Chamber Music* (London: Woburn Press, 1978), pp. 15–16]; Frye

identifies him with Pound [*T. S. Eliot*, pp. 88–9]; while Kenner, insisting on his "compound" nature, links him with "Yeats, Mallarmé, Hamlet's father, Ezra Pound, Dante, Swift, Milton," and Eliot himself (*Invisible Poet*, p. 274).

21. See Gardner, *Composition*, p. 195.
22. Jean-François Lyotard, "The Dream Work Does Not Think", trans. Mary Lydon, *Oxford Literary Review*, 6, no. 1 (1983), 13.
23. Eliot, Letter to Anne Ridler, 10 March 1941, cited by Gardner, *Composition*, p. 109.

PART II

Ezra Pound

CHAPTER V

"What part ob yu is deh poEM?"

O ye myriad
That strive and play and pass,
Jest, challenge, counterlie!

I ? I ? I ?

And ye?

Pound, "On his Own Face in a Glass."

A Little Crowd

Wyndham Lewis found it ironic that Ezra Pound should have appointed himself spokesman of the avant-garde. If Pound the pundit claimed to be resuscitating the dead art of poetry, Pound the lyricist merely disinterred its stiffened forms. "His fire-eating propagandist utterances were not accompanied by any very experimental efforts in his particular medium", Lewis remarks. "But this certain discrepancy between what Pound said—what he supported and held up as an example—and what he did, was striking enough to impress itself on anybody" (*TWM* 55). Later Pound himself was to dismiss his early verse as "stale creampuffs", and it is difficult to reconcile these nostalgic lyrics with his witty, vigorous polemics.[1] Between the minstrel and the demagogue, Pound's discourse breaks asunder, and not only does the practice flout the theory, but the theory is divided from within.

He contradicts himself most systematically when he attempts to circumscribe the author's powers. It would be an exaggeration to say that Pound had a "theory" of impersonality, for he prefers to send ideas straight into action: and slogans like "imagisme" and "vorticism" belong in manifestoes rather than in dissertations in philosophy. But it is under these rubrics that he legislates the self's domain. However, he scolds poets, as often as he praises them, for self-effacement. He agrees with Eliot, for instance, that Tennyson would have written better verse if he had been less "encrusted with impersonal ideas." He should have been *more* egotistical, not less: "It was that lady-like attitude to the printed page that did it—that something, that ineffable 'something', which kept Tennyson out of his works" (*LE* 276). At other times, however, Pound suggests that the work of art transcends the author's personality, whether he deliberately suppresses it or not. "It does not matter whether the author desire the good of the race or acts merely from personal vanity", he argues. "The thing is mechanical in action" (*LE* 22). What the author has to say is less important to his greatness than the language that the dead have fashioned for his use:

> it took two centuries of Provence and one of Tuscany to develop the media of Dante's masterwork . . . it took the latinists of the Renaissance, and the Pleiade, and his own age of painted speech to prepare Shakespeare his tools. It is tremendously important that great poetry be written, it makes no jot of difference who writes it. (*LE* 9–10)

It is the tradition, rather than the individual, which engenders poetry: and Pound demotes the poet to the secretary to his age. However, he also endorses Eliot's conception of tradition, in which the new work may alter the whole order of the past:

> Mr. Eliot and I are in complete agreement, or "belong to the same school of critics", insofar as we both believe that the existing works form a complete order which is changed by the introduction of the "really new" work.[2]

This view implies that "all ages are contemporaneous", as Pound asserts in *The Spirit of Romance* (*SR* 8). He is so convinced that the poet must address tradition, rather than his private feelings, that he often takes impersonality for granted. Poets serve as the antennae of their race, and their poetry can only blossom if the time is pure (*ABCR* 73).

Pound's critics urge impersonality more forcefully than he does, for they cannot reconcile the man who suffers with the mind that creates. Wyndham Lewis thought Pound a "parasite", bereft of all identity but that which he embezzled from the dead. "He receives", writes Lewis, "he is the *consumer*":

> Pound is that curious thing, a person without a trace of originality of any sort. It is impossible even to imagine him being any one in particular of all the people he has translated, interpreted, appreciated. . . . Ezra is a crowd; a little crowd. (*TWM* 85–6)

According to Lewis, Pound surrenders his originality to the dictation of the masters of the past. His mind is a hotchpotch, mixing "in exactly equal proportions Bergson—Marinetti—Mr. Hueffer (with a few preaphaelite 'christian names' thrown in), Edward Fitzgerald and Buffalo Bill" (*TWM* 38). Though other critics argue the proportions, even the most sympathetic separate the artist from the man, to counteract the scandal of his politics. Indeed, Donald Davie points out that American society asserted "an absolute discontinuity" between the poet and the man when Pound received the Bollingden Prize for the *Pisan Cantos* in 1949.[3] Pound himself has argued that one of the "great maladies of modern criticism is that first rush to look for the person, and the corresponding failure EVER to look *at* the thing" (*ABCR* 147). However, he has made his person so objectionable that his readers gladly turn their gazes to the thing.

Yet no gaze could even quite take in *The Cantos*. More like a life than an artifact, this "sprawling", "leviathanic", "cryselephantine" text grew longer with the poet's years, equally unable to revise its errors.[4] The poem, like its author, seems unable to speak in its own defence.[5] For it lacks consistency of motive, and therefore defies judgment according to the canons of literary law. Perplexed by the caprices of its form, critics delve underground to seek a hidden allegory, a "deep structure" (Bush), a "backbone"

(Watts), "the very core of what *The Cantos* are all about" (Pearlman).[6] By discovering the poem's hidden unity these critics hope to bring Pound's hidden rectitude to light: for no one seeks his unifying principle in his vitriol against the Jews, though here he is *maniacally* consistent.[7] According to George Dekker, for example, Pound's "evil is obviously peripheral . . .; the success or failure of the poem must be accounted for on other grounds."[8] Forrest Read devoted his life's work to proving that Pound had hidden the meaning of his work in a "kaleidoscopic pattern for the assiduous and intelligent to discover."[9] Unreadability is above all contagious. Dekker, for instance, takes precautions to avoid infection, and bears his liberalism like moly to guide him through the text's iniquities: "My own socio-political bias is more or less conventionally liberal; I detest Pound's anti-Semitism . . .".[10]

Ironically, these critics reassert the contradictions of the work in the very trouble that they take to disavow them. Noel Stock, however, condemns the poem for its inconsistencies, complaining that it fails to "communicate with the ground of realism which is naturally present in the human mind."[11] Indeed, the text's derangements hint that this humanist conception of aesthetic unity is drawing towards the expiration of its history. Charles Olson calls Pound the "tragic Double of our day" because his life mirrors the wreckage of his times.[12] But as Jean-Michel Rabaté has pointed out, he also means that Pound is the double of our doubling; that we participate in his duality; and that no prophylactic measures can preserve us from complicity.[13]

It is Pound's attitudes of personality that dramatise this doubling most persistently. He first attempted to transcend the self through the dramatic monologue, but in many ways his masks empower the personality that they conceal. For this reason, he subordinates the mask to the exigencies of Imagism (1912). Vorticism (1914) and the ideogrammic method (1927) also promised an escape from subjectivity, yet both retrieve the self in different forms. This chapter traces the fate of personality through his early poetry and criticism, and concludes with *Hugh Selwyn Mauberley*, his first epic deconstruction of the self.

A Chaplet of Instants

Pound begins to advocate impersonality as early as 1907, at the same time that he clings to a subjectivist aesthetic. In a letter to his girlfriend Viola Jordan in 1907, he situates his poetry in a tradition of "subjective personality analysis."[14] On the other hand, he chides his mother for interpreting his verse as self-exposure: "You mustn't take my stuff so personally. 'The Necklace' is perfectly fictitious. . . . If it is necessary for me to continue writing fiction, I shall probably commit murder and arson in the first person . . .". Here he implies that the first person is an empty function, serving merely to enhance illusion. Although he uses his own experience as "material", the act of writing transfigures that experience, for the poet's life can never be conflated with his words. Nonetheless, he adds, "I have to write from the inside."[15] Like Eliot, Pound presumes that poetry begins in the expression of emotion, though writing is a crucible which burns its privacy away. So he hints in another letter to Viola Jordan, where he appeals to her

> to pardon what is yet imperfect, looking rather to what I have striven to express than to the technicalities and minutiae of that expression, I give you that part of me which is most real, ~~fartherest distilled~~ most removed from the transient personality, (Persona, a mask), most nearly related to things that more [sic] permanent than this smoke wraith the earth. . . .[16]

Here Pound envisages the mask as a quintessential self, extracted by the alchemy of verse from the grosser elements of personality.

In his dramatic monologues Pound strives to capture sudden disclosures of the self, more valid for their very evanescence.[17] His masks compose a "chaplet of instants", to use a formula of Georges Poulet's.[18] As Pound explained to Williams:

> To me the short so-called dramatic lyric—at any rate the sort of thing I do—is the poetic part of a drama the rest of which (to me the prose part) is left to the reader or implied or set in a short note. I catch the character I happen to be interested in at the moment he interests me, usually a moment of song, self-analysis, or sudden understanding or revelation. And the rest of the play would bore me and presumably the reader. (*L* 3–4)

Purged of the intrusions of the author, these masks may seem impersonal, but they depict the moments when another subjectivity shines through most luminously. In this way they salvage personality, even though they hide the author's own.

In practice, however, Pound pays more attention to the act of speech than to the personal details of the speaker. His early poems sing of singing, write of writing: their speakers meditate the lyrics that they will or won't indite, and how to store them, destroy them or disseminate them. His troubadours are less concerned with the *content* of their poems than with their fortunes as objects of consumption. Often they withdraw their works from circulation to avenge themselves against their loves. In "Marvoil", Arnaut Daniel schemes to stuff his song into a hole in his lady's castle wall, to surprise her when she least suspects a serenade (*CEP* 95–6). This metonymy transforms the song into a symbolic phallus, with the advantage over the real organ that it rapes invisibly and through deferred effects. In "Le Fraisne", Piere Vidal stows his sorrows in the woods, as if they too were objects or part-objects: "I wrapped my tears in an ellum leaf / And left them under a stone . . ." ("La Fraisne", *CEP* 9). By association, the "leaves" of the text become the hiding-places where the poet's sorrows wait to be aroused, his powers unleashed. In "Famam Librosque Cano", Pound fantasies that his own books will be remaindered like Fitzgerald's *Rubaiyyat* (*CEP* 23). Again, the *content* of these books subsides into the question of their *physical trajectory*.

While these poems speculate about their distribution, others brood upon their own production. In "Silet", for example, the poet watches the ink dripping from his "deathless pen" (*CEP* 181). In 'To la Contessa Biazafior", the ink grows dim as night descends upon the poet's page (*CEP* 65). In "The Cry of the Eyes", the speaker's eyes admonish him for subjecting them to his own writing:

> Free us, for we perish
> In this ever-flowing monotony
> Of ugly print-marks, black
> Upon white parchment.
>
> (*CEP* 24)

It is the moment of inscription that interests these texts, rather than the words the ink indites. In each case, the subject-matter of the poem is another poem, which is hidden, hoarded, procrastinated, or aborted. "Na Audiart", for instance, is a song that promises another song which will preserve the lady's loveliness in "rose and gold" (*CEP* 14). Cino, on the other hand, disowns his former verse, and sallies out to seek new songs along the open road ("Cino", *CEP* 10–12). "Praise of Ysolt", like its predecessor, "Vana", is a song about the poet's incapacity to sing (*CEP* 79–80; 27). *Hugh Selwyn Mauberley* takes this theme to epic proportions, and becomes a lexicon of the impossibility of its own creation. Apart from the external impediments to poetry—the stupidity of the populace, the tyranny of the marketplace, and the gamy Romanticism of the 1890s—these poems hint at an impediment within, built into the structure of the enterprise.

In Pound, the purpose of the mask is to restore the existential link between the speaker and his words.[19] Therefore he subordinates the biographical details of his personae to the moment of enunciation, when song and self unite in the epiphany of utterance. At the same time, however, he complains that to write "I am" is to deny it, because the now when this was true has always passed. The text becomes the epitaph to that lost consciousness:

> When I behold how black, immortal ink
> Drips from my deathless pen—ah, well-away!
> . . .
> Time has seen this, and will not turn again;
>
> And who are we, who know that last intent,
> To plague tomorrow with a testament!
>
> ("Silet", *CEP* 181)

> Silent my mate came as the night was still.
> Speech? Words? Faugh! Who talks of words and love?!
> Hot is such love and silent,
> Silent as fate is. . . .
>
> ("Piere Vidal Old", *CEP* 110)

These words refer primarily to their performance, often botched and interrupted. For Pound can only simulate the living voice when it begins to lose its mastery, to spend itself in cries, expletives, or to stammer and to vanish into dots. In "Piere Vidal Old", for instance:

> Behold me shrivelled, and your mock of mocks;
> And yet I mock you by the mighty fires
> That burnt me to this ash.
> . . .
> Ah! Cabaret! Ah Cabaret, thy hills again!
> . . .
> Take your hands off me! . . . [*Sniffing the air.*]
> Ha! this scent is hot!
>
> (*CEP* 111)

These aphasic moments mark the "tragic doubling" of the act of writing, when the subject forfeits being, presence, speech—"To plague tomorrow with a testament!" The poems seem compelled to re-enact the tragedy of writing as division.

The most obvious of these divisions is the split between the author and his masks. Yet by giving voice to the poets of the past, Pound endorses *their* identities even while he temporarily forgoes his own. On scrutiny, however, his poetry unfolds into a battle for the voice where poet and personae struggle for mastery. Many of the early poems mix modern with archaic diction, and they jar upon the ear because they dispossess the speakers of their idioms. Like *The Cantos*, these poems "include history", but they include it in the form of difference, as the traces of another voice within the voice.[20] In "The Tree", for instance, the soul-in-timber figures forth the self-in-writing, and while the speaker turns into a tree his voice grows wooden in its atavism (*CEP* 35). The metamorphosis itself is an image of the poet's verbal transmigrations through personae. Indeed, Pound speculates that myths like these evolved as masks to screen their own creators:

> These tales of old disguisings, are they not
> Strange myths of souls that found themselves among
> Unwonted folk that spake an hostile tongue, . . .
>
> ("Masks", *CEP* 34)

Allegories of their own production, the disguisings that these stories *tell* shadow forth the masks they *are*. Pound believes that the tradition of metamorphosis provides a tutelage in time, by teaching us that "things do not remain always the same" (*LE* 431). These changes implicate the self: for Pound imagines personality as fire, a transformative power rather than a soul-substance:

> O thou anxious thou,
> Who call'st about my gates for some lost me; . . .
> If thou hast seen my shade sans character,
> If thou hast seen that mirror of all moments,
> That glass to all things that o'ershadow it,
> Call not that mirror me, for I have slipped
> Your grasp, I have eluded.
>
> (*CEP* 172)

"Sans character", the self eludes a fixed identity, so that the "mirror" of mimesis necessarily belies its mutability. Yet it is by evading representation that the self transcends its images, unsevered by the doubles it has left behind. Rather than endangering the self, Pound revels in its getaway, as if its slippage were the source of its resilience. It seems that he denies the self only to restore it elsewhere, in another guise.

"Imagism" was one of his most rigorous attempts to chasten poetry of personality. In his manifesto for the movement, "A Few Don'ts by an Imagiste" (1913), he urges "Direct treatment of the 'thing' ", implying that the artist must suppress himself in favour of the revelation of his subject-matter.[21] This "thing" may be "subjective or objective", but the poet must approach it like a scientist, patiently labelling his specimens.[22] However, this form of impersonality does not impugn the poet's mastery, for Pound assumes that the subject can be insulated from the "thing" that he subjects to words, from the "treatment" he performs upon the world. As Alan Durant has argued, Pound presupposes a transcendent subject and an object given in advance, rather than acknowledging the *work* which constitutes them both.[23] In spite of and, indeed, *because* of his impersonality, the poet remains the hidden lord of language, rather than the plaything of its machinations. But Joseph

Riddel, who shares Durant's poststructuralist bent, cites the same words from Pound to argue for the opposite interpretation. " 'Direct' implies immediacy", he writes, "but it is the 'treatment' which is direct, and a treatment is already a kind of doubling."[24] Though Riddel is quibbling with the syntax here, he is right to argue that Pound is less empiricist than Durant claims, and less seduced by the ontological pre-eminence of *things*.

For Pound is more preoccupied with *powers* than with objects, and he defines the image in kinetic rather than mimetic terms: "An 'Image' is that which presents an intellectual and emotional complex in an instant of time" (*LE* 4). In 1914 he transumes the image into the "vortex", which he defines as a ganglion of energies, rather than the replication of an object: "The image is not an idea. It is a radiant node or cluster; it is what I can, and must perforce, call a VORTEX, from which, and through which, and into which, ideas are constantly rushing" (*GB* 92). Riddel argues that Pound avoids idealising the subject or the object, for both are seized into the vortex, and they re-emerge as the effects rather than the origins of the creative process. He claims that Vorticism displaces "the authority of a commanding subject or creative force, of an *a priori* unity that commands linearity and resolves thematic or imagistic play."[25] However, Durant argues that the still point in the vortex, like "the central suction of a whirlpool", sneaks the transcendent subject back, in the guise of an impersonal centricity.[26] This subject still reclaims the eccentric forces of the maelstrom, untouched by the turbulence he has unleashed, so that no radical "decentring" occurs. While Riddel disavows the demagogue in Pound to fashion him a deconstructionist *avant la lettre*, Durant ignores the *oddities* of his epistemology to vilify his discourse of authority. Their argument exposes the divisions of the text itself, torn between the master's voice enunciating central verities, and the hesitations which undo those dictates from within.

Pound's attitude to rhythm is equally equivocal. Like Eliot, he privileges metre as part of a general campaign for time, but he regards it as the most and least impersonal domain of poetry. "I believe in an absolute rhythm", he declares in his

Imagist "Credo", "A man's rhythm must be . . . his own, uncounterfeiting, uncounterfeitable" (*LE* 9). Though one may steal the poet's thoughts and words, it is too difficult to forge his metric signature: "Rhythm is the hardest quality of a man's style to counterfeit" (*SR* 103). He agrees with Eliot that personality gets out of hand only when the voice surrenders to the letter. Speaking of an anonymous poem in the *ABC of Reading*, he argues that "The first effort of misguided ink-page scholars would be to FIND THE AUTHOR. Note that the author particularly refrained from signing the poem" (*ABCR* 147). The ghost of his own signature, the author only steals the stage when speech gives way to writing. His deeper self resides in rhythm, where it outlives this "ink-page" personality.

Like Bergson, therefore, Pound attributes voice to metre, self to time, yet he falls into the same paradox as the philosopher. For the hard edge that divides one selfhood from another melts under the influence of rhythm—or as Pound calls the poet's music, "melopoeia":

> In melopoeia we find a contrary current, a force tending often to lull, or to distract the reader from the exact sense of the language. It is poetry on the borders of music and music is perhaps the bridge between consciousness and the unthinking sentient or even insentient universe. (*LE* 25)

Just as Eliot sets music at the "frontiers of consciousness", at the border of the city and the jungle, Pound sets melopoeia at the intersection of the living and the dead. But if rhythm undermines such boundaries, how can it also bear the author's autograph? Ironically, Pound enshrines the self in the very music that foreshadows its extinction. In fact, he assures Helene Margaret in an unpublished letter that rhythm is the most efficient route to *im*personality:

> Impersonality VIA metre, (i.e. work on intractable metre) rather than via immitation [sic] or recollection of a "poem in a style", or of a mode of speech, which gives merely the loss of one's *own* personality without gain of impersonality.[27]

Here Pound advises this aspiring poet to transcend the ego, instead of forfeiting her own for someone else's; and he urges that the discipline of metre will enable her to supervene herself. Yet elsewhere he insists that it is metre which actually *creates* the poet's personality. His arguments grow circular, for he views impersonality as an extension of the self's domain: "Not un-man, my Estlin, but all-men", as he protests in *Canto* LXXXVIII (581).[28] He urges authors to attend to the temporal dimension of their verse to counteract both selfishness and self-perdition.

Poetic Anemometry

In his article on "Vorticism" Pound describes the composition of his famous poem "In a Station of the Metro", where he puts his speculations on impersonality to work. "The 'one image poem' ", he writes, "is a form of super-position, that is to say it is one idea set on top of another" (*GB* 89). Needless to say, the "prose parts" or discursive elements must be removed, for they are tainted with the author's subjectivity:

> I wrote a thirty-line poem, and destroyed it because it was what we call work 'of second intensity.' Six months later I made a poem half that length; a year later I made the following *hokku*-like sentence:—
> The apparition of these faces in the crowd:
> Petals on a wet black bough.

Pound adds that the poem is "trying to record the precise instant when a thing outward and objective transforms itself, or darts into a thing inward and subjective" (*GB* 89). His rhetoric implies that the thing remains a thing whether it is subjective or objective, and that either must be treated clinically. For it is the *thing* which must transform *itself*, without the lengthy interventions of the author. Reading the poem, however, it is hard to tell which line presents the outward vision, and which records the inward metamorphosis. Though the "faces in the crowd" seem to represent external data, the text records the "apparition" rather than the faces *per se*, and an apparition presupposes a perceiving consciousness. But the poem eliminates this residue of subjectivity in the moment of arriving at its metaphor. For the "Petals on a wet black bough" present themselves as an objective fact, although they rise from the imagination. Thus, *rhetorically*, the poem moves from the inward to the outward, from the "apparition" to the fact; *conceptually*, it travels in the opposite direction, because the petals image the imagination and the flowers of the poem's rhetoric itself. The result is a hesitation rather than a hierarchy, where it is impossible to tell the tenor from the vehicle. Most important, a literal effacement has occurred, because the petals overblot the faces at the very moment that the metaphor obliterates the mark of self. In this little poem, the poetics of disfiguration that Eliot explores in "Little Gidding" seem to re-emerge in miniature.

An earlier poem, "Histrion", implicates the self in these poetics more explicitly. Here Pound likens his personae to the faces stamped on coins, and images the poet's personality as liquid metal:

> 'Tis as in midmost us there glows a sphere
> Translucent, molten gold, that is the "I"
> And into this some form projects itself:
> Christus, or John, or eke the Florentine,
> And as the clear space is not if a form's
> Imposed thereon,
> So cease we from all being for the time,
> And these, the Masters of the Soul, live on.
>
> (*CEP* 71)

"Molten", amorphous, the self has no identity unless it takes the face of some dead master. Until "some form projects itself", the "I" remains "translucent," "a clear space": and the very centre of the self becomes the "work shop" of an otherness, a mint in which one mask outstamps another.[29] It is as if the writing subject were the legal tender of tradition, struck with the features of the dead. This numismatic metaphor suggests that Pound is less concerned with the stability of personal identity than with the distribution of poetic currency. Indeed, he praises plagiarism as a duty rather than a crime, because it keeps the word in circulation, encouraging the commerce of the living and the dead.

Curiously, this economy of influence reappears in Pound's

pastoral repertoire. In his early poems, winds and hills and streams become the loci of the lyric utterance: "White words as snow flakes but they are cold / Moss words, lip words, words of slow streams" (*CEP* 79). In "Vana", Pound envisages his words as autumn leaves, scattered by the breezes of the spring: "The words are as leaves, old brown leaves in the spring time / Blowing they know not whither, seeking a song" (*CEP* 27). In these poetics the search for self gives place to fanning the afflatus; and the winds that bluster through these texts diffuse the self abroad with its creations: "I being part of all", Pound writes, "the sky and the wind thereof is my body."[30] For it is through the winds that the tradition circulates, reducing the poet to a bellows or at best, a weather vane:

> *For man is a skinfull of wine*
> *But his soul is a hole full of God*
> *And the song of all time blows thru him*
> *As winds through a knot-holed board.*
> ("Make-strong old dreams lest this our world lose heart", *CEP* 52)

The speaker here becomes a passive embouchure, exhaling the spirit of the past. Similarly, in "Prelude: Over the Ognisanti" the speaker sees himself as the amanuensis of the wind:

> And hither float the shades of song they sing . . .
> Which shades of song re-echoed
> Within that somewhile barren hall, my heart,
> Are found as I transcribe them following.
> (*CEP* 59)

In *The Cantos*, Pound declares that "No wind is the king's wind", and the same unruliness applies to the worded breezes of these early texts (IV 16). Indeed, this verbal ventilation means that speech is always stolen, because the voice, as wind, can always be "spirited away."[31] Like Joyce, Pound sees the poet as a burglar and adulterer, "covetous of his neighbour's word", who loses any voice that he can call his own to loot the inspiration of the past (*Finnegans Wake* p. 172, line 29). For this reason he champions the troubadours for their adulterous verse, and praises every poet for his pilfering: "All bards are thieves save Villon, master-thief" ("Piazza San Marco", *CEP* 238). For the business of the writer is to sow the word, rather than to hoard the wind: and the author who demands a private speech is interfering with the distribution of the Logos. Words, like coins, lose all their value when their circulation is deranged—and this is the predicament that Pound explores in *Mauberley*.

A Consciousness Disjunct

"I am sure of *Mauberley*, whatever else I am sure of", T. S Eliot once stated, and many unexpected critics share his certainty.[32] Crisp, witty and urbane, *Mauberley* seems a changeling in Pound's oeuvre, too compact for the author of the "endless scripture" of *The Cantos*.[33] Indeed, the relationship between the author and the text provokes much controversy. For the poem bears a double signature: two names, E. P. *and* Mauberley, both loom over its "scattered Moluccas", coaxing and vexing identifications. John Espey insists that only "a complete divorce between Pound and Mauberley" can save the text from crumbling into "unrelated pieces arbitrarily patched together".[34] He argues that the confusion of the two personae arose from a misprint in the first edition, where E.P.'s initials were misplaced. In its rightful position, this acronym implies that Pound is speaking in his own voice in the first part of the poem, while it is only in the second half that Mauberley arrives.[35] Most critics have assented to this reading, and indeed Christine Brooke-Rose blames any lingering misunderstanding of the text on those who "refuse to read Espey".[36] However, Jo Brantly Berryman, in the most recent full-length study of the text, reverses Espey's interpretation. She insists that Mauberley enunciates the first half of the poem, Pound the second.[37] What is clear from these disputes is that the text divides the speaker from his speech, putting the integrity of voice itself in jeopardy.

Donald Davie sneers at Pound's impersonations, but he unwittingly reveals the polylogic element of *Mauberley*. "Hugh Selwyn Mauberly is a mask that continually slips", he complains. "How are we to know in which poems Pound speaks through the mask, in which he doesn't?"[38] It is the mischief of the text to make this question undecidable. Pound once said that "Mauberley is a mere surface"; and part of the confusion has arisen because readers try to penetrate this surface and to transform the mask into a fully realised personality. For he also said, "Of course, I'm no more Mauberley than Eliot is Prufrock" (*L* 180). The poem may be an attempt to bury his earlier, more personal poetics: to exorcise his "subjective hosannah" (353). For he shares his initials with E.P. and some of the details of his biography. But there are discrepancies between them too, not least that E.P. is dead and buried. In 1956, Pound wrote that "Mauberley buries E.P. in the opening poem; gets rid of all his troublesome energies."[39] Thus *Mauberley* begins by burying its own creator, and thereafter buries anyone who tries to take his place. In the place of a controlling voice, Pound creates "a consciousness disjunct", a "Series / Of intermittences". In the place of living speech, the poem offers its unliving writings, reducing its personae to posthumous fictions. For the only time the speaker uses the first person is to compose his own obituary:

"I was
"And I no more exist;
"Here drifted
"An hedonist".

(381–4)

Pound told Thomas Hardy that "the Mauberley is thin": and it is crucial to perceive the way he regulates this dearth and sculpts this silence.[40]

He thins out both of his main characters by introducing further, fugitive personae. The poem begins in a different language and another's voice, borrowing its first subtitle from Ronsard: "Ode pour L'Election de Son Sepulchre." Then Pound switches to his own frustrated years in London:

For three years, out of key with his time,
He strove to resuscitate the dead art
Of poetry; to maintain 'the sublime'
In the old sense. Wrong from the start—. . . .

(1–4)

The three years refer to 1914–17, when Pound was championing Vorticism. As early as the second line, however, E.P. begins to merge with Dante, who according to Boccaccio had also struggled to resuscitate "la morta poesi."[41] " 'The sublime' / In the old sense" may refer to Burke or the Romantics, or to the older sense in which Longinus used the word; but the scene shifts abruptly forward to the "half savage" country where Pound was born, in Idaho in 1885. "Out of date", he complains: as if he had arrived too early or too late for the renaissance that he might have instigated. The next mask is "Capaneus" (8), one of the seven against Thebes, who was struck down by Zeus for impiety, yet continued to defy him even in the fires of Dante's hell.[42] But this identification lasts no longer than the name. It is Odysseus, the most slippery persona of them all, who now becomes the poet's vehicle.[43] The last mask that E.P. assumes is Villon's, and he is forced to die his early death: "*en l'an trentusiesme de son eage*."[44]

Davie is correct, therefore, to complain that the mask continually slips, for almost every line in this first ode substitutes a new persona for the old, as fleeting and oblique as Mauberley's own cameos:

> Not the full smile,
> His art, but an art
> In profile. . . .
>
> (255–7)

Like the speaker of *The Waste Land*, Pound's speaker flits among the "battered books" of Western Europe, bespoken *by* the discourse of the past, and resorting to impersonation, forgery, pastiche, in the absence of a voice that he can call his own. And like *The Waste Land*, too, the poem is obsessed with its belatedness: too late to sift TO AGATHON, or forge Achaia; too late for Dionysus, mousseline, Pisistratus; too late even for the 1890s, which were themselves too late. The text itself seems doomed to obsolesce as it unfolds. For example, the second poem in the series begins, "The age demanded an image"; but in the third stanza, the " 'age demanded' " has been wrapped up in inverted commas, as if it were already trite, passé. While the poem mourns the loss of mousseline or

Eleusis or the barbitos, it participates in the same logic which supplanted them.[45]

The poem explodes its own pretensions, and even ironises its own ironies. It is this self-parody that leads Yvor Winters to complain that "Pound writes a lugubrious lament for the passing of pre-Raphaelitism, yet deliberately makes pre-Raphaelitism and himself appear ridiculous."[46] In "Yeux Glauques", for instance, Pound reviles "Foetid Buchanan" for slandering the pre-Raphaelites in his notorious review, "The Fleshly School of Poetry" (1871). He associates the "yeux glauques" of the title with the "clear gaze" of Elizabeth Siddal, Rossetti's wife and model; and he also misattributes these eyes to the woman in Burne Jones's *King Cophetua and the Beggar Maid*:

> The Burne-Jones cartoons
> Have preserved her eyes;
> Still, at the Tate, they teach
> Cophetua to rhapsodize; . . . (194–7)

Here the tone is elegiac, but in the fourth stanza the vision has begun to dissipate, and the eyes are now "Thin like brook-water / With a vacant gaze" (108–9). Having roused the reader's sympathy for the pre-Raphaelites, Pound seems to turn around and do a Buchanan on Burne-Jones himself. Berryman tries to solve this contradiction by arguing that it is Mauberley who repines for the pre-Raphaelites, while Pound knows that their feuds and dreams are out of date.[47] But these names merely stabilise divisions in the text itself, which mocks the very artists that it mourns, and even ridicules its own nostalgia. "All passes, ANANGKE prevails" in the structure of the text, as well as in the world that it reviles (264).

Elsewhere, Pound defines the *anangke* of modernity as "cash necessity", and he brands the era as the " 'age of usury.' "[48] In the third poem in *Mauberley*, he lists the usurious perversions of the age:

> The tea-rose tea-gown, etc.
> Supplants the mousseline of Cos,
> The pianola "replaces"
> Sappho's barbitos.

Christ follows Dionysus,
Phallic and ambrosial
Made way for macerations;
Caliban casts out Ariel.

All things are a flowing
Sage Heraclitus says;
But a tawdry cheapness
Shall outlast our days.

Even the Christian beauty
Defects—after Samothrace;
We see τὸ καλὸν
Decreed in the market place.

Faun's flesh is not to us,
Nor the saint's vision.
We have the press for wafer;
Franchise for circumcision.

All men, in law, are equals.
Free of Pisistratus,
We choose a knave or a eunuch
To rule over us.

O bright Apollo
τίν' ἄνδρα, τίν' ἥρωα, τίνα θεὸν,*
What god, man, or hero
Shall I place a tin wreath upon!

(33–60)

Pounds "usury" corresponds to Eliot's "heresy", for both consist of the compulsion to usurp, displace and disassociate. In this poem, usury reduces history to a systematic travesty of sacred rites. It is through usury, for instance,that Christian asceticism supplanted the erotic mysteries of Dionysus. According to Pound, "all the dogma worth a damn came from greek mysteries etc / everything that built the cathedrals."[49] In *Mauberley* he hints that Christianity still celebrates the flesh backhandedly by mortifying it with such enthusiasm. In the age of Mr Nixon, however, "Even the Christian beauty /

*Tín andra, tín héroa, tina theòn.

Defects." The cult of Eleusis, "phallic and ambrosial", surrenders to the tyranny of eunuchs. Though "the saint's vision" is a poor substitute for "faun's flesh", Pound still prefers it to the "press" that takes its place. Even macerations now give way to an emasculated, bland democracy.[50] At the end of the poem, Pound deliberately mistranslates Pindar's ode, imitating usury's procedures: for the "tin" wreath is a bilingual pun on τίν᾽ ἄνδρα, τίν᾽ ἥρωα, τίνα θεὸν.[51] Thus a tin wreath, rather than a laurel crown, rewards the modern poet for his tin ear and the tintinnabulation of his press.

According to Pound, usury vitiates the *pace* of history at the same time that it perverts the sacraments. The reason that E.P. is "out of key with his time" is that the whole time-signature has gone awry, producing haste without rhythm, novelty without duration—a mere *et cetera*. Even the "conservatrix", who accordingly to her title should conserve the past, consigns tradition to oblivion:

> No, 'Mileian' is an exaggeration.
> No instinct has survived in her
> Older than those her grandmother
> Told her would fit her station. (188–91)

Men like Mr Nixon who commercialise the arts destroy the rhythmic circulation of the word: and it is only in a living tomb that the artist can escape this merciless velocity. E.P., Monsieur Verog, the "Stylist", and Mauberley choose sepulchres in preference to the demonic tempo of the age. Their art, therefore, remains "still-born", "dumb-born", "pickled", "bottled", or at best, "in magic amber laid" (110, 220, 120, 232). The ideal of an immortal work of art perverts itself into a living death, a foetus bottled in formaldehyde. The artist, too, embalms himself alive: Lionel Johnson goes so far as to pickle his own tissue in alcohol!

> Johnson (Lionel) died
> By falling from a high stool in a pub . . .
>
> But showed no trace of alcohol
> At the autopsy, privately performed—
> Tissue preserved—the pure mind
> Arose toward Newman as the whiskey warmed. (126–32)

In the midst of this delirium, Mauberley is striving to create a face that could "brave . . . time", and brave that other face, the "accelerated grimace" of the age (235, 22). Indeed the poem teems with faces, in various stages of disfiguration; and as in "Histrion" or "Little Gidding", each face takes shape in the defacement of another. For instance, the "Half-ruin'd face" of "Yeux Glauques" is superseded by the "circular infant's face" of Brennbaum, and yet his features, too, are half-erased (113, 141):

> The heavy memories of Horeb, Sinai and the forty years,
> Showed only when the daylight fell
> Level across the face
> Of Brennbaum "The Impeccable".
>
> (144–7)

All these faces could be seen as Mauberley's creations, the fragmentary visions of his still-born art:

> —Given that is his "fundamental passion",
> This urge to convey the relation
> Of eye-lid and cheek-bone
> By verbal manifestation. . . .
>
> (281–5)

"Thin like brook water, / With a vacant gaze", every face is disappearing, outfaced and "overblotted" by another: "Quick eyes gone under earth's lid" (108–9, 93). The last face that emerges is the "sleek head" of the "Medallion", after its creator has already vanished in the cobalt of oblivions (389, 368). But even at the end it is "a face still forming" (*LG* II 48):

> Beneath half-watt rays,
> The eyes turn topaz.
>
> (399–400)

With its double signature, the text itself is two-faced, both half-ruined. One could say that they are two faces of the same coin: for there are many hints that Mauberley's art consists in striking coins, where the face is almost always shown in profile. At one point, for instance, Pound depicts him as a "Pisanello lacking the skill / To forge Achaia" (260–1).

Pisanello was a Veronese medallist who based his designs upon Greek coins, and in this sense the medals that he "forged" were "forgeries". Moreover, he reified these coins into high-class *objets d'art*, rather than a circulating currency.[52] Mauberley is labouring to counterfeit a Roman coin, itself a copy of the Greek. He is trying to recapture the "straight head / Of Messalina" (248–9) that appeared in profile on the coins struck in the early years of Claudius's reign.[53] The final poem in the sequence reveals the only work of art that he completes, and it is called "Medallion" because it is a coin no longer current. As in "Histrion", to strike a face is to forge one's own identity: but here it is impossible to rescue Mauberley's clear gaze from the ruined features that surround him.

Pound's obsession with the coinage of identity persists throughout his work. Its sources might be found in what Freud calls the "family complex" of his name: for a "pound" is both a unit of weight and a unit of money.[54] Moreover, his "Achaian" father, *Homer* Pound, worked as an assayer with the Mint, and in one of his earliest and strangest memories, Pound recalls men shovelling coins, half-naked in the gas-light, "with a gleam on tarnished disks" which had spilled out of their rotten money bags.[55] By 1933, Pound is "savin the woild by ECONOMIC propaganda", and his major platform is to mint new money, fighting the "obstructors of distribution" (XIV 63).[56] As late as the Rock-Drill Cantos of 1955, he singles Cleopatra out for praise, not for her infinite variety but simply for reissuing the currency (LXXXV 543). By forging old coins, Mauberley is yearning for a lost economy, but the tender he produces has already proved defunct, and it is impossible to resurrect the culture which bestowed life on his medals. Because he refuses to imprint his coins with the accelerated grimace of the age, he takes his faces out of circulation. Even his medallion is "caught in metamorphosis", like the still stone dogs that bite the empty air (295–8). As we have seen, to shun "the world's welter" condemns the artist to emasculation and a still-born art, whereas to join it condemns him to ephemerality (175).

Numismatic Onomastics

In the *ABC of Reading* Pound takes this economics further, suggesting that the poet's personality provides the backing for his cheques on knowledge:

> ANY general statement is like a cheque drawn on a bank. Its value depends on what is there to meet it.
>
> . . .
>
> The same applies with cheques against knowledge. If Marconi says something about ultra short waves it MEANS something. Its meaning can only be properly estimated by someone who KNOWS.
>
> You do not accept a stranger's cheques without reference. In writing, a man's "name" is his reference. He has, after a time, credit. . . .
>
> (*ABCR* 25)

Here, Pound is using "credit" in a double sense, as faithful testimony and financial guarantee. The word "reference" is equally ambiguous: for on the following page Pound asserts that "A general statement is valuable only in REFERENCE to the known objects or facts." Here reference may either mean the bank balance which supports the cheque, or it could mean *semantic* reference, the world to which the poet's word should correspond. In the course of time, Pound says, the author gains such credit that his *name* suffices as a "reference". He adds that "The INTEREST in a statement can be more or less durable": and the word "interest" has a monetary meaning, too. For the more facts the writer has accumulated in the bank, the greater the "interest" he is due (*ABCR* 26, 29). In the paranomasia of these terms, a strange equation is taking shape: facts have come to stand for money, money for credit, credit for reference, and reference has become the interest of the proper name. According to this logic, the poet circulates his name among his texts, and it is through this self-dissemination that he reaps the interest of his signature.

These metaphors make writing sound suspiciously like usury: for writing is the bank account in which the author gathers interest on his signature. Perhaps Pound condemns usury because it brings the hidden motivation of his verse to light, the restless proliferation of his name. It is perhaps to curb this pullulation that *Mauberley* begins by burying Pound's initials. But if a man's name is his reference, rather than the man the reference of his name, his signature cannot be bound to his identity. Rampant, prodigal, it errs among the many voices he has forged. Poetry becomes the cobalt of oblivions in which the author's name is set adrift, to odyssey forever through the alphabet.

The next chapter pursues that odyssey within *The Cantos*. But it approaches the theme of subjectivity obliquely: for although Pound's autograph bestrews itself throughout his work, it is never where he urges us to look. It is necessary, therefore, to explore the entire system of his thought in order to discern the name that haunts it. Nietzsche's axiom that "philosophy is autobiography" was never truer than for Pound, and never more inexorably self-destructive.

Notes

1. Quoted by J. B. Harmer, *Victory in Limbo: Imagism 1908–1917* (London: Secker and Warburg, 1975), p. 74.
2. Pound, "Praefatio", in *Active Anthology* (1933; repr. London: Faber, 1973), p. 9.
3. Donald Davie, *Ezra Pound: The Poet as Sculptor* (New York: Oxford University Press, 1964), p. 242.
4. Letter to John Quinn, 24 January 1917, *L* 104; letter to Milton Bronner, 21 September 1915, cited by Noel Stock, *The Life of Ezra Pound*, p. 184.
5. Parts of this argument appeared in my article "Floating the Pound: The Circulation of the Subject of *The Cantos*", *Oxford Literary Review*, 3, no. 3 (1979), 16–17.
6. See Ronald Bush, *The Genesis of Ezra Pound's Cantos*, p. 16; Harold H. Watts, *Ezra Pound and the Cantos* (London: RKP, 1952), p. 30; Pearlman, *The Barb of Time: On the Unity of Pound's Cantos* (New York: OUP, 1969), p. 279n.
7. However, Delmore Schwartz argued in a review of 1938 that although *The Cantos* "have no plot", they have "a wholeness based on certain obsessions and preoccupations, deriving . . . from the character of Pound's mind . . .". See Schwartz, "Ezra Pound's Very Useful Labors", *Poetry*, 55, no. 6 (1938), 324–39; cited in Ronald Bush, *The Genesis of Ezra Pound's Cantos*, p. 5n.

8. George Dekker, *Sailing After Knowledge: The Cantos of Ezra Pound* (London: RKP, 1963), p. xv.
9. Read, *One World and The Cantos of Ezra Pound* (Chapel Hill: University of North Carolina Press, 1981), p. xi.
10. Dekker, *Sailing After Knowledge*, p. xv.
11. Noel Stock, *Reading The Cantos* (London: RKP, 1967), p. 1.
12. *Charles Olson and Ezra Pound: An Encounter at St. Elizabeth's*, ed. Catherine Seelye (New York: Grossman, 1975), Canto 3, p. 53.
13. Jean-Michel Rabaté, "Pound's Art of Naming: Between Reference and Reverence", lecture delivered at the Ezra Pound Conference, London, 1982.
14. Letter to Viola Jordan, MS (? October 1907), Pound Archive, Beinecke.
15. Letter to Isabel W. Pound (January 1905), Paige Carbons no. 88, Pound Archive, Beinecke.
16. Letter to Viola Jordan, TS (24 October 1907), Pound Archive, Beinecke: published with corrections in Pound, "Letters to Viola Jordan", *Paideuma*, 1 (1972), 109.
17. See Jackson, *The Early Poetry of Ezra Pound* (Cambridge, Mass.: Harvard University Press, 1968), p. 15.
18. *Studies in Human Time*, p. 14.
19. See Rabaté, "Pound's Art of Naming", for this insight.
20. See Ch. VI.
21. First published in *Poetry* I, no. 6 (1913), 200–6; repr. in *LE* 3.
22. See "The Serious Artist" (1913), *LE* 46.
23. See Alan Durant, *Ezra Pound: Identity in Crisis: A Fundamental Reassessment of the Poet and his Work* (Brighton: Harvester Press; Totowa, New Jersey: Barnes and Noble, 1981), p. 23.
24. Joseph Riddel, "Pound and the Decentred Image", *Georgia Review*, 29 (1975), 574.
25. *Ibid.*, p. 575.
26. See Durant, pp. 28–9.
27. Postcard to Helene Margaret, TS, postmarked 19 February 1931, in Pound Archive, Beinecke.
28. He is thinking of the pseudonym ΟΥ ΤΙΣ (noman) with which Odysseus deceived the Cyclops.
29. See "Fifine Answers", *CEP* 19.
30. See "Invern", *CEP* 35; "Aegypton", *CEP* 37.
31. See Derrida, "La parole soufflée", in *Writing and Difference*, pp. 175–6, for a similar account of inspiration in Artaud.
32. Cited by Hugh Kenner, " 'Mauberley' ", in *Ezra Pound: A Collection of Critical Essays*, ed. Walter Sutton (Englewood Cliffs, New Jersey: Prentice-Hall, 1963), p. 43. See also F. R. Leavis, *New Bearings in English Poetry* (1932; Ann Arbor: University of Michigan Press, 1960), pp. 235–6.
33. See *The Translations of Ezra Pound*, ed. Hugh Kenner (London: Faber, 1953), p. 220.
34. John Espey, *Ezra Pound's Mauberley: A Study in Composition*

(Berkeley: University of California Press, 1955), pp. 62, 13.

35. *Ibid.*, pp. 17–21.
36. Christine Brooke-Rose, *A ZBC of Ezra Pound* (London: Faber, 1971), p. 159.
37. Jo Brantley Berryman, *Circe's Craft: Ezra Pound's Hugh Selwyn Mauberley* (Ann Arbor: UMI Research Press, 1983), Ch. 1.
38. Donald Davie, *Pound* (Glasgow: Fontana Modern Masters, 1975), p. 55.
39. Cited by K. K. Ruthven, in *A Guide to Ezra Pound's Personae (1926)* (Berkeley and Los Angeles: University of California Press, 1969), p. 126.
40. Cited by Davie, *Pound*, p. 46.
41. See Ruthven, p. 128.
42. See Dante, *The Inferno*, Canto XIV, 43–75, parallel text, trans. John D. Sinclair (New York: OUP, 1961), pp. 183–5. See also *SR* 123.
43. The syntax here suspends the referents of all these terms. Is E.P. Capaneus, and if so, is Capaneus the fisherman, the fish or the factitious bait? See Berryman, pp. 12–17, for a discussion of the sources and meaning of this line.
44. Villon's early death seems to have haunted Pound, for he returns to it in his poem "Salutation the Third": "Or perhaps I *will* die at thirty?" *CSP* 165.
45. According to Pound, it is *writing* which supplanted the barbitos. See *LE* 101: "When men began to write on tablets and ceased singing on the *barbitos*, a loss of some sort was unavoidable." The complicity between writing and usury is discussed fully in the next chapter.
46. Ivor Winters, "T. Sturge Moore", *Hound and Horn*, 6 (1933), 358.
47. See Berryman, p. 97.
48. *GK* 96; Ruthven, p. 143.
49. Pound, unpublished letter to Olivia Rossetti Agresti, TS [August 1949], Pound Archive, Beinecke.
50. Zielinski writes that "Greek is the language of the oldest Christian writings, and language is . . . the confession of a people. Yes, Christianity in the form in which it has come down to us drew strength from the Greek people, as the oak from the soil." Tadeusz Zielinski, *Our Debt to Antiquity*, trans. Strong and Stewart (London: Routledge, 1909), p. 123.
51. See Ruthven, p. 132.
52. *Ibid.*, p. 142.
53. See Espey, p. 99, and Berryman, pp. 92–4.
54. *The Psychopathology of Everyday Life*, SE VI 23–4.
55. Pound, letter to Sir Montague Webb, cited by Stock, *Life*, p. 7; see also *C* 79: 673 for a further recollection of this scene; and Marcelin Pleynet, "La compromission poetique", *Tel Quel*, 70 (1977), 22–5, for a fascinating psychoanalytic exploration of this memory.
56. Letter to Viola Jordan, TS (17 June [1933]), in Pound Archive, Beinecke.

CHAPTER VI

The Erasure of History

for this stone giveth sleep
staria senza più scosse
and eucalyptus that is for memory
Ezra Pound, Canto LXXIV

An Address in Time

Pound was fond of saying that an epic is "a poem including history", and *The Cantos* splice the history of his life with the evolution of the world. Here ancient China converges with Renaissance Italy and the founding years of the United States: while the story of money interlaces these and other epochs like the "gold thread in the pattern."[1] But *The Cantos* are themselves included in the history they include, for they record the way that Pound read Europe and the way that Europe, in revenge, read Pound. His poem tells the history of its author, an author who becomes a history in the interminable process of his own inscription. Poem and poet weave each other's destinies.

"History" can either mean the past as it happened or the past as it is reconstructed by historians, but Pound prefers to disavow this difference. In Canto IV the swallows cry, " 'Tis. 'Tis. 'Ytis!" (14): and the poem as a whole asserts "It *is*" of each historic fact that it incorporates. While he cuts and pastes his documents, Pound conserves their idiom, for the lessons of history can only be induced from a sufficient "phalanx of particulars" (LXXIV 441). History itself must speak from the pages of *The Cantos*, unencumbered by the judgments of the poet. His selections, however, are tendentious, for *The Cantos* urge his case against the usurers, and they represent a kind of legal dossier, stuffed with evidence.[2] This "rag-bag", as Pound called it, only *seems* impersonal, for it conceals the most imperious of authors: "lord of his work and master of utterance" (LXXIV 442). There is no innocent history, no matter what the swallows say; and there is no voice more monologic than the poet's when he rattles off the interest rates. By "usury", Pound means that these rates have grown extortionate: but he capitalises on the word itself until it implicates all forms of exorbitance.

Moreover, he believes that the usurers have been deleting history for centuries, and that our knowledge of the past is marred by "OMISSIONS of the most vital facts".[3] To rectify these misconceptions, he insists that history is a spiral rather than an evolution, in which the same errors teach the same lessons, and a handful of prototypes patiently repeat themselves through time. "We do NOT know the past in chronological sequence", he declares. "It may be convenient to lay it out anaesthetized on the table with dates pasted on here and there, but what we know we know by ripples and spirals eddying out from us and from our own time" (*GK* 60). Here Pound envisions history as a vortex, where the past whirls around the present with a kind of centrifugal energy. He insists that "A man does not know his own ADDRESS (in time) until he knows where his own time and milieu stand *in relation to* other times and conditions" (*GK* 83). Without addresses, men and letters err through time as Odysseus meandered through enchanted seas. An address implies a proper place, a boundary, and a destination; but it is paradoxical that Pound insists upon a fixed abode in the same breath that he asserts the relativity of history. Since a man can only know his place "*in relation to*" other places and conditions, the pattern must be new at every moment, and there can be no private property in time.

If personal identity depends on an address in time, the only way to write *oneself* must be to reconstruct one's history. Pound's personal biography, however, spills into the record of his times: the contemporary overflows into the past, the here into the elsewhere. Wyndham Lewis accuses him of Bergsonism for relinquishing the author's will to history's whimsy, because his personality unravels through these chronicles.[4] It is true that Pound reveals a taste for time, but he distrusts Bergson for his Jewishness and his "subjectivo-fluxivity". Yet in his Introduction to Cavalcanti (1912) and his Postscript to de Gourmont (1921) Pound denounces space, making time into the cornerstone of his cosmology. Like Bergson, he believes that personality inheres in time, and represents itself most faithfully in rhythm. Ernest Fenollosa's work on the Chinese ideogram convinced him that time governs nature and poetic language, too. In *Antheil and the Treatise of Harmony* (1924), he empowers time still further, enlisting music to its empery.

A preface, an edition, a postscript, and a promotion, these four essays supplement the work of others, rather than asserting their own case. For Pound subordinates his own authority to a confluence of powers drawn from many areas, works and writers, believing that the strength of theory lies in the energies it harnesses, rather than in its author's novelties. This economy of intellect prefigures his later obsession with the marketplace. For Pound's poetics, like Eliot's, develop in two phases, and by a kind of deferred action he revamps his earlier aesthetic theory in the 1930s as a panacea for the world's economy. In fact, he insisted that he had not deflected a hair's breadth from his lists of beautiful objects, "made in my head and held before I ever thought of usury as a murrain and marasmus" (*GK* 109). By the same token, he discovered "blobbiness" and "mess" in music and in painting long before he knew that they were caused by the degree of tolerance a culture showed to usury (*GK* 109; *I* 198). It is only in the 1930s that he comes to understand his early tastes as reactions to the history of the interest rate. But they were always implicitly reactionary. In his early work, for instance, he vilifies Romantic poetry because it overflows with adjectives and feelings, encouraging the individualism he had just abandoned.[5] Later he decides that this excess of personality colludes with the intemperance of usury.

Pound's obsession with the "usurocracy" was to lead to his

downfall. But it is important to perceive its ingenuity, the rigour of its blindness to itself. The anti-Semitism of the times enforced its logic, but the holocaust itself could be perceived as the obsessive ceremonial where Europe purged itself of Jews. *The Cantos* stage the confrontation of psychic and political economies. Starting with Pound's early essays and ending with the *Pisan Cantos*, this chapter investigates his blindness with the perspicuity of his own idiom, as if obsession could observe its own finesse. First we shall see how his economies of power question the foundations of identity; and finally how *The Cantos* both erase and reinscribe the self.

An Economy of Power

Throughout his opus, Pound's poetics seep into his economics in a kind of rhetorical contagion. In 1951, for instance, he argues that "Money is an articulation":

> Prosody is an articulation of the sound of a poem. Money an arti / of / say NAtional money is articulation of total purchasing power of the nation.[6]

The word "articulation" enacts what it implies, by hinging speech to economics. While money is the means by which the nation enunciates its power, it is through prosody that poems budget their expenditure of sound. Power must be cashed in words or coins to circulate among these currencies, for Pound distrusts potential energy. All his economies depend upon the "power to issue" (CXI 782): whether they issue forth in wisdom, banknotes, poetry or progeny, the rhythmical purgations of the flesh or the "holy mystery of fecundity."[7] Sometimes it is difficult to tell the body from the body politic, for Pound believes they implicate each other. One diversifying power races through them both, sluicing out impurities through sheer velocity.[8]

According to Pound, medieval thought detected these quicksilver energies, but modern consciousness has disregarded them for static forms:

> We appear to have lost the radiant world where one thought cuts through another with a clean edge, a world of moving energies "*mezzo*

> *oscuro rade*", "*risplende in se perpetuale effecto*", magnetisms that take form, that are seen, or that border the visible, the matter of Dante's *paradiso*, the glass under water, the form that seems a form seen in a mirror, these realities perceptible to the sense, interacting, "*a lui si tiri*" untouched by the two maladies, the Hebrew disease, the Hindoo disease, fanaticisms and excess that produce Savonarola, asceticisms that produce fakirs, St Clement of Alexandria, with his prohibition of bathing by women.[9]

This world has been forgotten, not annihilated, and its radiance still winks from time to time. According to Pound, its powers are forever becoming-in-a-form. He argues that medieval philosophers united force and form, and therefore that they "would probably have been unable to think the electric world, and *not* think of it as a world of forms."[10] Pound refuses to distinguish power from the paths it blazes or the forms it energises, for power *is* the trace of its trajectory. "Diseased" religions disembody energy, and their asceticism is a symptom of this error. Similarly, modern thought denies energy its borders, shape and loci, just as Judaism ("the Hebrew disease") denies its God His graven images. Pound insists that power must be seen as local, manifest and plastic, rather than as a shapeless mass of latent force.

In the domain of poetry, he inveighs against padding and adornment because they coagulate the poem's moving energies. When he tells poets to condense their outpourings, he is urging them to be impersonal, but this is part of an ecology of power: "Dichten = condensare", he declares (*ABCR* 36). Ideally, poetry should harness nature's effervescence to the page, for both partake of a creative impulse which transcends the individual. One name he gives this force is the "*virtù*" (*MN* 348). Among its other names are light and love. Following Cavalcanti, he argues that the *virtù* is the force that emanates from a person or an object, enmeshing them in subtle labyrinths of power.

> Virtù is the potency, the efficient property of a substance or person. Thus modern science shows us radium with a noble virtue of energy. Each thing or person was held to send forth magnetisms of certain effect. . . . It is a spiritual chemistry, and modern science and modern mysticism are both set to confirm it.[11]

These forces circulate in vision, for perception consists of an exchange of energies. As Pound says, vision is "not the homage of an object but the direction of a force": "light . . . moves from the eye . . .".[12] The world receives the gaze as if it were a lover, and the seer and the seen unite in a perpetual "*inluminatio coitu*" (XXXVI 180;; LXXIV 435). In this cosmology, the asceticisms that dishonour coitus thereby wrench observer from observed, and sterilise the intercourse of vision. They insulate the subject and give him the illusion that his eye is master of the visible.

According to Pound, Cavalcanti identified the light of intellect with love, and he derived this spiritual chemistry from Grosseteste's philosophy of light. Grosseteste argued that light confers corporeality on matter, being half-corpuscular itself: "Cette substance extrèmement tenue est aussi l'étoffe dont toutes choses sont faites . . ." (*MN* 359). Nature expresses this creative flow as a light-bulb expresses electricity, but Pound is careful to distinguish flow from overflow. "Flows", he writes, "but NOT as water down a drain-pipe, look at the first leaf you pick up."[13] He insists that flows define form rather than dissolving it: they trace the lines of force that vein the leaf, just as they wreathe the air with eyebeams.[14]

Personal identity also surrenders to this interplay of moving energies, rather than transcending its commotion. Pound came across the work of Richard of St Victor in 1909, and was later fond of quoting his formula of love: "The human soul is not love but love flows from it. Thus it cannot delight in itself, but only in the love pouring from it."[15] The subject here becomes the agent of desire; and Pound goes so far as to rewrite the *cogito* in terms of love: "Amo ergo sum, and in just that proportion" (*C* LXXX 493). I love, therefore I am; but love exceeds the bounds of personality, reducing self-identity to a delusion. He elaborates this amorous epistemology in his Postscript to Rémy de Gourmont's *Natural Philosophy of Love*. Here he proposes the extraordinary notion that the world began in a divine ejaculation. The same spermatic force still circulates through nature, dispensing incarnation as it moves. The poet inherits this priapic power, for the brain itself is a "clot of genital fluid", restless to enflesh a second cosmos (see PS 169–79). Rather than the origin, the artist is the last descendant of the "big bang" that initiated the creation. Pound traces this insight back to ancient Greece, rejecting later gods as parvenus. In Canto IV, for instance, Zeus unites the principles of light and the spermatic sea when he ravishes Danäe in golden rain:

> Thus the light rains, thus pours, *e lo soleills plovil*
> The liquid and rushing crystal
> beneath the knees of the gods. . . .
> Danäe! Danäe! . . .
> the god's bride, lay ever, waiting the golden rain.
> (IV 15–16)

Art, like nature, runs on phallic power; and Pound's spermatic economics determine his conception of the beautiful. He pleads that:

> the thing that matters in art is a sort of energy, something more or less like electricity or radio-activity, a force transfusing, welding, and unifying. A force rather like water when it spurts up through bright sand and sets it in swift motion. (*LE* 49).

One of the main reasons Pound changed his allegiance from Imagism to Vorticism was to align himself with phallic energy: for under Amy Lowell, "Amygism" had become too feminine, too flabby and subjective for his taste. In his lexicon, geysers, fountains, whirlwinds, cataracts, earthquakes and eruptions mark the resurgence of spermatic force, blasting the old fixities to weld new forms. Pound praises Wyndham Lewis's paintings because they harness this exuberance:

> the whole of it, beauty, heaven, hell, sarcasm, every kind of whirlwind of force, ££££££££ and emotion. Vortex. that is the right word for it, if I did find it myself. / Every kind of geyser from jism bursting up white as ivory, to hate or a storm at sea. Spermatozoon, enough to repopulate the island with active and vigorous animals.[16]

Rather than copying the forms of life, Lewis plugs into its *élan*, and his paintings thus transfuse the vital flow.

For the same reason Pound demands "transmittiability" in

poetry, and subordinates the meaning to the dynamism of the work (*ABCR* 27):

> There's no use in a strong impulse if it is all or nearly all lost in bungling transmission and technique. This obnoxious word that I'm always brandishing means nothing but a transmission of the impulse intact. It means that you not only get the thing off your own chest, but that you get it into someone else's. (*L* 23; cf. *C* LXXIX 486)

Though Pound agrees with Eliot that poetry begins in self-expression, he is less interested in the experiencing subject than in the kinetic power that his feelings represent. He conceives of feeling in thermodynamic terms, as a force projected on to a mass, which patterns matter as the magnet draws a rose out of the steel dust (to use his most seductive image of aesthetic form). "Emotion is an organiser of form", he says.[17] The poet is a node of intersecting energies, where power burns its trace upon the page. "Chemically speaking", Pound exaggerates, the human subject is nothing but "a few buckets of water, tied up in a complicated sort of fig-leaf" (*SR* 92). Moreover, poetry achieves its fullest meaning as it passes from author to translator: for Pound believes that meaning is the metamorphic essence of the language, rather than the product of the words themselves. "Don't bother about the WORDS, translate the MEANING", he commands.[18] Not that the words are accidental, for power must enflesh itself in the protoplasm of the language if it is to circulate at all. But the fewer words the poet uses, the less he blocks the transference of energies. It is important not to overload the switchboard.

In Pound, all the world becomes a switchboard. The poet, like the scientist, must study it by pinpointing its matrices of force. These Pound calls "Luminous Details". "These facts are hard to find", he argues, but once they are disclosed, "They are swift and easy of transmission. They govern knowledge as a switchboard governs an electric circuit" (*SPr* 21, 23). This theory was reinforced when he discovered Ernest Fenollosa's odd sinology. Fenollosa thinks that "Things are . . . the terminal points, or rather the meeting points, of actions, cross-sections cut through actions, snap-shots" (*CWC* 10). He objects to Western languages because they separate the subject from the action and the object. In the Chinese ideogram, these moments coalesce: for in reality a single movement envelops the doer and the deed. Chinese writing brings language and nature back together, because the same "entangled forces" throb through both. However, Fenollosa does not mean that *words* are more like *things* than we perceive, but rather that *things* are more like *tropes*. "Metaphor . . . is at once the substance of nature and of language", he claims (*CWC* 23). The ideogram reveals the metaphoric basis of reality, because the noun becomes a thing, the thing a power. When Western language shuffles bloodless categories to and fro, it blinds itself to nature's transformative energies. For Fenollosa, "all truth is the *transference of power*" (*CWC* 11).

Pound agrees with Fenollosa that "a thing only IS what it *does*", and he argues that the same holds true for personality (*SL* 82). He puts the case to Basil Bunting in the strongest terms:

> You bloody bullhea ded ape
> A man IS what he does/ that is
> guts
> the whole ~~gits~~ of the epic view.
> Mr Heinz settin round,
> like all damn kikes, dreamin
> they are J / bloody) hoover,
> dont epify.

> All this snotten and shitten belly=button P gazing etc . . . no fkn/ use. . . . and NUTS; bbbbbbbbdy ballzzz about Browning getting any further INTO [t]he mind than Homer . . ., that's the whole point about the Ọdysses / you go on iggurant thinking H. James and Browning did something NEW and then you bump smack onto here in the fkn/ greek.[19]

In the true epic, the agent is implicated in his action as deeply as the noun is entangled in the verb. Moreover, Pound agrees with Fenollosa that the "transferences of force from agent to object . . . occupy time" (*CWC* 7). For it is time which orchestrates Pound's multiverse of fluid force, while space obstructs its interchanges. By subordinating self to action, epic poetry restores the precedence of time.

Poets, historians, economists and rulers must all cooperate to liberate these energies from spatial blockages. In *The*

Cantos, for example, Pound praises princes who forge roads or cut canals to speed the circulation of commodities and news (XXII 101).[20] Canto XXXI pays homage to the canal as a "channel of correspondence" and a "water communication" (153, 156): for it *articulates* one region with another and encourages the trade of words as well as money. These canals retrace the text's topography, and engrave the landscape with the channels that *The Cantos* forge through history. The poem superposes "luminous details", plucked out of the flux of history, and the poet's art lies in the silences that canalise the text, suturing one era to another (*SPr* 21).

Pound described this technique as the "ideogrammic method": for in his view the Chinese written character juxtaposes images that fuse into concepts in the reader's mind (*SPr* 239). "The Chinaman is to define red", he proposes in the *ABC of Reading*:

> How can he do it in a picture that isn't painted in red paint?
>
> He puts (or his ancestor put) together abbreviated pictures of
> ROSE CHERRY
> IRON RUST FLAMINGO (*ABCR* 22)

The meaning of the character arises from the friction between its images. In fact, the pictogram itself becomes a tiny switchboard where meaning circulates like electricity. By analogy, Pound argues that juxtaposing *histories* should shock the reader into recognition of the moral that unites them. Because all truth is the transference of power, the poet drives the lines of force through history which enable past and present to redispose their meanings and intensities. And the less the author intervenes, the keener his impact.

Lords of the Lyre

Canto IV illuminates this method. The following diagram provides a road-map to the intersecting histories of the text:[21]

Canto IV

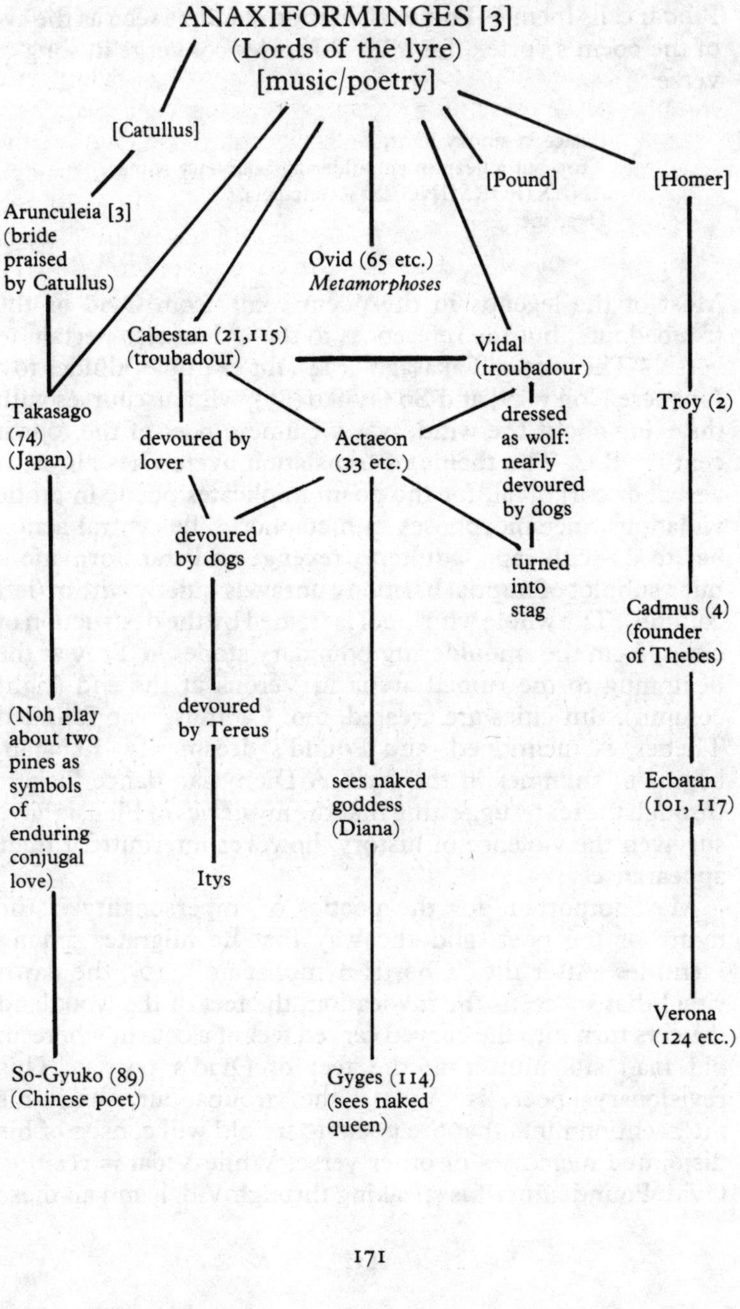
ANAXIFORMINGES [3]
(Lords of the lyre)
[music/poetry]
[Catullus]
Arunculeia [3]
(bride
praised
by Catullus)
Takasago
(74)
(Japan)
(Noh play
about two
pines as
symbols
of
enduring
conjugal
love)
So-Gyuko (89)
(Chinese poet)
Cabestan (21,115)
(troubadour)
devoured by
lover
devoured
by dogs
devoured
by Tereus
Itys
Ovid (65 etc.)
Metamorphoses
Actaeon
(33 etc.)
sees naked
goddess
(Diana)
Gyges (114)
(sees naked
queen)
[Pound]
Vidal
(troubadour)
dressed
as wolf:
nearly
devoured
by dogs
turned
into
stag
[Homer]
Troy (2)
Cadmus (4)
(founder
of Thebes)
Ecbatan
(101, 117)
Verona
(124 etc.)

The poem opens with an invocation of the masters of the past: "ANAXIFORMINGES!" ("lords of the lyre") as Pindar calls them.[22] This exclamation could be seen as the eye of the poem's vortex, for all its histories converge in song or verse:

> Palace in smoky light,
> Troy but a heap of smouldering boundary stones,
> ANAXIFORMINGES! Aurunculeia!
> Hear me.
>
> (1–4)

Most of the legends in the poem come from Ovid or the troubadours, but the references to the Orient also pertain to verse. "The pine at Takasago" (74), for example, alludes to a Japanese Noh play; and So Gyuko (89), who discourses with the King about the wind, was a Chinese poet of the fourth century B.C. The theme of translation overarches all, be it verbal or corporeal, for the poem implicates poetic in erotic violations, metamorphoses in metaphor. The central action has to do with rape, adultery, revenge and transformation; but a subplot of nuptial harmony unravels quietly within (left column). The whole whirlpool is framed by the destruction of cities, from the smouldering boundary stones in Troy at the beginning to the ruined arena in Verona at the end (right column). But cities are created, too: Cadmus, who founded Thebes, is mentioned, and Pound's dream-city, Ecbatan, begins to shimmer in the dust. A Dionysian dance flickers through the text, suggesting that the mysteries of Eleusis have survived the violence of history, however intermittent their appearances.

Most important for the poetics of impersonality is the figure of the poet, and the way that he migrates among identities. After the "Chorus nympharum" (10), the dawn ritual that succeeds the invocation, the feet of the woodland dancers turn into the curved carved feet of a couch, where an old man sits muttering the feet of Ovid's poetry. This revisionary poet is Vidal, the troubadour, and his intervention hints that the poem to unfold will consist of his disjointed memories of other verse. While Vidal is reciting Ovid, Pound himself is speaking through Vidal, and all these voices overlap, "ply over ply" (79). The first of Vidal's memories is Ovid's Procne. In the *Metamorphoses*, Procne took revenge upon her husband Tereus when she learnt that he had raped Philomela by feeding him a literal *pièce de résistance*: the flesh of their own son, whose name was "Itys". But the text (itself a kind of maw) incorporates Itys into Cabestan, a troubadour consumed by love. For Cabestan was murdered by a jealous husband, who fed his heart to Soremonda, his unknowing wife: "It is Cabestan's heart in the dish . . ." (21). (In this line, "It is" should be heard as "Itys", especially because it follows so closely on his name.) In both these stories, sexual transgression ends in cannibalism. In the meantime, esemplastic power circulates between the poets—Ovid, Cabestan, Vidal and Pound—much as these lovers and relations jostle through the alimentary canal. Actaeon provides a variation of the menu, for his only sexual offence was to surprise Diana bathing. In revenge, she transformed him into a stag, so that the dogs pursued him and devoured him:

> The dogs leap on Actaeon,
> "Hither, hither, Actaeon,"
> Spotted stag of the wood. . . .
>
> (57–9)

In textual terms, Vidal engorges Actaeon, for they fuse in the coincidences of their histories. Vidal fell in love with a lady called Loba, meaning She-Wolf: and to stage his seduction by the metaphor he dressed up as a wolf himself. The hounds were taken in by the disguise, and he narrowly escaped the fate of Actaeon.

In this case, the change of shape images a change in rhetoric, in which the proper name reverts into a common noun. This figure is known as antonomasia. In Canto IV, Pound combines it with "paranomasia": the puns that abound within the text. When Itys becomes "It is", for example, both a pun and an unnaming have occurred. Curiously, it is the swallows who concoct this pun, and they themselves are puns, for they swallow his name into their cry as Soremonda swallowed up her lover. In the poem puns become a verbal form of gluttony, and digestion a fleshly *jeu de mots*. The poet, too, becomes a living pun, confected of himself and his precursors. These lines reveal how some of these personae overlap:

> The dogs leap on Actaeon.
> Stumbling, stumbling along in the wood,
> Muttering, muttering Ovid:
> "Pergusa . . . pool . . . Gargaphia
> "Pool . . . pool of Salmacis".
>
> (IV 15)

Here, muttering could be taken as an adjective, meaning that Ovid is muttering. But it could also be taken as a verb, for Vidal is "stumbling" over Ovid's words, lost in the woods of his memory. Since this stumbling alludes to Actaeon careening to his death, all three figures interpenetrate. Personal identity has turned into a porous membrane restlessly traversed by phantoms.[23]

This poem offers a foretaste of *The Cantos* as a whole, for they are polygluttonous in their consumption of the past. Yet everything they swallow up remains unchewed and undigested, alive within its ventral tomb, dyspeptically other. This tension is crucial to Pound's aesthetics, for he images poetic form as a diversity in unity, where all the elements converging must remain discrete, unblurred. The ideogram, for instance, unites a set of shorthand pictures without conflating them into a single *eidos*. Similarly, the magnet draws a rose out of the iron filings without denaturing their elemental form:

> Hast'ou seen the rose in the steel dust
> (or swansdown ever?)
> *so light is the urging*, so ordered the dark petals
> of iron.
>
> (LXXIV 449: my emphasis)

In *The Pisan Cantos*, Pound praises counterpoint in music as another model of aesthetic form: for each melodic line remains intact—it *is*—even though they all proceed in unison. The poet, too, must keep his urging light, so that the "facts", inviolate, achieve their own epiphanies. But Pound perceives these facts as movements, which are always turning into something other than themselves. It is the moment of their transformation that his lyrics strive to capture, when they tremble between being and unbeing. The "Void air taking pelt" in Canto II is an example, or the translucencies of Canto LXXIX: "When the pomegranate is open and the light falls / half through it . . ." (490). Similarly, the dance that flickers in and out of Canto IV intimates that forms are in the making and powers are still dawning in their forms: "Dawn, to our waking, drifts in the green cool light . . ." (4:13). Such instants figure the diastases within the text itself, as its voices interpass and penetrate (LXXX 520). Incorporation without digestion, unity without homogeny, discrimination without distintegration: these are the "unwobbling pivots" that Pound must find.[24]

Canto IV figures poetry as a kind of Eucharist, in which word becomes flesh, flesh food, and food text.[25] This gastroeconomics soon begins to influence the body politic. For the poem devours histories much as its inhabitants ingurgitate each other's words and bodies. When Cabestan merges with Itys, or Vidal with Actaeon, or Pound with Ovid, they create an infinite polyphony: but they also mark the matrices or *puns in time*. (In these cases, Pound is mingling history with fiction, oblivious to their conventional distinction: for Truth and Calliope can slang each other all they will [VIII 28].) Since personal identity depends upon a home in history—an "address in time"—it is important that history "includes" poetry as epic includes history. The "repeat in history" corresponds to the refrain in song; the "subject rhyme" to rhyme in poetry (*L* 210). Because it aspires to the condition of poetry, history also has a melopoeic and a phanopoeic—a rhythmic and figural—dimension (*LE* 25–6). "Run your eye along the margin of history", Pound urges, "and you will observe great waves, sweeping movements and triumphs which fall when their ideology petrifies." "Ideas petrify", he adds for emphasis (*GK* 52). Rhythm is the "fundamental drive", Pound argues: and *The Cantos* strive to rescue history's "margin" of rhythm, its waves and movements, from the anaesthetic of chronology and the petrifaction of ideas (*A* 48). Time must not be etherised upon a table: for it is through rhythmic movement that history purges its canals of the "clog" or "blockage" Pound calls hell.

While rhythm is "a form cut into TIME", the image is time's pigment (*ABCR* 198). Pound contrasts the *idea* which petrifies history to the *image* in which history is stored. "Tradition inheres . . . in the images of the gods, and gets lost in dogmatic defintions", he argues. "History is recorded in monuments, and *that* is why they get destroyed."[26] Images and monuments transport the past into the present, and thus make history possible at all: for history is not the past as such, but the force that sweeps the past into the present, "in ripples and spirals eddying out from us and from our own time." Pound insists that tradition *inheres* in images, for it is in these living forms that the *power* of the past survives. The image is history incarnate.

Ideas inhibit history's rhythms, but they also threaten to erase its images. The same sorcery that petrifies history "putrefies" its monuments and symbols. "The power of putrefaction aims at the obfuscation of history", Pound rages:

> it seeks to destroy not one but every religion, by destroying the symbols, by leading off into theoretical argument. Theological disputes take the place of contemplation. Disputation destroys faith, and interest in theology eventually goes out of fashion. . . . Suspect anyone who destroys an image, or wants to suppress a page of history. (*SPr* 317; see also 306)

Ideas deny the poetry of history, imposing theory in the place of phanopoeia, melopoeia. The "petrifaction of putrefaction" (XV 64): this is how the Hell Cantos execrate the power that effaces history. And hell is just another name for Usura.

In Canto XIII, Kung remembers:

> A day when historians left blanks in their writings,
> I mean for things they didn't know,
> But that time seems to be passing.
>
> (XIII 60)

The blanks in history are not truth itself, but these historians affirm the truth, because they know they do not know it. They figure truth as absence. *The Cantos* try to bring the blank back into history; but they must cancel cautiously, because the blank that stands for truth has been supplanted by another blank that stands for usury. "The one history we have NOT on the news-stands is the history of Usura", Pound fulminates. "All this is still blank in our histories" (*GK* 115). It is usury that supplements the living image with inert ideas, and entrammels history with theory. What tops it all is that *Usura has no history*. By vandalising images and rhythms, it threatens to destroy the address book of the past, engulfing selfhood into its amnesia. At once erased and erasing, usury designates a suicidal mechanism whereby history would obliterate itself. To defeat Usura, *The Cantos*, paradoxically, must blank the blank, erase erasure.

Pound's time-propaganda begins in earnest in 1928, as part of his promotion of Antheil, but he tells Louis Zukofsky in 1936 that "The second vol of MAKE it NEW wd/ have dealt with TIME/ ."[27] For Pound opposes time to space, and his concept of usury is riddled with antitheses. The next part of this chapter will explore these oppositions: and if the question of the subject momentarily recedes, this is just because its traces are so omnipresent. For it is in the terms that he excludes that Pound inscribes himself within his texts, till he becomes the very effigy of all exclusions. His mission of erasure implicates him in the darkness that he struggles to efface, and drives him towards a violent impersonality.

Darkness

"The element most grossly omitted from treatises on harmony up to the present is the element of TIME" (*A* 9). So Pound launches his campaign for Georges Antheil, the avant-garde composer whom he met in 1923.[28]

> The early students of harmony were so accustomed to think of music as something with a strong lateral or horizontal motion that they never imagined any one, ANY ONE could be stupid enough to think of it as static; it never entered their heads that people would make music like steam ascending from a morass. (*A* 11)

Pound believes that the deepest life of music lies in measure rather than harmonics, for measure has the nobler pedigree.

It originates in "the age-lasting rhythms of the craft, cloth-clapping, weaving, spinning, milking, reaping" (*A* 88). These crafts still move to nature's rhythm, rather than the dead tick of the metronome. Pound implies that rhythm has escaped miscegenation, so that the stamp of the original survives, "uncounterfeiting" and "uncounterfeitable" (*LE* 9).[29] Though one may steal the poet's words, it is impossible to forge the inkless signature that he inscribes in time. Because it testifies to parentage and origin, rhythm guarantees both racial and personal identity.

In the twelfth century, however, "steam" began to ooze from the "morass", and to settle over poetry and music, where it has thickened through the centuries (*A* 11). This steam, Pound thinks, disfigures rhythm. Wagner, for example, "produced a sort of pea soup, and . . . Debussy distilled it into a heavy mist, which the post-Debussians have desiccated into a diaphanous dust cloud" (*A* 40). All these gases rose out of the chord, and have asphyxiated rhythm since the Middle Ages. Chords, Pound says, are spatial. Only the gross omission of the element of time enabled them to seep out of the swamp where they belong. Space congeals music, and Pound compares the study of the chord to examining "the circulation of the blood from corpses exclusively" (*A* 23). Like Bergson, he believes that everything went wrong when space usurped the precedence of time.

In music, "slushy chords" betray that space has ousted time; in painting, colour is the stigma of its usurpation. "Chords are like colour", Pound declares, and he uses the same metaphors of obfuscation and incontinence to denounce them both as spatial "heresies" (*A* 18, 19, 40, 48, 62). Like Blake, he censures colour in favour of the line, which he regards as a form of rhythm (*A* 33). Through the line, the plastic arts dispel the fumes of space, for the line pays tribute to the element of time. "The line is unbounded", he writes: "it marks the passage of a force, it continues beyond the frame. . . . all our ideas of beauty of line are in some way connected with our ideas of swiftness and easy power of motion . . .".[30] Like the canal, the line provides a path for energies to flow along, while colours block the arteries of power. Yet Pound even measures colours in temporal terms, calculating their duration and their frequency, in order to acquit them of their spatiality. For it is when the painter slights the "razor edge" of time that he permits his pigments to besmirch the line (*A* 148). Pound admires Wyndham Lewis's parsimony with colour, and suspects that he should leave his lines alone:

> I don't see why he should paint pictures, his gift as I see it is so much in invention, it is so much a matter of almost speech in form, that I myself would probably keep him at drawings if I had any control over him.
>
> Hȩ h££££££££ himself is very apt not to finish or to fill in the colour of his drawings. I feel this is a real indication that the job is finished, that the creation is finished when he has draw~~i~~an in his figure, or indicated a few tones.[31]

Pound identifies the line with "speech in form" because he sees both speech and line as arts of time. It is only with the supplement of space that both degenerate.

"Clogs are spatial", he announces to Zukofsky in a letter of 1936 (which he dates "anno XIV" in honour of the fascist calendar). He is speaking of the clog of usury: and it is through such metaphors as these that his allergy to space creeps into his later economics. In fact "usury" comes to signify the witchcraft that perverts time into space. "You will have to pry up at least ONE eyelid to the changed status of Ez", he warns Zukofsky; for he has now discovered that "monetary reform occurs in TIME." This is the same "YELLYment of TIME" which "inheres in etc/ music etc." When time can overcome the ravages of space, power flows and money moves like music. "Whereas clogs (as the German railway signs tell us, are SPATIAL. raumlich)."[32] Space produces clogs and constipation on the one hand, incontinence and foetor on the other. And these are the two sides of usury.

Usury rose from the morass at the same time that space polluted rhythm and the line. By "1200/ or after 1221", at the latest, "it ALL went to rot . . .".[33] Space erases time from music with the same miasmal mist that usury erases history with. Both rely upon a fatal trope which Pound calls "satanic transubstantiation":

> Only spoken poetry and unwritten music are composed without any material basis, nor do they become "materialised".
> The usurers, in their obscene and pitch-dark century, created this satanic transubstantiation, their Black Mass of money, and in so doing deceived Brooks Adams himself, who was fighting for the peasant and humanity against the monopolists.
> ". . . money alone is capable of being transmuted immediately into any form of activity."—This is the idiom of the black myth! (*SPr* 307)

Because spoken poetry and unwritten music unfold in time, they cannot be corrupted into the materiality of space. The same majestic rhythm that articulates their movement should also regulate the flow of cash.[34] Pound agrees with Major Douglas, the economist who invented Social Credit, that money should be treated as ticket. Temporality is crucial here, because tickets are "timed", and, according to Pound, the "timing of budgets" is essential to economic rhythm.[35] Instead, money has decayed into a fetish. It hoards power, when it should merely mark the passage of a force, and trace a path for power. In their obscene and pitch-dark century, the usurers spatialised money and, ever since, it petrifies and putrefies.

Writing hoards the energies of music and the spoken phrase in the same way that the bankers hoard the powers of production. As soon as writing intervenes, poetry and music undergo satanic transubstantiation, for they stagnate in space when they should lilt in time. In fact, the more Pound worries about usury, the more telegraphically he writes. It is as if he feared the words should be fetishised like money if the reader were to linger too tenderly upon their substance:

> in
> discourse
> what matters is
> to get it across e poi basta
>
> (LXXIX 486)

In Pound's "world of moving energies", writing must transport thought with the "greatest possible despatch", to mimic speech in its electric grace.[36] This is why the author must restrain, or at least "condense" his own emotions, for too much self-expression clogs the interlocutory canals.

Pound urges speed, impersonality and speech because he fears that writing, in so far as it is spatial, must be tainted with the incremental "ooze" of usury. Rome Radio attracted him because it kept his "language [in] the air", avoiding the satanic transubstantiation of the page (*ABCR* 19). For writing is the usury of speech, as space is the usury of time.

In every sphere of culture, usury defaces signs of time. It destroys the rhythms of the craft, where the music of poetry originates, rusting the chisel, blunting the needle, gnawing the thread in the loom:

> with usura the line grows thick
> with usura is no clear demarcation. . . .
> Stonecutter is kept from his stone
> weaver is kept from his loom
> WITH USURA
> wool comes not to market . . .
> Usura is a murrain, usura
> blunteth the needle in the maid's hand
> and stoppeth the spinner's cunning. . . .
> Usura rusteth the chisel . . .
> It gnaweth the thread in the loom . . .
> It hath brought palsey to bed, lyeth
> between the young bride and her bridegroom
> CONTRA NATURAM . . . (XLV 229–30)

In painting, the line grows thick, as colours clog its moving energies. In music, the chord befouls time. In language, the sudden incandescence of the spoken word succumbs to the "palsey" and the usury of writing. "All things that are are lights", quotes Pound, in homage to Scotus Erigena (LXXIV 429): but all these lights are quenched in Usura's Black Mass.[37] Silently, invisibly, it takes possession of the world of light, and substitutes the dazzle of its deathly gold. "Pecuniolatry" supplants the contemplation of the mysteries (*SPr* 348). Satanic transubstantiation mocks the incarnation of a god or of a thought, while the fetish is the diabolic double of the image. With its gross materialisations, the Black Mass mocks art and travesties enfleshment.

These doubles ooze into all economies. "Ooze" itself is usury's parodic supplement to Pound's Heraclitean principle of flow. "Properly understood capital is liquid", urges

Pound: but usury derides fluidity with sludge.[38] Even the rhythms of the flesh pervert themselves, as the human frame turns upside-down in hell:

> Standing bare bum,
> Faces smeared on their rumps,
> wide eye on flat buttock,
> Bush hanging for beard,
> Addressing crowds through their arse-holes,
> Addressing the multitudes in the ooze. . . . (XIV 61)

If the face, like the signature, betokens personal identity, both these tokens sink into the slime. In defiance of Pound's principle of "clear demarcation", the anus takes the place of mouth and genitals at once, and substitutes its ooze for speech and sperm. Usury has seized "Control of the outlets" (CIV 738): be they the outlets of the market, the organs of the news, or the very orifices of the human body. A new idolatry has superseded the spermatic thrust, "phallic and ambrosial": for the anus has become creator of the universe—"a continual bum-belch / distributing its productions" (XV 65).

This bum-belch is a non-origin, which parodies the very notion of a source. To purify the currencies of words of flesh or finance, it is necessary to return to sources, be they the classics, time, the mint, the phallus or the sun. But usury is money "created out of nothing", as Pound quotes wrathfully from Paterson, the founder of the Bank of England.[39] It corresponds to the attempt, in discourse, "to lift zero by its own bootstraps" (*GK* 78). Having no origin, it also has no destination, and thus defies the very principle of teleology in history. Instead, it festers in the sty of the between. This is why Pound lumps usury with sodomy (as Dante did), and creates a hell in which to damn them to each other to eternity. For both neglect the ends to imitate the means of generation. In a footnote to the Usura Canto, Pound defines usury as "A charge for the use of purchasing power, levied without regard to production; often without regard to the possibilities of production" (XLV 51–4). Sodomy disdains production, too, endangering Pound's shibboleths of labour, history and natural fecundity. *The Cantos* mourn the "*coitu inluminatio*" which has given way to this usurious excess (LXXIV 435). In a benevolent economy, " 'any note will be paid' ": "the deposits", Pound repeats, "will be satisfied" (LXXXVI 564; XXXVIII 190). But neither sodomy nor the "buggaring bank" is ever satisfied, nor cashed into the pulchritude of nature (LXXVII 468). Teeming in darkness, they create an excremental universe, exuberant as the spermatozoic one they imitate.

Pound vilifies betweenness more than any other crime of usury, because it undermines the principle of evolution. "Entering all things", usury *defers*. It comes between the stonecutter and the stone; "between the young bride and her bride-groom":[40]

> . . . between the usurer and any man who
> wants to do a good job
> (perenne)
> without regard to production—
> a charge
> for the use of money or cedit.
>
> (LXXXVII 569)

This passage suggests that any form of interest interrupts production, breeding difference and delay where union should occur. But Pound insists that even interest has a base in nature before it is corrupted into usury. Nothing can come of nothing, no matter what the wretched Paterson might say.

> The idea of Interest existed before the invention of metal coin.
> And there is MUCH more justification for collecting interest on a loan of seed, on a loan of she-goats and buck-goats, than on a loan of non-breeding, non-breedable metal. (*RS* 176–7; see also *SPr* 318)

Since living things increase and multiply, interest reflects their future productivity. "INTEREST", Pound declares, "is due teleologically to the increase in domestic animals and plants."[41] He insists that money should "represent something . . . such, namely AS rams and ewes" (*RS* 176; cf. *SPr* 347). Here the questions of time and meaning coincide, for interest refers to things as they *will be*, not to things as they are. Under usury, however, teleology and reference both decay. Now money represents itself alone, its own perverse immaculate conception. Instead of *representing* future sheep, it fattens on its own tautology, indifferent to the destiny of meaning. "Money is now the NOTHING you get for SOMETHING before you can get ANYTHING", writes Frederick Soddy, an economist whom Pound admired despite his name.[42]

Even in ordinary circumstances, money is a kind of go-between, "the middle term" that mediates between the vendor, the consumer and the goods (*SPr* 342: LXXXVII 574). Similarly, language mediates between the speaker and the world. But usury blights both currencies, impeding distribution and bloating the between. By imitating generation, it destroys the boundaries of the living and the dead, confounding animal and vegetable and mineral (see *SPr* 341, 346, 349). This confusion undermines the very means of representation. Moreover, money which is created out of nothing remains unrepresentable, because there is no need for "credit slips" at all. Soon, the power of the nation rots away because there is no currency to embody it. Silvio Gesell, one of Pound's economic gurus, argues that the "coined money of a nation is a drop in the ocean of uncoined money." Similarly, Douglas hints that "real purchasing power is not represented by figures anywhere, but can be materialised by those in possession of the secret of the process, as and when required."[43] To represent this power is to let it forth to purge the clogs from the economy; but usury proscribes representation, so that the banks emasculate the powers of production. Since Pound believes that history inheres in images, and power only comes to life within a form, this discarnation is particularly scandalous. Thus he endorses Douglas's argument that "*under the present system* there are never enough credit slips to deal with the product; to distribute the product; to conjugate any of the necessary verbs of a sane economics and decent and agreeable life."[44] This metaphor suggests that Usura descends on language, too, depriving "verbs" of definition and exactitude. Indeed, Pound believes that economic mess is both the cause and the result of "muddling and muddying terminology" (*GK* 31). Clear definition unblocks the economy, cleaning the canals of communication and exchange. When word and world disband under the influence of usury, the economies of language, history, finance and the flesh can no longer articulate themselves. Pound fumes:

> MESSES of cliche supplied by Iouce and the restuvum to maintain the iggurance spewed out by the OOzevelt Anschauung.
> AND the OOze was possible because writers did not keep the language clean.[45]

Is it usury that defiles definition? Or did the writers unleash usury's marasmus when they failed to purify the dialect of the tribe? Whether the ooze originates in money or in language now becomes impossible to tell, for both succumb to hell's black alchemy. The sewers take the place of the canals. The "infamy which controls English and U.S. finance", Pound declares, "has made printing a midden, a filth, a mere smear . . ." (*GK* 184). Money seethes in the "usurers' dunghill" (LXXVIII 481). Language has been transsubstantiated, too, and festers in the "piles of books" that line the "great scabrous arse-hole" of the Hell Cantos.[46] "Gold bugs against ANY order", the usurocracy begrimes the currencies of finance, word and flesh alike with its excremental signature, its "smear" (LXXXVII 572; *GK* 184).

It is through the smear that usury disseminates itself through history, and it betrays itself wherever monuments and records are destroyed. The word "smear" expresses the calumny of usury, in addition to its filth and its erasures. For if the world was created by an ejaculation, hell's bum-belch is busy decreating it by blotting out its history. "My generation was brought up ham ignorant of economics", Pound frets in a radio broadcast. "History was taught with OMISSIONS of the most vital facts. Every page our generation read was overshadowed by usury" (*RS* 339). It is by "destroying the symbols" that Usura spreads her empire of forgetfulness, and she even keeps herself under erasure. An "octopus", she disappears behind her ink.[47] For it is in the "ugly print marks" of the written page that she at once impresses and deletes her signature.[48] Pound argues that the "press" erases history, by which he seems to mean the newspapers, but he could also mean the printing-press itself: "The press, your press, is a machine for destroying the memory, the public memory. For effacing, for washing out the memory of yesterday and the day before yesterday" (*RS* 339).

However, there are secrets of light as well as secrets of the darkness. Pound is hard put to distinguish the mysteries of usury from those of Eleusis: the cult of Dionysus which he believes in as the hidden inspiration of the West. "Secret history is at least twofold", he writes:

> One part consists in the secret corruption, the personal lusts, avarices, etc. that scoundrels keep hidden, another part is the "plus," the constructive urges, a *secretum* because it passes unnoticed or because no human effort can force it on public attention. (*GK* 264)

A handful of men like Avicenna, Scotus Erigena, Grosseteste, Dante and Cavalcanti preserved Greek joy through the centuries of darkness.[49] They form a "conspiracy of intelligence" which has outlasted usury's erasures and survived its degradation of the flesh (*GK* 263):

> Dionisio et Eleutherio
> Dionisio et Eleutherio
> "the brace of 'em
> that Calvin never blacked out
>
> (XCV 647)

According to Pound, the "mysteries are self-defended, the mysteries *can* not be revealed" (*GK* 145). But usury creates a pseudo-mystery, an ersatz reticence, as self-defended as the genuine article. In the same way, the blanks in history that stand for secret truths surrender to the blank that stands for usury.

This blank cannot be kept at bay, but threatens to engorge both self and world into the nothing out of which it was created. More than a blank, it is a black hole, lodged:

> in hell's bog, in the slough of Vienna, in
> the midden of Europe in the black hole of all
> mental vileness, in the privy that stank Franz Josef
> in Metternich's merdery in the absolute rottenness,
> among embastardised cross-breeds. . . . (*L* 245)

Here Pound makes Vienna the capital of hell because the "Jewish science" flourished in its slough. (He probably feared the "kikiatry racket" because it might detect his confusion of the sphincter with the usurer: a confusion he kept secret even from himself.[50]) As the refuge of the Jews of "middle" Europe, Vienna is a "midden", for it stinks of usury's betweenness; and a contagion of the signifier turns "middle", "midden", "mud" and "muddle" into synonyms for one another in Pound's idiom. The Jews not only practise usury, but they refuse to represent or even name their god. Their taboo against the graven image instigates the drive to disidentify, erase, unname, unrepresent that Pound excoriates in usury. "Without gods, something is lacking", he states, laconically (*GK* 126). And it is from this lack that usury creates its anti-cosmos out of nothing.

"The Semitic", Pound declares, "is excess. The Semitic is against any scale of values" (*I* 125). The Jews destroy the tools of representation: with Usura, the line grows thick, and categories leak across their boundaries. The term "Semitic" comes to *mean* erasure in Pound's writing, and particularly the erasure of history: "Time blacked out with the rubber" (VII 25). But he does not restrict the epithet to Jews. Protestantism is nothing more than "jewdianity . . . renewed jewdianity, reJEWed whichianity"; and both these religions conspire "semiticly to obliterate values, to efface grades and graduations" (*GK* 185).[51] If Canto C proclaims that usury is "beyond race and against race", this is because the Semitic must at least erase *itself* by rotting boundaries and embastardising breeds (C 798).

"Name 'em, don't bullshit ME"[52]

Of all of usury's assaults on definition, the last and consummate is the erasure of the proper name. Personal identity dissolves into the slime. There is no one, Pound mourns, "whom the ooze cannot blacken", for "the stench of the profit motive has covered their names" (XCVI 662). No name is proof against the smear. Moreover, the law of libel forces Pound himself to collude in the destruction of the name, and many of the Semites he castigates sneak through *The Cantos* under pseudonyms. "That ass Nataanovitch", for instance:

> Or some better known—ovitch
> whose name we must respect because of the
> law of libel
>
> (XXXV 172)

Pound attacks the law of libel in the *Guide to Kulchur*: "The purpose of law is to eliminate crime not to incubate it and cause it to pullulate" (186). This law flouts Pound's first principle of poetry and economics: "to call things by their right names—in the market" (XXXIV 168; cf. *SPr* 333). While the act of definition purges the economy, withdrawing names from circulation only helps to breed the crimes they designate. Like interest, they pullulate in darkness.

Unnamed and unnaming, smearing names with their Semitic ooze, the Jews defy the very notion of identity. They uncreate the universe that the Australian demigod Wanjina creates by naming it in Canto 74:

> and Rouse found they spoke of Elias
> in telling the tales of Odysseus   ΟΥ ΤΙΣ
>   ΟΥ ΤΙΣ
> "I am noman, my name is noman"
> But Wanjina is, shall we say, Ouan Jin
> or the man with an education
> and whose mouth was removed by his father
>   because he made too many *things*
> whereby cluttered the bushman's baggage
> vide the expedition of Frobenius's pupils about 1938
>   to Auss'ralia
> Ouan Jin spoke and thereby created the named
>   thereby making clutter
>
> (LXXIV 426–7)

In aboriginal legend, Wanjina named the world, and thereby brought it into being; but his father, like an incarnation of the law of libel, removed his mouth and his capacity to name. As if to sympathise with this unlucky onomast, the poem stammers on Odysseus, and his name degenerates into its alias, Elias. W. D. Rouse figures here because he travelled the itinerary of *The Odyssey*, and discovered that the Greek islanders still told Odysseus's stories under the name of the Jewish prophet Elias.[53] Thus, by identifying with Odysseus, Pound implicates himself with Elias and with the race responsible for all "historic black-out" (LXXXVIII 595). Better noman than Elias: better to be unnamed and unmanned than to be named after the prophet and the profit-motive. Yet the smear that usury casts over personal identity returns in every pseudonym, from Mauberley to noman, in which Pound struggles to erase his name: Bastien von Helmholtz, Hermann Karl George Jesus Maria, John Hall, Walter Villerant, B. H. Dias, William Atheling, M. D. Adkins, T.J.V., J.L., B.L., Hiram James, Abel Saunders, A. Watson, Alfred Venison.[54] In his typescripts Pound uses the £-sign to blot his errors out, turning his own signature into a nomadic cancellation. And indeed, it is in the act of self-erasure that he gives his name most unmistakably away.

He discloses it, for instance, in his reading of *Ulysses*, where he disapproves of Bloom's cloacal pleasures. Coyly, he writes to Joyce, "I don't arsk you to erase . . .": and breaks the thought mid-sentence.[55] It is the arse that Pound would like to arsk Joyce to erase, but the arse invades the very letters of the word "erase". Maybe this is why Pound thinks the arse provides the ooze that usury erases history with. Joyce spotted another word secreted in the letters of erase: for in *Finnegans Wake* he spells Ezra with an "s", turning the name into an anagram of "arse", and also of "erase" (*FW* 116). Is it possible that Esra is another name for Usura?

In the character of Bloom, Joyce equates Odysseus with the wandering Jew, and Pound was well aware of this when he chose Odysseus for his persona. The choice suggests an unconscious identification with the Jews. Indeed, Pound admits his wanderlust, and adds that "It is not for me to rebuke brother semite for similar disposition" (*GK* 243). A wanderer in life, he is equally nomadic in his verse, for *The Cantos* prolong his odyssey through space and time. They make him master of "a hundred tongues", like Geryon, the queen of fraud in Canto LI (251). By Pound's own logic, to be polyglot is to put oneself "beyond race and against race", as embastardised as fraud or as a Jew. It seems that there is more than a fraternal bond between the poet and the race—the anti-race—that he abominates.[56] Could it be that Ezra the wanderer, Ezra the prophet, and indeed, Ezra the Pound, is the Semitic incarnate? And if, as *The Cantos* say, "there is/ no end to the journey" (LXX 477), how could Ez defeat ooze, or Ezra erase usura? How could the self obliterate the self?

* * *

In Pound's hell, the anus has displaced the mouth, just as writing has supplanted speech, for the letter is the ooze that issues from the baser orifice. It is to stop the spread of ooze that Wanjina, the creator, must be silenced. How his mouth could be removed is something of a mystery, since the mouth already hollows out a void: one might as well erase Esra. His father would have had to seal it shut, and semiticly obliterate its cleft, so that Wanjina gains the only face in hell that cannot smear. However, his broken name, Ouan Jin, transliterates a Chinese ideogram meaning "man of letters", "literary gent."[57] This pun suggests that Wanjina stands for the voicelessness of textuality itself, which unfaces and unnames its own creator. Blank, mutilated, the "man of letters" represents the work of Thanatos in language, and the author's own remorseless decreation of himself.

In the first Canto, Tiresias foretells that Odysseus will lose all his companions. In the *Pisan Cantos*, this curse uncannily comes true:

> but I will come out of this knowing no one
> neither they me
>
> (LXXXII 526)

"This" may mean the cage at Pisa, where the Americans incarcerated Pound; but it may also mean the prison of the text itself, and its compulsion to erase erasure. Neither will they know me, Pound mourns—because his name itself has now become the blank in history.

The Gold Thread in the Pattern

"The celestial and earthly process can be defined in single phrase: its actions and its creations have no duality. (The arrow hath not two points)", Pound declares.[58] The powers of darkness do not amount to the antithesis of light, for he denies erasure the *prestige* of a negation. He abhors the dialectic, because the Semitic is "schizophrenic essentially", and the labour of the negative must therefore bear the stain of usury (*I* 140). Rather than a dialectic, history consists of a single principle of light, which darkness merely counterfeits without dissevering.

But it is because Pound rejects duality that *The Cantos* sink under the darkness they are striving to obliterate. Usury and history ooze through the partitions that he draws between them. A rhetorical marasmus infects time with space, rhythm with chords, line with colour, speech with writing, interest with usury: until it is impossible to purify the truths of history from their mockeries. The purest principles of Pound's poetics become accomplices to usury's satanic logic. Canto IV, for instance, rejoices in puns as the luminous matrices of history. Yet the puns confusing Ezra with erasure, arse and ooze become the agents of usury's destruction of the past. Similarly, Pound revels in antinomasis as the figure of Ovidian metamorphosis, in which the proper name materialises as a common noun. For instance, Arachne turns into an "arachnid" (and incidentally, her web resembles the arachnean script that Esra—Pound's satanic double—spins out of his arse or hinter-face). But this is the same trope that debases Pound into a pound of flesh, sentencing his name to endless usury. *The Cantos* envelop Pound in his own darkness, and entoil all his values in their antonyms. If the "middle" is the midden of usury, it also stands for his beloved principle of balance. If usury was created out of nothing, Pound praises emptiness elsewhere as "the beginning of all things" (LIV 281). Similarly, the "gold thread in the pattern" represents "the sun's cord unspotted"—"light tensile immaculata"—the filament of light which flickers faintly through the centuries of darkness (CXVI 797; LXXIV 429). But gold is the colour of extortion, too. The gold thread marks the vein of death that usury has woven through the tissue of the text, poisoning the images of time.

Pound urges a return to "Sagetrieb, or the oral tradition", where the past rejuvenates itself perpetually (LXXXIX 597).[59] He would sign his name in speech, in writing, on the air, rather than in any medium corrupted by the usury of writing. But his names are both compounded in all that *The Cantos* denounce. Pound himself is the infected currency; and Esra is the other face of the same coin, the face that belches into hell. Secretly, the smear of Esra overwhelms the blank of truth. What is more, the text itself falls foul of usury's between, and pullulates when it should circulate, unable to conclude or to cohere. Like sodomy and usury, it endlessly defers a fulness of meaning or a simple satiety. For *The Cantos* are themselves created out of nothing: out of the ruins of the excremental pound.

Notes

1. *LE* 86; Canto CXVI 797.
2. The term "dossier" is Rabaté's in "Pound's Art of Naming".
3. *"Ezra Pound Speaking": Radio Speeches of World War II*, ed. Leonard J. Doob (Westport, Connecticut and London: Greenwood, 1978), p. 339.
4. Pound's contempt for Bergson is belied to some extent by his unbounded esteem for his disciples, like T. E. Hulme and Henri Gaudier-Brzeska. Hulme, however, abandoned Bergsonism for the same political reasons as Eliot and Pound (see Introduction). For Gaudier's discipleship of Bergson, see H. S. Ede, *Savage Messiah* (1931; repr. Bedford: Gordon Fraser, 1971), p. 98.
5. See Introduction.
6. Letter to Agresti, TS [5 July 1951], Pound Archive, Beinecke.
7. "Heaven AND earth/ nothing cd/ be more idiotic than a religion which has put corsets on the holy mystery of fecundity. In fact Xtianity is one of the worst hoaxes." Pound, letter to Agresti, TS [August 1949], Pound Archive, Beinecke. See also *I* 94.
8. As in the "Project for a Scientific Psychology", where Freud maps out a similar economy of power, it is impossible to abstract form from force, or trace from tracing. See Freud, "Project for a Scientific Psychology", in *The Origins of Psychoanalysis* (New York: Basic Books, 1954), pp. 349–455; see also Jacques Derrida, "Freud and the Scene of Writing", in *Writing and Difference*, pp. 196–231.
9. "Cavalcanti: Medievalism" (1934), *MN*, p. 351.
10. *MN*, p. 352.
11. Pound, Introduction to *Cavalcanti*, pp. 3–4.
12. *Ibid.*, p. 5; *MN* 350.
13. Letter to Sister Bernetta Quinn, TS [28 June 1950?], in Pound Archive, Beinecke.
14. See Kenner on Pound's poetic thermodynamics in *The Pound Era*

(London: Faber, 1975), pp. 145–72.

15. Letter from Pound to Abbot, TS (18 June [1954]), in Pound Archive, Beinecke. See also *C* XC 609.
16. Letter to Quinn, TS, 10 March 1916, in Quinn Collection, New York Public Library.
17. See *LE* 48 and Pound, "Affirmations: IV. As for Imagism", *The New Age*, 16 (1915), 350.
18. See Michael Reck, *Ezra Pound: A Close-up* (New York: MacGraw Hill, 1967), facsimiles preceding p. 99; cited by Kenner, *Pound Era*, p. 150.
19. Pound, Letter to Bunting, TS, 17 January 1935, in Pound Archive, Beinecke.
20. I owe this insight to my student Tom Furniss, Southampton University, 1983.
21. Line references given in round brackets.
22. Olympian Ode II.
23. It is a curious coincidence that Pound's wolf-man, Vidal, should resemble Freud's so closely, for both reveal the link between the pun and the incorporation of the dead. In fact, the analysts Abraham and Torok have disclosed a whole "cryptonomy" within the wolf-man's lexicon. Just as he entombs the desire of the other in the pervious walls of his ego, so he ensepulchres one word, one language in another, in a limitless paranomasia (see Nicolas Abraham and Marie Torok, "Deuil ou mélancolie, introjecter—incorporer", Ch. 4, Section 3 of *L'Ecorce et le noyau* [Paris: Flammarion, 1978]; Derrida, "Fors", Preface to Abraham and Torok, *Cryptonomie: Le Verbier de l'homme aux loups* (Paris: Flammarion, 1978), pp. 1–73; trans. by Barbara Johnson as "Fors: The Anglish Words of Nicolas Abraham and Marie Torok", *Georgia Review*, 31 (1977), 64–116; see also Derrida, "Me—Psychoanalysis: An Introduction to the Translation of *The Shell and the Kernel*", *Diacritics* 9, no. 1 (1979), 4–12.) Pound peppers his poetic language with bilingual puns, like those that haunted the unconscious of the wolf-man, and wolfs the languages of others into his translations. See, for instance, Kenneth Sisam, "Mr. Pound and 'The Seafarer' ", *TLS*, no. 2734 (25 June 1954), 409; and W. G. Hale, "Pegasus Impounded", *Poetry* 14, no. 1 (1919), 52–5. See Pound's response to Hale in letter to Orage (April? 1919), *L* 148–50.
24. Cf. Pound, *Confucius: The Great Digest and the Unwobbling Pivot* (1952; repr. London: Peter Owen, 1968).
25. This ritual element reasserts itself in the pagan rite at the beginning and the Catholic procession that concludes the text, with its hints of mariolatry.
26. Pound, *A Visiting Card*, Money Pamphlets by £, no. 4 (London: Peter Russell, 1952), p. 18; repr. in *SPr* 322.
27. Letter to Zukofsky, TS [March? 1936], in Pound Archive, Beinecke.
28. For information about Pound's association with Antheil see R. Murray Schafer, *Ezra Pound and Music: The Complete Criticism* (London: Faber, 1978), p. 242ff. and *passim*.

29. See Donald Davie, *Ezra Pound: The Poet as Sculptor*, for discussions of Pound's quotations of metres.
30. Introduction to *Sonnets and Ballate of Guido Cavalcanti* (London: Stephen Swift, 1912), p. 11.
31. Letter to Quinn, TS, 13 July 1916, in Quinn Collection, New York Public Library. Pound uses the £-sign as a form of deletion.
32. Letter to Zukofsky, TS [March? 1936], Pound Archive, Beinecke.
33. Letter to Boris de Rachewilz, TS [31 May? 1954], Berg Collection, New York Public Library.
34. Pound, *Gold and Work*, Money Pamphlets by £, no. 2 (London: Peter Russell, 1951), p. 12; repr. in *SPr* 346.
35. See *I* 91–2; and *The Douglas Manual*, ed. Philip Mairet (London: Stanley Nott, 1934), p. 13; *SPr* 291; XCIX 706; "You forget the timing of budgets / That is to say you probably don't even know that / Officials exist in time." For discussions of Pound's economic sources see Earl Davis, *Vision Fugitive: Ezra Pound and Economics* (Lawrence, Kansas, and London: University of Kansas Press, 1968).
36. *MN* 351; *LE* 50. Cf. *SPr* 313.
37. See Walter B. Michaels, "Pound and Erigena", *Paideuma*, 1 (1972), 37–54.
38. Pound, *Social Credit: an Impact. Money Pamphlets by £*, no. 5 (London: Peter Russell, 1952), p. 14.
39. XLV 233; LXXIV 468; see also *SPr* 290, 308, 338; and Christopher Hollis, *The Two Nations* (London: Routledge, 1935), Ch. 3.
40. XLV 230; Addendum for C 798.
41. Quoted from Alexander del Mar, *The Science of Money* (London: George Bell, 1885), p. 101, in Pound, letter to Maverick, 9 September 1957, Pound Archive, Beinecke.
42. Frederick Soddy, *The Role of Money* (1934), in Montgomery Butchart, ed., *Money* (London: Stanley Nott, 1945), p. 268.
43. Silvio Gesell, *The Natural Economic Order*, trans. Philip Pye (1929; London: Peter Owen, 1958), p. 185; *Douglas Manual*, p. 34. See Del Mar, *The Science of Money*, p. 13; and Pound, *ABC of Economics* (London: Faber, 1933), p. 47; repr. in *SPr* 237. See also Earl Davis, *Vision Fugitive* for discussions of Pound's economic sources.
44. Pound, *ABC of Economics*, p. 33.
45. Letter to Sister Bernetta Quinn, TS [1954], Pound Archive, Beinecke.
46. CXII 784; IV 15; XIV 63; XV 64.
47. See XXIX 145: "She is submarine, she is an octopus, she is / A biological process." Here Pound is describing "woman", but the images of femininity, usury and excrement all converge in his visions of economic chaos.
48. See "The Cry of the Eyes", *CEP* 49.
49. See Leon Surette, *A Light from Eleusis: A Study of Ezra Pound's Cantos* (Oxford: Clarendon, 1979).
50. Pound, letter to Sister Bernetta Quinn, TS, (5 August [1954]), Pound Archive, Beinecke.
51. Letter to Boris de Rachewilz, TS (10 August [1954]), in Berg

Collection, New York Public Library.

52. LXXIV 430; LXXVII 473.
53. See Guy Davenport, "Pound and Frobenius", in *Motive and Method in The Cantos of Ezra Pound*, ed. Lewis Leary (New York and London: Columbia University Press, 1961), pp. 49–52.
54. See Noel Stock, *The Life of Ezra Pound*, pp. 44, 151, 163, 203, 209, 210, 212, 226, 229, 234–5, 246, 329, 330, 443.
55. *Pound/Joyce: The Letters of Ezra Pound to James Joyce, with Pound's Essays on Joyce*, ed. Forrest Read (London: Faber, 1966), p. 157.
56. See my "Floating the Pound: The Circulation of the Subject of *The Cantos*", *Oxford Literary Review*, 3, no. 3 (1979), p. 26; see also Daniel Pearlman, "Ezra Pound: America's Wandering Jew", *Paideuma*, 9 (1980), 461–81.
57. Davenport, p. 50.
58. Pound, *Confucius: The Great Digest and the Unwobbling Pivot*, p. 183; *SPr* 306.
59. Sagetrieb is a word coined by Pound, literally meaning "say-drive", or as David Gordon argues, "Pass on the tradition." See also LXXXV 557 and Carroll Terrell, *A Companion to the Cantos of Ezra Pound*, Vol. II (Berkeley and London: University of California Press, 1984), p. 479.

Coda

"I am I by memory", says Stephen Dedalus. Thus he asserts that personal identity depends upon the power to recall the past. According to this formula, the best way to achieve a self is to embark on one's confessions. In *Finnegans Wake*, however, Joyce makes fun of autobiographers, when Shaun the Postman mocks his brother's logorrhoea. "Spun from the bowels of his misery", Shem the Penman writes with his own excrement on "the only foolscap available", his own flesh:

> Then, pious Eneas, conformant to the fulminant firman which enjoins on the tremylose terrian that, when the call comes, he shall produce nichthemerically from his unheavenly body a no uncertain quantity of obscene matter not protected by copriright in the United Stars of Ourania or bedeed and bedood and bedang and bedung to him, with this double dye, brought to blood heat, gallic acid on iron ore, through the bowels of his misery, flashly, faithly, nastily, appropriately, this Esuan Menschavik and the first till last alshemist wrote over every square inch of the only foolscap available, his own body, till by its corrosive sublimation one continuous present tense integument slowly unfolded all marryvoising moodmoulded cyclewheeling history (thereby, he said, reflecting from his own individual person life unlivable, transaccidentated through the slow fires of consciousness into a dividual chaos, perilous, potent, common to allflesh, human only, mortal) but with each word that would not pass away the squidself which he had squirtscreened from the crystalline world waned chagreenold and doriangrayer in its dudhud. (*Finnegans Wake*, pp. 185–6)

Here Pious Eneas (Pius and Aeneus, but also an anal pseudonym for Shem) literally writes *himself*, scrawling his flesh upon his flesh. His identity unfolds into a hundred histories, and the obscene matter that he spins out of his bowels turns into an Orphic explication of the earth. This parable suggests that autobiography (self-life-writing) is the excrement of life, its nightly or "nichthemerical" emission. To write is to evacuate the self; to sever self from self; to reinscribe the self upon a self that hides itself behind itself only to expose itself most flagrantly. Self-born and self-begotten, Shem's creation parodies the immaculate conception. Yet his idiography becomes impersonal despite its onanism: "reflecting from his own individual person life unlivable . . . common to allflesh." And rather than confirming his identity, his writing prospers as his self declines, for he waxes "doriangrayer" with every word.

If *The Cantos* could dream, they might hallucinate their own creation in the form of Shem. Like Eliot, Pound stages his disfiguration in his verse, but it is the self that overblots the self: the "squidself", as Joyce would say, is "squirtscreened" by its own ink. Pound reinscribes himself with every effort to delete himself, and even his jeremiads against the usurers surreptitiously repeat his name. For usury becomes the demonic image of his "endless scripture", and represents his own ill-gotten gains: the incontinent dissemination of his signature.

What could be more "personal" than Pound's writing, his "corrosive sublimation" of himself? By this point, however, the terms "impersonal" and "personal" have probably outlived their usefulness. For both assume that personality is something unified, consistent, self-contained: something that exists *outside* the text, even if it intervenes from time to time. The autobiographical insistence in *The Cantos* has nothing to do with this theology of self. When Pound becomes £, the subject is reduced to a linguistic function—a sign in circulation—a locus of exchange and transformation. The name that haunts his poem is a roving cancellation rather than a personality.

Eliot, on the other hand, insists that poets should suppress their egoism, and keep their poetry and personalities distinct. But his arguments recoil against themselves. The very terms that frame his doctrine of self-abnegation—time and space—are steeped in the antitheses that they repress. Besides, his theory hints that personality is the inevitable consequence of writing, as opposed to the impersonality of speech. Thus he can never quite dispose of self, because it haunts the very grammar of its ostracism.

Eliot and Pound both show that it is impossible to overcome the self, but this does not mean that their work is merely a disguise for their biographies. Their poetry should be regarded neither as their mirror nor their hiding-place, but as the laboratory for the fabrication of themselves. As we have seen, Eliot's early poems explore the complicities of sexuality and personal identity. Saint Narcissus falls in love with his own doubles; Prufrock cruises the deserted streets, searching for a nameless love; and Gerontion shrinks into a sleepy corner, which explodes through the pressure of his own denials.[1] In *The Waste Land*, this explosion continues to reverberate: and the speaking subject is dispersed among the fragments of its shattered history. But its harrowed voice is superseded by another tone in *Four Quartets*, languid, assuaging and avuncular. Here Eliot discards the "I", but only to adopt a royal "we", complacently assuming the burden of humanity. But even this transcendent voice is not impregnable, for it echoes with quotations from the dead: and the strange inhuman logic of disfiguration overcomes the shibboleth of self. In different ways, both Eliot and Pound become their own self-exorcists, even as they struggle to invent themselves. On the other hand, they both reveal that subjectivity is never more indelible than in its passion for its own extinction.

"Impersonality" is often understood as a purely aesthetic category, but the term embraces many cultural domains. Although its politics became explicit only in the 1930s, the doctrine of impersonality was born conservative. It began as an attack against the individualism that Eliot and Pound had both rejected. For this reason it remained complicit with its opposite, and with the past it was deputed to forget. Moreover, the doctrine exemplifies the philosophical, aesthetic, and political assumptions which inspired the reactionary fervour of the modernists. Eliot inveighs against personality for much the same reasons that he ostracises the Jews from his Anglo-Catholic utopia. Similarly, the question of the self in Pound opens up the whole psychopathology of fascism. To some extent, critics have used the doctrine of impersonality to rescue modernism from its racism and homophobia: to purify the poems of their authors' politics, and hence to insulate aesthetics from history. For it is when the poems are most "personal", when the author is inscribed most visibly within the text, that the scandal of their history re-emerges. However, the closer one examines the theory of impersonality, the more its ideological objectives reappear; and it becomes impossible to separate its politics from its poetics. The innocence of the aesthetic domain perishes in Eliot and Pound.

Note

1. I owe Eve Sedgwick these suggestions.

Index

Poulet, Georges, 6, 66, 87, 139, 159